OCT 14, 1971

Money
and
Markets
A Monetarist View

Money
and
Markets

A Monetarist View

BERYL W. SPRINKEL, Ph.D., C.F.A.
Senior Vice President and Economist
Harris Trust and Savings Bank
Chicago, Illinois

1971

RICHARD D. IRWIN, INC.
HOMEWOOD, ILLINOIS 60430
IRWIN-DORSEY LIMITED, GEORGETOWN, ONTARIO

FIRST PRINTING, MAY, 1971

LIBRARY OF CONGRESS CATALOG CARD No. 79–149898

PRINTED IN THE UNITED STATES OF AMERICA

To my wife Barbara,
the most lovable and
loving Aquarian of them all

Preface

The purpose of this book is to explain the increasingly popular monetarist theory of aggregate demand and to relate changes in money to such important economic variables as business cycles, inflation, economic growth, and stock and bond prices. Emphasis is placed on practical application of the monetarist concepts to the prediction of economic and financial trends and to the formulation of profitable investment policies.

Monetarists contend that the major independent force determining changes in demand for goods, services, and assets is fluctuation in the growth rate of the money supply. The monetarist theory is compared and contrasted with conventional Keynesian or "new economics" doctrine which emphasizes changes in autonomous investment expenditures, including capital spending and the full employment budget, as the prime motivator of total spending. The predictive record of these two competing approaches is compared over recent years, and it is contended that the monetarist approach compiled the better score.

The factors determining fluctuations in the money supply are carefully analyzed, including both the commercial banking system and the monetary policy pursued by the Federal Reserve Board. Alternative measures of monetary change are considered, and it is concluded that data point to the desirability of using monetary aggregates like the money supply rather than credit factors such as free reserves and interest rates.

Empirical evidence points to a strong predictive relation between monetary change and such related economic variables as business cycles, leading indicators, inflation, stock and bond prices, and economic growth. Hence, monetary analysis can make useful contributions to the understanding of important economic issues as well as provide practical guidance to the management of personal investments.

The text utilizes analytical disciplines from the areas of monetary theory, business cycles, and investments. The ideas and method of analysis can be of use to laymen, students, and professional economists interested in the important economic debates of the day; it can also be of value to investors, including both professionals and the small investor managing his own funds. A serious attempt is made to avoid technical economic and financial jargon comprehensible only to professional practitioners.

I am grateful to many former teachers, students, and colleagues for stimulating my interest in the relation between monetary economics and practical finance. My largest intellectual debt is owed to Professor Milton Friedman of the University of Chicago, who taught me much about money. He also made many useful suggestions for improving the arguments and exposition presented in this book. Nancy Rosenberg, Robin Barnes, and Virginia Klarquist have my gratitude for gathering and processing most of the data; Grazina Juodelis has my appreciation for her assistance in my research; and my secretary, Terese Nauman, has my grateful thanks for typing many drafts of this manuscript.

I am also appreciative of publisher and author permission to quote various published works.

April, 1971   BERYL WAYNE SPRINKEL

Contents

List of Charts

xv

CHART

List of Tables

TABLE

Introduction

Since the fall of 1969, *Time* magazine has assembled a "Board" of economic experts several times a year and has reported their judgments about the economic outlook. The members of the board share a rather common outlook, with one conspicuous exception. The maverick is Beryl Sprinkel, who repeatedly has expressed views at sharp variance with the views of his fellow board members. In the fall of 1969, for example, the majority view was that the economy would continue to expand fairly rapidly. Only Sprinkel was warning of an impending recession. By December 1969, the majority view was being shaded toward Sprinkel's earlier view but remained more optimistic. Sprinkel was the only one who flatly predicted a recession in 1970. He forecast that real output in 1970 would be the same as in 1969; in fact, it fell by 0.4 percent. He forecast that unemployment would average 4.8 percent and reach a peak of 6.0 percent; in fact, it averaged 4.9 percent and reached a peak of 6.2 percent. His error in predicting output and unemployment was less than that of the other six members of the board who also recorded numerical predictions (one member of the board did not record a numerical prediction). The one place he went astray was on inflation: he anticipated that the recession would reduce the rate of rise in prices from the 6 percent of 1969 to 4 percent in 1970; in fact, the rate of rise in prices fell only to 5.3 percent. The inflationary inertia was stronger than he expected.

What explains the difference in predictions? The members of the board are all able and prominent economists. They include two former Chairmen of the Council of Economic Advisers, and all are experienced and competent analysts of economic activity. How is it that six men should hear one drummer and one man a very different drummer?

The answer is that they were following different theories. The majority were following the Keynesian theory which, first promulgated in the 1930s, became the orthodoxy in the economic profession in the 1940s and 1950s, the period when the members of the board became fully trained professional economists. This theory, as Dr. Sprinkel explains more fully in his book, stresses the effect of autonomous spending on short-run economic developments and gives little attention to the quantity of money. Autonomous spending is regarded as consisting primarily of private capital spending (plant and equipment, residential housing, etc.) and government spending. In the fall of 1969, business was planning heavy capital expenditures in 1970, and the government budget, which had shifted sharply in a restrictive direction as a result of the 1968 surtax, was stabilizing and indeed gave some signs of becoming more expansionary—as interpreted by this theory. High capital expenditures plus a minor assist from government spending spelled continued expansion. Hence the forecast for 1970.

Dr. Sprinkel, on the other hand, was following an older theory that has recently been experiencing a great revival: what used to be called the quantity theory of money but is now called monetarism. Despite the revival, the proportions on the *Time* board—6 or 7 to 1—are probably not very different from those in the economic profession at large, though the ratio is changing so rapidly that this may no longer be the case. This theory, as Dr. Sprinkel explains more fully in his book, stresses the role of changes in the quantity of money, not in autonomous spending, on short-run economic developments. In 1969, there had been a sharp reduction in the rate of monetary growth. Hence, Sprinkel's prediction of a recession.

Dr. Sprinkel was dramatically correct in his predictions for 1970, as he had been in earlier predictions. But that alone clearly does not prove that he is hearing the right drummer. One swallow does not make a spring. If the monetarist theory deserves confidence it is not because it enabled him to make a few good predictions but because it has a solid foundation in economic analysis and conforms to economic experience for many countries and over long periods of time. A great merit of Dr. Sprinkel's book is that it makes crystal clear the broad basis for confidence in monetarism.

There is another reason why a few good predictions are not by themselves a satisfactory basis for confidence in monetarism. As in the old saying, the monetarists need more protection from their friends than from their enemies. The economic world is full of many things and our knowledge of it is still very far from satisfactory. I have great confidence that the monetarist view as outlined by Dr. Sprinkel is correct *on the average* and *in the main*. But it does not provide any magic formula for predicting the precise course of economic activity in any one episode—any more than knowing that a pair of dice is far more likely to show 4 to 11 spots than 2, 3 or 12 can enable you to predict with complete confidence that a particular throw will not come up "craps." There is much variation in any particular episode. If Dr. Sprinkel's prediction for 1970 had not been fulfilled, that would not have reduced substantially my confidence in the monetary relations that I have studied for many countries and many decades. Similarly, the correctness of a few predictions can only add a mite to my confidence in those relations.

The importance of these predictions and their outcome is different: they illustrate the difference that the economic theory adopted can have on one's views of the immediate future; and their dramatic character calls the attention of the nonspecialist to the iceberg that underlies the tip that impresses him—if I may switch metaphors.

The nonspecialist could hardly have a better guide to the iceberg than Dr. Sprinkel. A native of Missouri, he has never taken things on faith but has always insisted on being shown the evidence. He early came under the influence of Harry Gunnison Brown, a coauthor and student of Irving Fisher, the greatest American economist of all time and a major contributor to the quantity theory of money. He received his graduate training at the University of Chicago, one of the few academic centers in the United States that did not succumb fully to the Keynesian revolution but remained an active center of research in money and banking and continued to teach the quantity theory as well as the Keynesian theory.

Since 1952, he has been applying monetarist principles in practice as an economist for the Harris Trust and Savings Bank and at the same time contributing to the scientific literature on monetary relations. His independence of mind has enabled him to keep from being bowled over by the prevailing fashion. His analytical ability combined with his empirical bent and the needs of his employment have led him to investigate how the monetarist counterrevolution could be used to guide business forecasting and investment practice. In this area, he has been a real pioneer, as is attested by his 1964 book on *Money and Stock Prices,* which appeared at just about the date when Keynesian views were at the peak of widespread public acceptance (although already losing ground in the academy).

The present book presents Dr. Sprinkel's considered judgment on a wide range of issues involving money. It is written primarily for the intelligent layman, interested in better investment of his assets, not for the professional economist. Yet it presents a sophisticated analysis of monetary relations that embodies results at the very frontier of scientific research. Professional economists—whether they are greatly concerned with how to invest their assets or not—have much to learn from this book.

There are cycles not only in the economy and the stock market but also in scientific views about the economy, though the scientific cycles tend to be of much longer duration. The bull market in monetarism has only recently begun. It has much farther yet to go.

Chicago, Illinois   Milton Friedman
April, 1971

CHAPTER 1

The Monetarists and
the New Economists

Introduction

This may be the Age of Aquarius; certainly it is the day of the monetarist. But some still argue that the one, like the other, is pure stargazing. It is the thesis of this book that understanding the monetarist view not only aids greatly in illuminating the important economic issues of the day but also provides useful insights into the ever-challenging task of managing personal investments, both stocks and bonds. This book explains the growing support for the monetarist view about money and monetary policy and the relation between money and such economic variables as inflation, business cycles, stock and bond prices, investment policy, and economic growth. Although monetarism cannot and does not explain all economic relations, it makes a major contribution toward understanding the connections among the above phenomena. The term "monetarist" may be used interchangeably with such frequently used terms as the "modern quantity theorist" and the "Chicago school of money theorists."

1

Public and private views about important economic issues seldom undergo so dramatic a shift as has occurred in the past few years. Keynesian economics became fashionable shortly after publication of *The General Theory of Employment, Interest and Money*[1] in 1936. Yet it wasn't until 25 years later that the basic tenets of Keynesian public policies were adopted in the United States. The basic elements of the modern monetarist view were first espoused by Irving Fisher in the latter part of the 1800's and the first two decades of this century, with antecedents going back at least to David Ricardo and Henry Thornton in the early 1800's. Although monetarism was popular and influential during the 1920's, the doctrine received scant attention after the Great Depression until the 1960's when the research of Clark Warburton, Milton Friedman, Anna Schwartz, and others became increasingly persuasive. It is tempting to argue that the perceptive research of modern-day monetarists and its persuasive and articulate presentation accounts for the major shift in views. But that explanation is too easy. Persuasive empirical evidence has long been extant. A better explanation is offered by the several recent head-on tests of the predictive power of Keynesian, or "New Economics," doctrines versus monetarism, combined with the emergence of monetarists in major policy-making roles in Washington. Episodic events offer limited scientific evidence for one view over another. Yet when backed up by voluminous basic research encompassing economic events over the past century, recent experience was a highly efficient and persuasive teacher.

UNDERSTANDING THE "NEW ECONOMICS"

The "new economics" preached and practiced in Washington from 1961 through 1968 was an attractively packaged ver-

---

[1] John M. Keynes, *The General Theory of Employment, Interest and Money* (New York: Harcourt, Brace & World, Inc., 1936).

sion of Keynesian economics first developed by John Maynard Keynes in his 1936 classic. Keynesian economists are frequently referred to as "new economists" or "fiscalists." The new economists adopted an activist role often described as "fine tuning" of the economy. Few quarrel with the objective of using monetary-fiscal and related economic policies to exert a stabilizing influence upon economic activity. A stabilizing set of economic policies would encourage high and relatively steady economic growth, low unemployment, and price stability. However, the record indicates that far from being "a step toward stability," as so frequently claimed, the new economics produced instability. Analysis of the theoretical underpinnings of the new economics doctrine reveals that the results were negative because of inherent weaknesses in the concept, not because of lack of dedication or lack of professional competence of responsible officials.

The hallmark of the new economics is the view that economic policy makers know enough to design and implement economic policies that will continuously give the right amount of economic stimulus or restraint. The new economics, based as it is on the Keynesian analytical framework, assigns star billing to fiscal policy and relegates monetary policy to at best a minor supporting role. Autonomous investment expenditures and federal tax and expenditure policies are regarded as exerting an important influence on private spending decisions. Hence, fiscal policy is the major policy tool available for influencing economic activity. Although there are several ways of measuring fiscal impact, new economists usually prefer to cite changes in the "full employment budget" as the best indicator of changing fiscal impact upon the economy.[2] An in-

---

[2] Arthur M. Okun, *The Political Economy of Prosperity* (Washington, D.C.: The Brookings Institution, 1970), pp. 45–46; Walter W. Heller, *New Dimensions of Political Economy* (Boston: Harvard University Press, 1966), p. 72.

It is interesting to note that although new economists utilize changes in the full employment budget to measure fiscal impact, the full employment budget concept

crease in the full employment deficit or a reduction in the full employment surplus is regarded as exerting an expansionary impact on the economy; a decreased deficit or an increased surplus, a restrictive effect. Monetary policy is considered an accommodating force at best, whose main task is to keep interest rates low in the cause of encouraging economic growth while providing favorable credit conditions for the housing industry. Furthermore, new economists typically measure monetary policy by the level of, and changes in, interest rates and free reserves rather than by such monetary aggregates as the money supply, bank reserves, or even total bank credit.[3]

Finally, the new economics warmly embraces the view that the economy is rife with monopolistic power both in industry and labor, and that wage-price guidelines effectively lower the inflation threshold and contribute significantly to the attainment of economic stability. Activism, emphasis on fiscal policy, de-emphasis of monetary policy, and application of "moral" suasion upon the marketplace were the essence of policies pursued.

THE MONETARIST VIEW

Economists subscribing to the monetarist view present a contrary doctrine. They argue that economic knowledge is imperfect and that frequent attempts to adjust economic stimulus or restraint emanating from government actions are more likely to destabilize the economy than to contribute to tranquillity. First, it is difficult to determine how fiscal or

---

was independently developed in the early postwar period by the Committee for Economic Development in *Taxes and the Budget: A Program for Prosperity in a Free Economy*, November, 1947, pp. 22–28; and by Milton Friedman in "A Monetary and Fiscal Framework for Economic Stability," *American Economic Review*, Vol. 38, No. 3, June, 1968, pp. 245–64.

[3] *Economic Report of the President* (Washington, D.C.: U.S. Government Printing Office, January, 1966), pp. 49–52.

monetary change should be measured.[4] Should fiscal change be measured by changes in the full employment budget, as frequently argued, or, alternatively, by changes in govenment spending, changes in the uniform budget, or changes in the national income budget? Should monetary change be measured by changes in interest rates or free reserves, as often contended by new economists; or by monetary aggregates preferred by monetarists, such as change in bank reserves, monetary base, the narrow money supply including demand deposits and currency; or the broader money supply also including time deposits of commercial banks? Not all these measurements of fiscal or monetary policy yield similar answers; hence, they are not likely to be equally valid.

Second, changes in policy affect the economy with a lag, and unfortunately the lags are somewhat variable. Even if we could specify the proper measurement of policy change, it would be impossible to predict when the change in policy would affect the economy. And even if the timing could be estimated satisfactorily, the magnitude of the effect on total spending would be uncertain. Reputable economists clearly disagree about the relative efficacy of monetary versus fiscal change. But they also disagree about the impact on spending of any particular policy change. Fiscalists usually estimate that a $1 billion change in fiscal stimulus would change spending by between $2 and $3 billion, but monetarists contend that the change would be near zero if monetary policy were unchanged. Monetarists usually estimate that a $1 billion change in the money supply would change spending by $5 to $6 billion, while fiscalists contend that the change would be much less.

Finally, even if the impact on spending could be estimated properly, frequent changes in policy would be stabilizing

---

[4] Beryl W. Sprinkel, "Techniques for Measuring the Impact of Monetary Policy," *Financial Analysts Journal*, September–October, 1967.

only if policy makers could predict correctly how much stimulus would be required at the future date when today's policy has its effect. Unfortunately, predicting the future trend of the economy is a hazardous business, especially at turning points of the business cycle, as will become evident in subsequent discussion. In other words, the period for which reliable forecasts can be made is frequently shorter than the lag between a policy change and its effect.

Therefore, most monetarists believe that a steady, persistently pursued policy of moderate monetary stimulus consistent with longer run growth needs of the economy will produce a greater degree of economic stability than an activist policy of fine tuning based on tenuous estimates of the future. Since most monetarists regard changes in the money supply as the best measure of monetary stimulus or restraint, which in turn is the major factor influencing total spending, policy prescriptions are frequently couched in terms of encouraging a relatively stable growth in the money supply ranging from 3 percent to 5 percent per year.

Monetarists interpret the empirical evidence as strongly suggesting that monetary change has a larger, more predictable, and quicker impact upon the economy than fiscal change and, indeed, as showing that fiscal change is not an important factor affecting aggregate demand.[5] Monetary change has a major effect on aggregate demand which, in turn, is related to such variables as GNP, prices, employment, profits, interest rates, and equity prices. Monetarists do not assert that fiscal change is unimportant, but merely that *by itself*—i.e., if the quantity of money is not affected—it has only minor effects on total spending and, hence, national income. Fiscal policy has important effects on the incidence of taxation, public versus private usage of resources, allocation of resources within the public

---

[5] Leonall C. Andersen and Jerry L. Jordan, "Monetary and Fiscal Actions: A Test of Their Relative Importance in Economic Stabilization," *St. Louis Federal Reserve Bank Review,* November, 1968, pp. 11–23.

sector, and similar issues. Furthermore, the size of the government deficit may influence the rate of monetary expansion, since Secretaries of Treasury are usually tempted to prevail upon the Federal Reserve to help finance a deficit; and the Fed often bends to the pressure. Monetarists maintain that the effect of a deficit on subsequent spending and income change depends critically on how the deficit is financed. If a deficit is financed by new money creation leading to a rapid increase in the money supply, subsequent spending and income creation will be speeded up. If a deficit is financed out of an existing money supply, the subsequent effect on total spending will be nominal.

Finally, most monetarists believe that the economy is highly competitive; therefore wage-price guidelines or controls are neither desirable nor effective. They argue that income creation, production, prices, and interest rates will respond to monetary change and that stable and moderate monetary growth will induce a high degree of economic stability conducive to real economic growth.

This cursory summary of the new economics and of the monetarist view has left out many relevant nuances. Monetarism and fiscalism are espoused by equally brilliant, logical, and articulate spokesmen. How then can the interested economist and observer choose? Philosophy, taste, prior training, vested interests resulting from years of teaching and researching often determine the choice. Yet there must be a better way, and the way has become increasingly evident in recent years. Economic research on these issues has been extant for many years. Yet it has been only in recent years that many observers began to change their minds about the relative efficacy of monetary and fiscal change. Surely the change did not emanate primarily from scholarly research efforts, even though research efforts played the critical role of offering an attractive alternative to doctrine underlying an unsuccessful policy. Much of the recent change in views within and without the economics profession has arisen from dissatisfaction with the predictive power of the Keynesian analytical system.[6] Doctrinaire views cannot long survive and prosper unless accompanied by performance. Since 1966 there have been at least four clear tests of the relative predictive power of the two approaches, and in each case monetarism yielded the better predictions. Let us briefly review these recent episodes.

MOMENTS OF TRUTH

A test of the relative predictive power of alternative ways of viewing the future requires that crucial variables point in opposite directions. For the monetarist-fiscalist debate, a satisfactory test requires that changes in the money supply on the one hand, and changes in the full employment budget on the other, predict opposite patterns of economic change. If both monetary and fiscal indicators point in the same direction, as has happened many times in the past, it is much harder to choose between the monetarist contention that monetary change caused the subsequent economic and financial market changes and the fiscalist contention that fiscal change was responsible. Fortunately for science as well as for future policy makers and investors, four episodes in the years spanning 1966–70 permit a reasonably definitive post mortem evaluation. Of course, it is impossible to prove that either view is the "ultimate truth." Yet the evidence during this time period is highly suggestive.

The first test occurred in 1966 and 1967. It will be recalled that the Viet Nam war began to heat up in earnest about mid-1965. Federal spending on the war and also on Great Society programs rose rapidly. The full employment budget shifted from a modest deficit of $0.2 billion in the first half of 1966 to a sizable deficit of $4.5 billion in the second half (see Chart 1). According to the gospel as espoused by Keynesian economists,

---

[6] Harvey D. Shapiro, "The Chicago School: Apostles of the Money Supply," *The Institutional Investor*, February, 1970, p. 36.

CHART 1

Full Employment Budget
(quarterly totals at annual rates, seasonally adjusted)

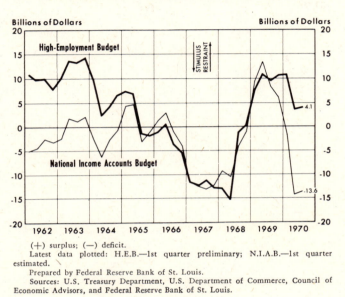

(+) surplus; (—) deficit.
Latest data plotted: H.E.B.—1st quarter preliminary; N.I.A.B.—1st quarter estimated.
Prepared by Federal Reserve Bank of St. Louis.
Sources: U.S. Treasury Department, U.S. Department of Commerce, Council of Economic Advisors, and Federal Reserve Bank of St. Louis.

this trend meant that the fiscal stimulus was increasing, since the government was spending much more than it was "taking out" of the economy in taxes. Therefore, those economists expected the economy to continue to expand rapidly and foresaw a very real possibility of acceleration of the inflation that had first become clearly evident in the last half of 1965.

A small fringe element in the economics profession took a diametrically opposite view, predicting that the economy would shortly enter a pause at best or a recession at worst. This expectation was based on the view that the restraining monetary impact upon the economy would prove more important than the expansive impact of a growing deficit. In the spring of 1966 the Federal Reserve became quite concerned about the accelerating inflation. Already in December 1965, the Federal Reserve raised the discount rate amidst widespread opposition by the administration, which argued that any move toward tightening should be delayed until the implications of the forthcoming budget message were evident. Despite the discount rate rise, expansion in the quantity of money continued unabated until about May 1966, when the Fed sharply slowed the rate of monetary growth. Monetary growth declined from a 5 percent annual rate in the first five months of 1966 to approximately zero from May 1966 to November 1966 (see Chart 2). Mone-

CHART 2

Money

(amount and turnover)

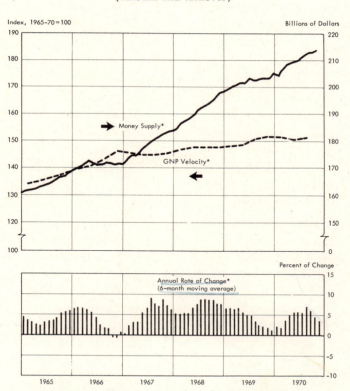

* Money supply = all comm'l. banks dem. dep. adj. + currency (seas. adj.).
Source: Dept. of Commerce, Federal Reserve Board.

tarists, true to their view about economic forces, predicted a significant slowing in economic activity in the first half of 1967.

What was the outcome? The economy moved into a period of pause or mini-recession in the first six months of 1967. Current GNP rose an average of $6.9 billion per quarter in those six months, compared to $15.2 billion per quarter in the prior year. Industrial production declined at an annual rate of 4.8 percent in the first six months of 1967, compared to a 3.8 percent annual rate of rise in the last six months of 1966. Prices, as measured by the Consumer Price Index, rose at the annual rate of only 1.1 percent in the first half of 1967, compared to 1.6 percent in the last half of the preceding year.

Monetary policy was eased in early 1967, and by the third quarter of 1967 economic expansion resumed with accompanying accelerating inflation. Both monetarists and fiscalists predicted a resumed growth at that time, since both monetary and fiscal change pointed toward expansion.

Clearly, the monetarist expectations for the first half of 1967 more closely approximated the actual trend of events than did the fiscalist expectations. But, of course, it is always possible for imaginative and articulate analysts to explain away a temporary aberration, and the fiscalists did. Few persons at that time were convinced that an important test had occurred which would shed light on later experience. In fact, considerable ridicule was poked at one prominent monetarist who had predicted a recession when, in fact, only a mini-recession occurred.

The 1966–67 exchange of arguments and epitaphs was only a warm-up for the much greater confrontation that occurred in 1968. After long deliberations within the administration, it was finally decided to ask for a large tax increase in order to cool a clearly overheated economy. Accordingly, in January 1967 President Johnson requested a large tax increase whose stated objective was to slow the rate of rise in the economy, reduce inflation, and lower interest rates. Since 1968 was an election year, this request for higher taxes displayed considerable political bravery. Congress was of course aware of the adverse political impact of a large tax increase in an election year and accordingly debated the request for 17 months, but finally in June 1968 enacted the surtax requested by the President. President Johnson signed the bill into law, and everyone sat back and waited for the widely advertised economic goodies to arrive. Unfortunately for the fiscalists, it was a long wait, even though there was ample reason for expecting an imminent slowdown if the budget really did exert an important independent effect on economic conditions. The full employment budget moved from a deficit at the annual rate of $15 billion in the second quarter of 1968 to a $10.7 billion surplus by the second quarter of 1969 (see Chart 1). A $25.7 billion restraining swing in the full employment budget was indeed a massive change. Little wonder that fiscalists almost uniformly predicted a significant slowing in the economy, reduced inflation, and lower interest rates.

Monetarists once again differed. They contended that, despite the dramatic shift in fiscal stimulus, monetary evidence pointed to full steam ahead. Monetary policy, as measured by growth in the money supply, had turned highly expansive throughout 1967 and through the first half of 1968 (see Chart 2). Unless they were to abandon their way of viewing the immediate future, they were forced to predict no significant slowing of the economy in response to the tax increase. The average annual rate of growth in the money supply averaged 6.0 percent in the last half of 1967 and 6.7 percent in the first half of 1968. They stuck to their theory and argued against a slowdown in the last half of 1968.

The Federal Reserve Board, according to later testimony,[7]

---

[7] "Record of Policy Actions of the Federal Open Market Committee," *Federal Reserve Bulletin,* November, 1968, pp. 910–19.

greatly feared "overkill" resulting from the dramatic fiscal change. Accordingly, in August 1968 the discount rate was reduced, and for a brief period of time, monetary growth accelerated further. Again the fat was in the fire. The August 1968 action of the Federal Reserve Board made the monetary-fiscal confrontation more decisive, although, as the test turned out, it also increased the overheating of the economy and greatly accelerated inflationary pressures, as monetarists expected. The scientific gain was bought at the nation's expense!

As the last half of 1968 unfolded, it appeared for a brief period that fiscal medicine was indeed having its predicted effect. Interest rates dropped sharply, and one of the major eastern banks reduced the prime rate, presumably in anticipation of a slowing economy. But the economy did not stick to the fiscal script. Again it danced to the tune of the dollar, inflation accelerated, interest rates rose, and the annual rate of GNP rose only $3.7 billion per quarter less in the last half than in the first half.

Monetarists explained the lack of significant economic slowing in the last half of 1968 by the prior and continued rapid growth in the money supply. They also argued that there was no *a priori* reason why a large tax increase with unchanged (or increased) monetary growth should deter spending. It is true, as fiscalists argue, that a tax increase reduces disposable income. That follows from the rules of arithmetic not economics. Will a sharp decrease in disposable income lead to a reduction in consumer spending? That all depends—sometimes it does and sometimes it doesn't. Consumer spending is usually believed to be determined by expected permanent income. If a tax increase is billed as a temporary affair, as was the 1968 tax bill, then there is little reason to expect a dramatic reduction in consumer spending. Reducing one's standard of living is a painful affair and is to be avoided at nearly all costs, especially if the income reduction is likely to be temporary.

Why not continue spending and finance that outlay by increased borrowing, reduced saving, and conversion of assets into spendable form? The continued rapid growth in consumer outlays in 1968, accompanied by a decreased savings rate and stepped-up consumer borrowing, suggests that is what happened.

It is necessary to trace the impact of the tax increase somewhat further. Again, arithmetical reasoning suggests that after the tax increase the federal government will have a smaller deficit to finance. This means that investors who would have bought the increased supply of government bonds now have funds available for other purposes, including purchasing other debt instruments such as corporate bonds, assuming that monetary policy remains unchanged. The freeing of additional funds for other purposes will offset, in dollar amounts, the tax increase or the reduction in the deficit. To a first approximation, will not the one offset the other? The monetarist answer is yes. Any possible restraining effect of the tax increase has to be sought at a much deeper level, in terms of its effects on interest rates and on rates of spending. But these effects are likely to be minimal. Therefore, in the judgment of the writer, there is no presumption that a temporary tax increase will restrain spending significantly if monetary policy remains unchanged. Of course, if monetary growth is also reduced at the time that taxes are increased, there is reason to expect spending to be restrained. However, much the same effect would follow from reduced monetary growth even if taxes were not increased. The monetarist regards the disposition of a surplus and the method of financing a deficit as critical in determining their impact on spending. But these matters reflect monetary, not fiscal, policy.

By early 1969 it was clear that the economy was not cooling. Even so, another interesting confrontation occurred. Although fiscalists were discouraged by the slowness of the economic response to the recommended fiscal medicine, their confidence in ultimate success was undiminished. The outgoing Council of Economic Advisers, in preparing its last economic report for the Johnson administration, predicted that the rate of rise in GNP would taper significantly in the first half of 1969 but would accelerate in the last half of the year because of an easing fiscal policy:

The fiscal restraint contained in the Revenue and Expenditure Control Act of 1968 will have its major impact on the economy early in 1969. . . . The first part of 1969 should see a slowing of economic expansion. . . . At mid-'69, a substantial pay increase for Federal Government employees is scheduled. Beyond that, only a slight increase for Federal Government employees is anticipated. The tax burden on consumers will also be reduced at that time as final settlements on 1968 taxes are completed in the first half of the year, although consumer spending should continue to feel the lagged effects of final settlements. These fiscal elements, together with a continued increase in private investments, are expected to lead to slightly more rapid economic expansion in the second half of the year.[8]

Monetarists, unimpressed by the fiscal evidence, predicted that the business pattern for the year ahead would be the exact opposite. They expected economic activity to be strong in the first half in response to the expansive monetary policy in 1968. But they expected activity in the last half to slow if monetary policy were tightened in the first half of 1969 according to the policy intent outlined by the incoming Nixon administration. In fact, monetary growth was sharply reduced in the first half of 1969; the economy remained strong in the first half of 1969, but then industrial production began to decline in August, and real GNP declined in the fourth quarter; unemployment began to rise; and the profit squeeze intensified. Again, forecasters relying on changes in the money supply

---

[8] *Economic Report of the President* (Washington, D.C.: U.S. Government Printing Office, January, 1969), pp. 55–56.

predicted the trend in the economy more accurately than did forecasters relying on fiscal change.

The most recent test developed in late 1969 and early 1970. Keynesian economists, relying on a projected reduction in the full employment surplus due especially to two scheduled tax cuts and a sharp projected rise in autonomous plant and equipment expenditures, predicted a strong economy in 1970 with only a modest slowing in the rate of rise in GNP and only a slight increase in unemployment. Monetarists, however, impressed with the considerable monetary restraint dating especially from the spring of 1969 and to a lesser extent as far back as the third quarter of 1968, flatly predicted a recession with declining real output at least in the first half, sharply rising unemployment, reduced corporate profits, and, with an appropriate lag, a lessening of inflationary pressure. As the year ended with unemployment near 6 percent of the labor force, industrial production off 7.5 percent from the July 1969 high, and the real GNP off slightly for the year, it was evident that the monetarists' expectations had again been largely realized, even though the rate of inflation was slightly more than expected.

SUMMING IT UP

To what does the recent evidence add up? One swallow does not make a spring, and four successes are hardly decisive. Four successive and successful tests cannot and should not convince everyone that the monetarist position is correct. If these episodes were the only evidence supporting the monetarist view, there would be little reason to be confident that money would continue to have the same relation to economic activity. However, recent confrontations were a major factor influencing observers to take seriously the monetarist interpretation. Yet these experiences are only a very small part of the total evidence available. Much more detailed and long-term evidence for the United States, as well as many other nations of the world, support the monetarist interpretation of income creation and financial market adjustments.

Indeed, recent events may have exerted too much influence on men's minds. Careful researchers have, for years, been compiling convincing evidence of the truth in the monetarist view of economic and financial events. Yet the public turned a deaf ear, as did most members of the economic profession. One should not conclude that the prior theorizing and research were in vain; its time simply had not arrived. Attention shifted toward an available alternative only when the fiscalist interpretation was found sadly lacking in predictive value. Fortunately, a carefully developed and researched body of theory and fact was readily available. If it had not been, economics would have slipped even further in the minds of the laymen as well as policy makers. Because of the success of recent monetarist tests, there is a danger that too much confidence will be placed in the monetarist relation. Although we can be confident that monetary change will have subsequent major effects on economic activity and financial markets, there is no reason to believe that nonmonetary factors have zero influence, or that the monetary effect will be uniform. We do not yet fully understand the adjustment process that accounts for the lag in effect and cannot predict the lag at all precisely. Although money clearly matters, it does not follow that only money matters. There are enough unknowns to provide ample room for further research by the current and prospective crop of students of money. But at long last the correct questions are being asked, some answers are available, and further answers can be expected.

2

The Explanation
in a Nutshell

What Are the Facts?

Economists are primarily interested in the monetarist explanation because of its distinct implications for economic policy, and ultimately economic performance as measured by economic growth, employment, and inflation. But the theory also has important implications for investors interested in changing asset values such as stock and bond prices. Only recently have economists plied their trade with some success to analysis of change in financial markets, and this tendency has received considerable impetus from the growing support for the explanation offered by the monetarist. It turns out that the modern quantity theory offers an adequate explanation of changes in income creation which, when combined with existing capacity of labor and capital resources, can be used for predicting employment changes and the probable degree of inflation. Volatility in monetary change has been in the past, and presumably will be in the future, closely related to the degree of

18

instability in economic performance as measured by such diverse aggregates as income creation, employment, prices, industrial output, and corporate profits.

But monetarism also offers a useful insight into the fluctuation of market prices closely related to the hearts of investors. Bull and bear stock markets have been closely associated with prior and coincident monetary change. Bond prices are also connected with monetary change through change in inflationary expectations. These expectations in turn appear to be correlated with past price changes which are influenced directly by earlier changes in monetary growth.

The empirically observed pattern of economic and financial events over a typical business cycle appears to be consistent with the explanation offered by the modern quantity theory. First we note that all business expansions have been preceded by increased growth in the money supply. If, in fact, expanding growth in the money supply causes subsequent acceleration in income creation, the modern quantity theory explains the ascending phase in a typical business recovery. Also, since income growth slows or actually becomes negative in an economic contraction, the prior reduction in monetary growth is consistent with a monetarist explanation. An acceleration in monetary growth during a recession or depression explains the tendency for income creation to recover beginning at the lower turning point of the economic contraction.

But inflation also has a cyclical characteristic. During the early phase of an economic expansion inflation is usually quite subdued. An increase in income creation is accompanied by an increase in real output, and prices do not rise significantly. So long as sufficient productive capacity is available, more rapid dollar income growth is typically accompanied by more rapid real growth. But after the economy approaches full employment of resources so that higher income creation cannot be accompanied by similar real income growth, expanding de-

mand is accompanied by rising prices. Even after income
growth slows near the peak of a business expansion, prices tend
to continue rising for a few quarters, but after the first or
second quarters of a recession, the rate of price rise typically
tapers as excess demand is removed from the economy. Inflation does not again become a serious problem until the subsequent recovery has proceeded to the point where rapid income
creation cannot be matched by equal real output gains.

Bond prices or their opposite (interest rates) tend to be at
their low (high) near business cycle highs when inflation is
near its peak. As inflationary fires cool in the subsequent recession, bond prices (interest rates) typically rise (fall). When
inflationary fears are renewed somewhere in the subsequent
recovery, bond prices (interest rates) typically go down (up) as
the demand for funds rises.

But stock prices typically lead business cycle turning points.
In other words, stock prices generally decline prior to the beginning of a recession, just as they usually rise in a recession
period well before the trough in the economic contraction has
been reached. Therefore, stock prices are a leading indicator of
economic activity. Knowing what is happening to business
activity and profits is not sufficient for predicting stock prices,
since prices move first. Chart 3 presents a schematic view
of the usual relations between business peaks and troughs and
such related variables as monetary growth, inflation, stock
prices, and bond prices.

The search for a method of anticipating major movements
in common stock prices has been eagerly pressed forward; but
success has been as elusive as the search for the fountain of
youth. Stock price trends are particularly difficult to predict,
since they appear to have no close and simple relation to the
general pattern of business and profits. It is true that economic
activity and stock prices go in the same direction about two-
thirds of the time, but it is the other third that is most interest-

CHART 3
Monetary Change and Markets

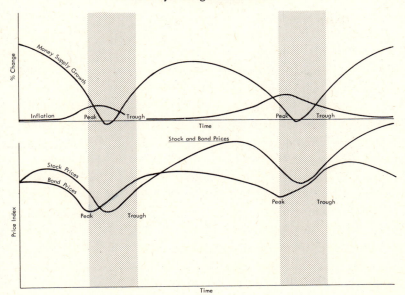

ing, and potentially most profitable. Usually, stock price changes move well ahead of subsequent business changes so that economic activity and share prices are moving in separate directions at the turning points in the market. Occasionally, stock prices forge a pattern all their own, apparently unrelated to the underlying business and profit trend. Even if predictions of future business trends were usually reliable, it would not be possible to detect turning points in stock prices unless business cycle turning points could be projected several months into the future. Unfortunately, business cycle forecasting is a hazardous art, particularly near turning points, and the longer the forecast period, the greater the probability of error.

Some market analysts have recognized the tendency of stock price changes to lead business cycle turning points, and have argued that the explanation for this relationship lies in the sagacity of the few analysts who foresaw the subsequent business change and achieved the appropriate action in the market prior to the change. Stock prices and business data are usually consistent with such an interpretation, but this hypothesis provides no guide to less farsighted observers. Furthermore, this explanation is not subject to test, for even though we may not know of anyone who consistently took the proper market action prior to subsequent economic changes, such a person or group of persons may exist. To complicate matters further, it is difficult to segregate fact from fancy. It always appears easier to locate investors who by their own testimony made the proper investment decision prior to a *past* market change than it is to find investors who announced their investment moves prior to predicted market movements which subsequently occurred. The leading stock price-business cycle relation has existed as far back into history as data are available; therefore, if someone knew the secret in the past, it was handed on to his successors. But the leading relation has been so stable over such a long period of time that we can be reasonably certain that something of more basic economic significance than a few successful forecasters explains the consistency.

Although economists have long been concerned with attempting to explain changes in general economic activity, relative prices of competing goods and services, and the general price level, until recently very little attention was given to explaining broad price changes in assets such as common stocks. In fact, most economists contended that changes in stock prices were not amenable to economic analysis. It was apparently believed that equity prices are determined more by chance than by reason. The oldest theory, and the most valid, as will be argued subsequently, purporting to explain changes in aggregate monetary demand relies on changes in the stock of money as the independent or causal factor. This theory is generally called the modern quantity theory of money, or monetarist explanation.

If, in fact, changes in the stock of money influence the will-ingness of consumers and investors to exchange money for goods and assets, there should be a demonstrable relation be-tween monetary change on the one hand and business and stock price changes on the other. Chart 4 relates peaks and

CHART 4

Liquidity Changes and Stock Prices

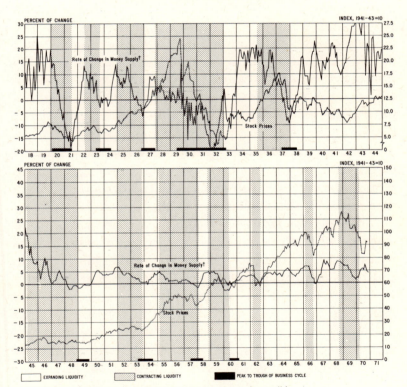

* All commercial banks demand deposits adj. + currency (seas. adj.).
† Annual rate of monthly change, 6-month moving average.
Price index scale different on upper and lower charts.
Source: Standard & Poor's Industrial, National Bureau of Economic Research, Inc., Federal Reserve Board.

troughs in the rate of change in the stock of money—demand deposits of commercial banks plus currency—to changes in stock prices and the underlying business trend. It is readily apparent that contracting liquidity usually precedes both declining stock prices and sagging business activity. The average time span between declining monetary growth and weak stock prices has been about nine months, whereas weaker liquidity has preceded a business contraction by sixteen months on the average. Therefore, stock prices have usually declined an average of seven months prior to a weaker business trend. Recently there has been a sporadic tendency for the lead of money over bear markets to shorten.

In the past 52 years, however, there have been three sizable market breaks that were not preceded by contracting liquidity or shortly followed by a business decline. These breaks occurred in 1939–40, 1962, and 1966, the latter two followed by a pause in economic activity. Clearly, factors other than money occasionally influence equity prices, and sometimes the impact of monetary change is registered on equity prices more quickly than at other times. The beginning and spreading of World War II undoubtedly destroyed confidence in stock prices in 1939 and 1940, despite the underlying favorable monetary trend. In both 1962 and 1966 monetary contraction occurred at about the same point in time that stock prices peaked, and a bear market continued until monetary growth was increased. Although contracting monetary growth trends were closely associated with both the 1962 and 1966 breaks, the usual lead before bear markets did not exist. Perhaps a growing realization of the impact of reduced monetary growth on equity prices accounted for the sharply reduced lead. Prior to the 1969 bear market, monetary growth declined for a longer period than in either 1962 or 1966. In fact, if the highest rate of monetary growth occurring in October 1967 is chosen as the peak, changing money led the stock market peak by fourteen months. Only an unfolding of the future will determine whether the recent tendency for a shortening lead of monetary growth over bear markets will continue. Since investors as well as economists appear to be paying more attention to changes in monetary growth, such a development appears possible. In other words, it may continue to be more difficult for a monetary analyst to get a jump on his competitors in the investment market. It may still be worth the effort, however, since the returns are inevitably high. Chart 4 also clearly indicates that rising liquidity trends precede a recovery in stock prices and an expansion in economic activity. But the elapsed lead time is less. Expanding money typically precedes a rise in stock prices by about two months, whereas it precedes an expanding business trend by about eight months. There appears to have been no significant exception to this leading relation in the past 52 years. Following the bear markets of 1962, 1966, and 1969–70 monetary expansion gave an adequate indication of an imminent bull market for the careful monetary analyst to make appropriate investment decisions.

It therefore follows that an investor who based his stock market decisions over the past 52 years upon expanding and contracting monetary growth would have participated in all bull markets. He would have avoided most bear markets but, in recent years, only if he recognized the shortening lead of monetary growth over bear markets. Investors searching for and realistically hoping to find the magic touchstone which will bring certainty in all future stock market timing decisions should cease reading at this point. Those wishing to improve the probability of being right on future investment decisions may find this book of continuing interest.

If an investor can properly measure and interpret changing monetary trends, the correct investment action is usually indicated in advance of the time for action. Therefore, an investor can develop an additional safeguard against the hazard to which many investors are prone—buying at high markets when optimism is at a peak and selling at the low when pessimism is rampant. But before a new investment technique can be used successfully, it must be understood. Understanding is the first hesitant but necessary step toward developing confidence. Without confidence, the temptation to abandon an investment approach when doubts first arise is irresistible. It is, of course, much easier to state the above principle than to follow it in practice.

The remainder of this book will deal with such questions as the following: What is money? Why should monetary change influence economic activity and bond and equity prices? What determines changes in monetary trends? How do the Federal Reserve and commercial banking systems fit into this picture? How can monetary change best be measured? What are other useful approaches to business cycle prediction? Why is monetary change a major causal factor in business cycles? Why does "too much" money cause inflation? What are the hazards of applying monetary analysis to the timing of stock market action? What does monetary change and inflation do to bond prices? What effect should tax factors have on investment timing decisions? How can monetary expertise be applied to investment policy decisions? Why is inflation bad for both stock and bond prices? If monetarism is to rule the 1970's, what are the implications for economic growth and investment performance? These questions are not exhaustive, but are meant to be suggestive of the discussion to follow. Now let us briefly consider the sixty-four-dollar question: Why should monetary changes make a difference?

It is an easy task for an imaginative analyst to "explain" past business, and stock and bond price trends by resorting to *ad hoc* reasoning. Unfortunately, there are frequently as many explanations as there are imaginative analysts. Clearly, the objective of a careful student of economic affairs should be to isolate a simple and ubiquitous explanation which is consistent with factual trends over a long period of time and under widely varying circumstances. To fabricate a tailor-made explanation for each event may create the impression of ingenuity or freshness of approach, but provides little enlightenment on future events. Many observers apparently feel that to be satisfactory an explanation must be highly descriptive of the event under analysis. This method dotes on citing many variables and their possible influence. The eclectic approach gives the impression of being exhaustive, but because of the limitations of both the human mind and mathematical formulations, the results are frequently of limited use.

The approach taken in subsequent analysis may appear limited in scope and narrow in concept. But it will attempt to isolate a major variable which offers a plausible explanation consistent with most empirical patterns of business cycle trends, inflation, and stock and bond prices. The viewpoint taken is that the usefulness of a theory is not measured by its ability to describe but by its ability to predict. A theory which does not describe in detail the results under question may in one sense be labeled unrealistic, but may at the same time be extremely useful if it is capable of predicting many later events. In other words, a theory may properly be rejected if it is incapable of yielding useful predictions, but cannot be disproven by questioning the "reasonableness" of underlying assumptions. A theory capable of yielding useful predictions concerning economic events must concentrate on the most basic underlying relations, and will, therefore, be as simple as possible and narrow in scope, but broad in terms of useful implications.

WHAT IS MONEY?

Money is easily the most sought after, the most frequently condemned, and the least understood element in our complex world. Confusion over the concept of money is partly due to lack of agreement on definition of the term. To the poor man pursuing money so that he may buy the basic necessities of life, it may represent the only means of survival in a cold, competitive world. To others more fortunate, money may represent the means of acquiring the material and spiritual extras in life that make living easier and more rewarding. To the miser, money may not represent a means to an end, but rather an end in iself. To the social philosopher who does not approve of letting the free market determine how money is spent, it may be roundly condemned because it stands as a symbol of greed and inequity. To a few members of the "turned on" generation, it is an object of derision so long as a sufficient quantity is provided by doting parents.

Since some form of money or credit is used in the production, sale, and exchange of all goods and services, it is clear that money is a pervasive phenomenon in our free, competitive economy. Because of its widespread use and influence, it is not difficult to imagine that money can be a force for great good or evil in the economy as a whole. A proper understanding of its effect on the economy can be used for both public and personal gain. Specifically, a proper understanding of the influence of money can contribute greatly to our understanding of changes in the business cycle and the financial markets. Although it would be irresponsible to contend that such an understanding makes perfect predictions of business and market changes possible, monetary analysis can provide useful guidance. Imperfect though our understanding may be, enough is now known about the role of money and its effects on economic activity in general, and the financial markets in particular, to enable an astute investor to take these factors into consideration.

To the economist, when considering it from an analytical viewpoint, money represents a medium by which goods and services can be exchanged conveniently, and because of its widespread acceptance in trade, it frequently acts as a liquid medium for storing value, as do other forms of assets. Money performs so many roles in our economy, some of which are performed by all assets, that it is impossible to specify uniquely on mere *a priori* grounds what the term covers. Clearly, cash in circulation (representing liabilities of the U.S. Treasury and the Federal Reserve banks) is money. Demand deposits in banks also are money, since they are readily acceptable in most circumstances, even though it may be difficult to write a check against a demand deposit when you have no satisfactory means of identification. Certainly, time deposits in commercial banks partially serve the liquidity role of money, as do shares in savings and loan associations, deposits in mutual savings banks, U.S. government savings bonds, and short-term U.S. government securities. To a lesser extent, other less liquid assets such as long-term bonds, stocks, and real estate act as a store of value. There is, clearly, a continuum of assets which more or less meets the store-of-liquidity specification for money, even though such assets do not serve as a medium of exchange.

The selection of a meaningful definition of money must be based on empirical evidence rather than theoretical arguments, since the *a priori* approach does not yield a clear-cut answer. The definition selected should be the one which bears the most consistent relationship to subsequent economic events.

Several studies have investigated the relation of money to the economy, and each attempted to determine the "proper" definition of money by use of empirical evidence.[1]

Meltzer, Feige, Andersen, and Jordan concluded that money should be defined to include demand deposits and currency.

---

[1] Milton Friedman and David Meiselman, "The Relative Stability of Monetary Velocity and the Investment Multiplier in the United States, 1897–1958," *Stabilization Policies,* prepared for the Commission on Money and Credit (Englewood Cliffs, N.J.: Prentice-Hall, 1963), pp. 165–268; Allen H. Meltzer, "The Demand for Money: The Evidence from the Time Series," *Journal of Political Economy,* June, 1963, pp. 219–46; Edgar L. Feige, "The Demand for Liquid Assets: A Temporal Cross-Section Analysis" (Ph.D. thesis, University of Chicago, 1963); Leonall C. Andersen and Jerry L. Jordan, "Monetary and Fiscal Actions: A Test of Their Relative Importance in Economic Stabilization," *Federal Reserve Bank of St. Louis Review,* November, 1968, p. 14. Also Milton Friedman and Anna Schwartz, *Monetary Statistics of the United States* (National Bureau of Economic Research, Columbia University Press, 1970), pp. 89–197.

The Friedman-Meiselman and Friedman-Schwartz studies concluded that time deposits of commercial banks should be added, since their money-income correlations were improved moderately. Each study rejected the inclusion of still broader assets such as savings and loan shares.

If we observe the changes in monetary growth of the two series in the postwar period we find they usually move up and down together (see Chart 5). In recent years volatility in the broader series, including time deposits in commercial banks, has been greater than in the narrow series including only demand deposits in commercial banks and currency. This is due to the fact that in recent years of high and rising interest rates, Regulation Q, which establishes legal ceiling rates that banks can pay for time money, has frequently prevented commercial banks from competing for the saver's dollar with open market instruments such as Treasury bills and commercial paper. Hence, during such periods, time money grew much less rapidly than demand money. Therefore, the narrow series displayed a steadier growth. During periods when commercial bank ceiling rates became fully competitive with open market instruments, time money grew more rapidly than demand money. Hence, greater volatility occurred for the broader series. But periods of savings outflow from commercial banks do not mean that liquidity in the total economic system is being reduced by that amount since the funds flow into open market instruments and frequently are ultimately converted to demand deposits. Users of the broader series usually eliminate the disintermediation effect in such periods by subtracting corporate certificates of deposit. Once Regulation Q is eliminated as an important market influence there appears to be little reason for choosing one series over the other. The two series would give equally valid interpretations of changing monetary impact upon the economy. In the meantime, the narrow series appears to be least distorted by artificial market impediments.

CHART 5

Flows of Money and Credit

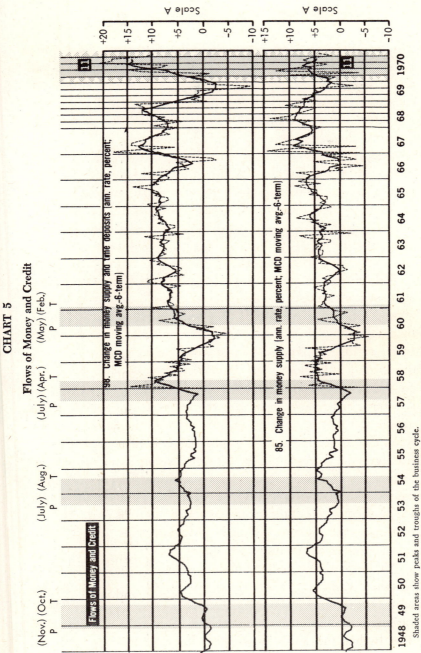

Shaded areas show peaks and troughs of the business cycle.
Jagged edge denotes a slowdown in business which may possibly be defined as a recession.
Source: U.S. Department of Commerce, *Business Conditions Digest*, December, 1970.

When the word "money" is used later in this text, it will refer simply to the total of the public's holdings of coin, currency, and demand deposits in banks. Money will, therefore, consist of private demand deposits subject to check and cash. The only defensible reasons for thus arbitrarily restricting our definition are that the concept is simple, money so defined is apparently as closely related to subsequent economic events as money more broadly defined would be, and in recent years it has been a better indicator of changing monetary impact.

HOW DOES MONEY INFLUENCE THE ECONOMY AND ASSET PRICES?

The impulse of changing money influences the economy and asset prices through its impact on total demands for assets, goods, and services. Potential economic production is determined by real supply factors such as the size and quality of the labor force, average hours of work, the stock and quality of capital, the state of technology, and the efficiency with which resources are combined. The degree of utilization of economic resources is determined primarily by the volume of total demand—that is, whether or not demand is large enough to utilize available resources at existing prices. In other words, the actual production of goods and services will depend not only on real supply factors but also on changes in total demands. With given supply conditions, the volume of total demand will determine the amount of actual production, income, and employment attained in the economy. But how does changing money influence aggregate demand?

Although the amount of money actually circulating in the economy is largely beyond the control of private spending units, the demand for money tends to be a stable relation varying only with such factors as real income and interest rates. The higher the levels of income, the larger the amount of money spending units desire to hold. Also, the lower the level of interest rates, the greater the amount of money spending units are willing to hold, since the cost of maintaining liquidity is reduced. Individuals and business firms will attempt to distribute their holdings of assets in such a way that the income or satisfaction from like units will yield the same benefits. If individuals and businesses feel they have inadequate liquidity, they will attempt to convert nonliquid assets into liquid funds. Also, by reducing expenditures relative to incomes, individual spending units will attempt to build up their liquidity. But these actions will tend to place downward price pressure on less liquid assets such as common stocks and bonds. The attempt to reduce spending relative to income will have the effect of reducing total demand and, consequently reducing incomes, employment, and, eventually, the general price level if spending declines enough. Therefore, decreased liquidity resulting from reduced monetary expansion or monetary contraction contains the forces to prevent further increases in total demand and, hence, increases in real economic activity.

Conversely, a rapid rise in overall liquidity resulting from an increase in monetary growth tends to have the opposite effect. As "excessive" liquidity develops, spending units are induced to exchange money for less liquid forms of assets. This action tends to place upward pressure on the prices of less liquid assets such as common stocks and bonds. Also, spending units are inclined to attempt to reduce liquidity by increasing spending on goods and services relative to the current flow of income. This action raises the overall level of monetary demand, resulting in either a higher level of production of goods and services if unemployed resources are available, or upward pressure on the general price level if full employment of resources exists.

Not only does monetary change influence asset prices directly by changing liquidity incentives, but also the indirect effects may be even more important. Excessive money creation inevitably creates serious inflation, which results in higher interest rates that adversely influence bond prices and stock prices as well, unless inflation adds commensurately to profits. A tighter monetary policy designed to bring an inflation under control also exerts short-run pressure toward even higher interest rates and hence lower asset prices. But a tighter monetary policy also slows the growth in total spending and places downward pressure on corporate profits, which further depresses equity prices. Of course, reduced inflation followed by lower interest rates and an expanding economy accompanied by rising corporate profits exert a positive influence on both stock and bond prices.

Now to briefly recapitulate the argument. It was demonstrated that changing monetary growth typically precedes changing equity prices which, in turn, usually move in advance of overall business fluctuations that tend to coincide with interest rate changes. Liquidity change, as defined, consists of changes in money—that is, demand deposits of commercial banks and currency. A condensed version of a long-lived and recently revived theory, generally labeled the modern quantity theory of money or monetarist explanation, was presented to show that this explanation is consistent with observed trends in money, stock prices, bond prices, inflation, and business cycles. Although this explanation may at first blush appear unrealistic in a descriptive sense, readers are cautioned not to reject the point of view unless it yields inadequate predictions. The next major step is to understand the forces which cause a change in the stock of money and, hence, trigger the chain of responses in the equity market, the bond market, economic activity, and price levels. Unless the major causal forces can be isolated, a developing monetary trend cannot be understood, nor can a prospective change be detected.

CHAPTER 3

What Causes the Money Supply To Fluctuate?

The simple and essentially correct answer to this question is that monetary policy as formulated and executed by the Federal Reserve Board establishes the prevailing trend in the stock of money. But adequate comprehension of the answer must be based on knowledge of the elementary structure of the banking system, an understanding of the process of money creation and destruction, and the ability to analyze changes in the sources and uses of commercial bank reserve funds. Although mastery of these matters is inevitably somewhat tedious, the results will hopefully be worth the effort.

Basic Structure of the Banking System

Approximately 43 percent of the nation's 13,700 commercial banks are members of the Federal Reserve System. But these member banks are the larger institutions and account for about 82 percent of total demand deposits. Furthermore, nonmember banks are either directly or indirectly influenced by Federal Reserve policy. The Federal Reserve Board is thus able to determine changes in the stock of money because of its ability to regulate banks which contain most demand deposits, the major component of the money supply.

Member banks of the Federal Reserve System assume certain obligations in return for receiving privileges of membership.[1] The primary obligation with regard to monetary change is maintaining legal reserves on deposit without interest at the reserve bank (except those reserves held as vault cash). Other subsidiary requirements include: (1) the remittance at par for checks drawn against them when presented by a reserve bank for payment; (2) compliance with various federal laws, regulations, and conditions of membership concerning the adequacy of capital, mergers with other banks, establishment of branches, relations with holding companies, interlocking directorates, and loan and investment limitations.

From the point of view of monetary control, the most important privileges extended to member banks are the following: (1) the privilege of borrowing from the reserve bank, subject to criteria for discounting set by statute and regulation, when a temporary need for funds arises; (2) the privilege of using Federal Reserve facilities for collecting checks, settling clearing balances, and transferring funds to other locations. Subsidiary privileges include: (1) obtaining currency from the reserve bank when required; (2) sharing in the informational facilities provided by the system; (3) participation in the election of six of the nine directors of the Federal Reserve bank for their district; (4) receiving a dividend of 6 percent on the paid-

[1] For greater detail, see Board of Governors of the Federal Reserve System, *The Federal Reserve System, Purposes, and Functions* (Washington, D.C., 1963).

in capital stock of the Federal Reserve bank which each member bank is required to purchase as a condition of membership.

There are twelve Federal Reserve districts across the nation with a Federal Reserve bank located in each district. Several of the Federal Reserve banks also have branches. While the Federal Reserve banks earn an income, largely from the U.S. government securities owned, their operations are not carried on primarily for profit, but for the purpose of conducting monetary policy. Income is used for paying expenses and maintaining a proper surplus. The remainder of the earnings is paid to the U.S. Treasury.

The top policy-making body of the central bank is the Board of Governors of the Federal Reserve System, with offices in Washington, D.C. It consists of seven members appointed by the president of the United States and subject to confirmation by the Senate. Board appointments are for terms of fourteen years, with terms expiring every two years. The Board's main functions are to formulate and execute monetary policy and supervise the operations of the Federal Reserve System. It has full authority over changes in reserve requirements, and also "reviews and determines" discount or borrowing rates established by each of the twelve Federal Reserve banks.

The federal Open Market Committee has responsibility for changes made in the System's portfolio of government securities. It decides the amount and timing of purchases and sales of government securities in the open market. The authority to buy and sell government securities is one of the most important monetary controls exercised by the Federal Reserve System. Membership on the Open Market Committee is comprised of the seven members of the Board of Governors and five of the twelve presidents of district Federal Reserve banks. Actual purchases and sales of securities for the federal Open Market Committee are made through the facilities of the Federal Reserve Bank of New York.

The Federal Reserve System once had a reserve requirement in the form of gold certificates held as reserves—a stipulated proportion of its liabilities in the form of Federal Reserve notes and deposits. Although President Kennedy once contemplated eliminating this gold reserve requirement, the deluge of mail from "gold" sensitive citizens was so large that scheduled hearings were canceled and the idea was discarded. Years later after further gold loss and many billions of dollars accumulated deficits in the balance of payments, President Johnson quietly requested and received authority to eliminate the gold reserve requirement of the Federal Reserve in a two-stage phase out. The time for removal of this anachronism had arrived. Existence of the gold reserve requirement had never significantly influenced monetary policy, but it remained a potential source of instability until it was removed. The U.S. Treasury remains the custodian of all monetary reserves held in the form of gold, and the Federal Reserve still carries gold certificates which represent the actual gold in its balance sheet, but there is no required gold reserve ratio.

To summarize, the Federal Reserve System exercises control over the nation's commercial banking system primarily through its influence on member banks which hold about 82 percent of total demand deposits, the major component of the money stock. Member banks must hold the bulk of their reserves with the district Federal Reserve bank. The Federal Reserve System influences the amount and cost of acquiring bank reserves by use of three major tools: (1) changes in reserve requirements, (2) changes in the discount rate, and (3) open market operations. The Board of Governors has complete authority in determining reserve requirements; discount rates are established by each of the twelve Federal Reserve banks, and the Board of Governors "reviews and determines" the rates; finally, the federal Open Market Committee consisting of the seven Board members and five of the twelve

regional Federal Reserve bank presidents determines purchases and sales in the open market from the System's portfolio of government securities. By far the most important
control technique is open market operations as measured either
by frequency of use or magnitude of effect.

Money is an asset of its holder, but it is a liability of some
financial institution. The various components of the stock of
money, consisting of demand deposits and currency, are liabilities of either commercial banks, the U.S. Treasury, or Federal
Reserve banks. Most demand deposits included in the money
stock are liabilities of commercial banks; U.S. notes and coins
are liabilities of the U.S. Treasury, while Federal Reserve
notes are liabilities of the Federal Reserve banks. Therefore, it
is apparent that the stock of money can vary only as the liabilities of various financial institutions change.

In developing an understanding of the U.S. banking system
and the process of monetary change, it is useful to observe
partial balance sheets or T-accounts of three institutions—the
U.S. Treasury, the Federal Reserve System, and the commercial
banking system. We are interested in only those portions of
total assets and liabilities closely related to the monetary system.

First let us consider the U.S. Treasury, which is the custodian of the monetary gold stock. Most changes in the country's
gold stock are the result of transactions with foreign countries.
On December 31, 1969, the U.S. gold stock amounted to $10.4
billion, as indicated in Table 1, and gold certificates had been
issued to Federal Reserve banks amounting to $10.0 billion.
Gold is an asset of the Treasury, and gold certificates are a
noninterest-bearing liability. Also, Treasury deposits with Federal Reserve banks appear as an asset. In addition, $6.8 billion
of Treasury currency, which is part of the stock of money, had
been issued by the Treasury and was, therefore, another noninterest-bearing liability.

The Federal Reserve System holds all the gold certificates

TABLE 1

Partial Balance Sheets, December 31, 1969
(billions of dollars)

U.S. Treasury

Gold	$ 10.4	Gold certificates	$ 10.0
Deposits with Federal Reserve banks	1.3	Treasury currency outstanding	6.8

Federal Reserve System

Gold certificates	$ 10.0	Federal Reserve notes	$ 47.3
		Deposits of member banks	22.1
		U.S. Treasury deposits	1.3
		Foreign deposits	0.1
		Other deposits	0.8

71.6

Commercial Banking System

Deposits with Federal Reserve	$ 22.1	Demand deposits adjusted	$167.3
		Time deposits adjusted	192.4

Holders of Money

Currency in circulation	$ 46.3
Demand deposits adjusted	167.3

203,6

issued by the Treasury, so this item appears in the Federal Reserve partial balance sheet as an asset. Federal Reserve liabilities directly related to the money supply on December 31, 1969, amounted to $71.6 billion, consisting largely of $47.3 billion Federal Reserve notes, which are a part of the money stock, and $22.1 billion of member bank deposits which serve as member bank reserves. Most U.S. Treasury payments are made by checks written on a Federal Reserve bank, so U.S. Treasury funds are on deposit with Federal Reserve banks. The relevant portions of the commercial banking system's balance sheet consist of the asset representing deposits with the Federal Reserve banks, vault cash holdings of currency and coins, and liabilities consisting of deposits. The reserve requirement ratio for country banks at year-end 1969 amounted to 12½ percent for demand deposits under $5 million and 13 percent for those over $5 million; reserve city banks had a required reserve ratio of 17 percent for deposits under $5 million and 17½ percent for those over $5 million. The weighted average demand deposit required reserve ratio is now about 15.1 percent. All commercial banks have a required reserve ratio of 3 percent against savings deposits and other time deposits under $5 million and 6 percent for other time deposits in excess of $5 million. On December 31, 1969, excess reserves of the commercial banking system amounted to only $528 billion—that is the difference between total reserves and required reserves.

Finally, the stock of money consisting of currency outstanding and demand deposits is at all times held by some owner and, therefore, appears as an asset in the combined partial balance sheet of money holders.

THE PROCESS OF MONETARY CHANGE

Since demand deposits of commercial banks are the largest and most readily controlled component of the stock of money, it is imperative that students of money understand how demand deposits change if they are to understand the process of money creation and destruction.[2] For the moment, we will suspend consideration of *how* total reserves change and concentrate on the response of the commercial banking system to a change in total reserves. As a useful first approximation, it may be stated that the maximum amount of demand deposits that can be outstanding at any time is fixed by the average required reserve ratio and total reserves held by commercial banks. Commercial banks are required to maintain reserves in the form of either deposits with Federal Reserve banks or cash in their vaults of not less than a specified fraction of commercial bank deposits. Therefore, commercial bank deposits cannot exceed the amount their total reserves will support.

---

[2] See Federal Reserve Bank of Chicago, *Modern Money Mechanics*, May, 1961, for a more elaborate treatment of this subject.

For example, if we assume the average required reserve ratio is 15 percent and total reserves (available to support demand deposits) $16 billion, total demand deposits could not exceed $106.67 billion. In other words, each $1.00 of reserves could support $6.67 of demand deposits. An amount of demand deposits in excess of $106.67 billion would create a reserve deficiency which would require either an increase in reserves or a reduction in demand deposits.

But banks may maintain what are called excess reserves—in excess of the required minimum—and deposits may, therefore, be less than the amount supportable by total reserves. However, since banks enjoy no return on excess reserves—that is, the Federal Reserve pays no interest on commercial bank deposits —the profit motive insures that *most* excess funds will be loaned or invested except in very unusual circumstances such as those during the Great Depression. However, institutional and economic factors result in some excess reserves even in more normal periods. For example, excess reserves averaged $257 million or 0.9 percent of total reserves in December 1969. Most reserves are fully utilized, since banks have an incentive to convert excess reserves to required reserves by expanding loans and/or investments and, hence, deposits. With a fixed required reserve ratio, factors that change total bank reserves will also tend to change the total stock of money in the same direction, but by a multiple amount.

But what is the process by which a given increase in total reserves results in a multiple expansion in demand deposits? An example would perhaps clear up the matter. Let us again assume an average required reserve ratio of 15 percent for all member banks, and let us further assume that the Federal Reserve System increases total reserves by an amount of $1 million which ends up as reserves of commercial bank A.

Assume, also, that the initial increase in total reserves was brought about in a way that did not affect required reserves in the first instance. Therefore, excess reserves of commercial bank A rose $1 million also, since total reserves — required reserves = excess reserves. We will not now inquire into the means by which the Federal Reserve increased total and excess reserves, but will concentrate on the effect this action might have on commercial banks.

Since commercial bank A now has excess reserves on which no return is being earned, there is an incentive to either loan or invest the funds. The effect on the stock of money would be the same regardless of whether the funds were *loaned* or *invested*. If business activity is strong, the funds would probably be loaned, since the rate of return tends to be higher, and a bank usually feels a strong responsibility to meet the credit demands of its customers. In making a loan, a bank typically accepts a promissory note in exchange for credit to the borrower's deposit account. Hence, bank A's loans (assets) and deposits (liabilities) both rise by $1 million. Total reserves are unaffected by the above transaction, but excess reserves decline by $150,000, since demand deposits, against which a 15 percent required reserve ratio prevails, rose by $1 million. Excess reserves are now $850,000. Up to the present, the increase in the stock of money (demand deposits in this case) has been $1 million, the same as the initial increase in total reserves and excess reserves. But 85 percent of the initial excess reserves remain in the banking system.

Bank A did not expect to retain the deposits created through its loan operations. Borrowers acquired the funds for spending, and checks are drawn against the new funds and deposited in other banks. Although banks typically require that compensating balances be maintained in the lending bank, this complication will be ignored, for it does not affect the essential nature of the multiple expansion process. When the funds are transferred to another bank, they are not extinguished but remain in the banking system. Whichever bank receives the new deposits will also hold an equal amount of reserves, of which all but 15 percent will be excess, that is, $850,000. We will assume that bank B, which received the deposit, also wants to get its excess funds to work earning a return, and that the amount of the excess reserves, $850,000, is loaned to a customer. Bank B will accept a promissory note equal to $850,000, and will in return credit the borrower's deposit account for a like amount. Bank B will now have $1 million reserves more than prior to the deposit from bank A—$1.85 million deposits more than previously—and still have excess reserves amounting to $850,000 × 85 percent, or $722,000. Bank A at this point will have lost the initial reserve and deposit, but loans would be $1 million higher. It is important to recognize that $722,000 excess reserves still remain in the banking system, even though total deposits are already increased $1.85 million on the basis of the initial increase of $1 million in total and excess reserves.

Let us trace these transactions through bank A and bank B with the aid of partial balance sheets or T-accounts (Table 2).

TABLE 2

Partial Balance Sheets

	Bank A	
(1)	Loans + $1 million	Demand deposits + $1 million
(2)	Reserves − $1 million	Demand deposits − $1 million

	Bank B	
(3)	Reserves + $1 million	Demand deposits + $1 million
	Loans + $850,000	Demand deposits + $850,000

Remember that bank A made the initial loan and deposit credit because it had $1 million excess reserves. The initial deposit made in bank B is usually termed a primary deposit, whereas the deposit resulting from the loan is called a derivative deposit. Note that when bank B's derivative deposit is withdrawn, deposits and reserves each will decline by $850,000, and bank B will then have zero excess reserves, even though total reserves are $150,000 higher than prior to the primary deposits of $1 million. If the derivative deposit is made with bank C, that bank will then have excess reserves of $722,000 and can make a loan and deposit credit of that amount. At that point, total deposits will be $2.572 million greater than initially, and $614,000 excess reserves will remain in the banking system.

When the remaining excess reserves of $614,000 are converted into required reserves in the manner described above, the total increase in demand deposits, that is, the money stock resulting from the initial increase of $1 million in excess reserves, will be $6,666,666.67. Therefore, it is correct to say that with a given increase in excess reserves, there will be an ultimate multiple expansion in loans and/or investments which results in a multiple demand deposit expansion. The size of the potential multiple expansion will depend on the average required reserve ratio for demand deposits. The smaller the average required reserve ratio, the larger the ultimate expansion. The multiple will be equal to the reciprocal of the average required reserve ratio, that is, multiple $= 1/$average required reserve ratio. In the above case, the expansion factor $= 1/0.15 = 6\frac{2}{3}$. Table 3 summarizes the response of the commercial banking system to the initial $1 million.

As a practical matter the preceding example overstates the expansion factor since a rise in demand deposits is usually accompanied by a rise in currency in circulation (internal drain). Each one dollar rise in currency in circulation reduces commercial bank reserves by a like amount and hence limits ultimate increases in the money supply. Nonetheless the practical expansion factor is sizable.

It is important to recognize that it was the *banking system* and not a *single bank* that achieved a multiple demand deposit expansion on the basis of a given amount of excess reserves. A single bank could make loans and/or investments equal only

TABLE 3

Monetary Expansion Process

	Assets (in Thousands of Dollars)				
	Reserves				*Liabilities,*
				Loans and/or	*(Demand*
Total			*Required*	*Excess*	*Investments*	*Deposits)*
Initial reserves provided	1,000	......	0	1,000		
Expansion—Stage 1	1,000	......	150	850	1,000	1,000
2	1,000	......	278	722	1,850	1,850
3	1,000	......	386	614	2,572	2,572
4	1,000	......	478	522	3,186	3,186
5	1,000	......	556	444	3,708	3,708
6	1,000	......	623	377	4,152	4,152
7	1,000	......	680	320	4,529	4,529
8	1,000	......	728	272	4,849	4,849
9	1,000	......	769	231	5,121	5,121
10	1,000	......	803	197	5,352	5,352
Final stage	1,000	......	1,000	0	6,667	6,667

to the amount of excess reserves, and, hence, derivative demand deposits could rise only by a like amount. Reference to Table 2 will clarify this distinction. Bank A which began the process with $1 million excess reserves made a loan of only $1 million and credited demand deposit accounts by a like amount. At that instant, bank A still had $850,000 excess reserves, which would suggest that a sizable further loan and deposit expansion was possible. Yet, if additional loans had been made and demand deposit accounts credited accordingly, the bank would have ended up in a deficit reserve position after the derivative deposits were transferred. It should be noted that after the initial derivative deposit of bank A was transferred, the bank no longer had excess reserves, since total reserves were decreased by $1 million consisting of a decrease of $850,000 in excess reserves and a reduction of $150,000 in required reserves as demand deposits declined by $1 million. Only if the derivative deposits were placed back in bank A would excess reserves remain after the transfer occurred. Therefore, although the banking system can achieve a multiple deposit and loan expansion, no individual bank can achieve that result. Expansion of loans and investments by an individual bank must remain in step with the System's expansion. Otherwise, a deficit reserve position develops which requires either the liquidation of loans and/or investments or the acquisition of additional reserves, either by borrowing from the Federal Reserve bank or by borrowing reserves from other commercial banks.

It should also be understood that the stages of expansion do not occur simultaneously. An individual bank cannot participate in the expansion process until it acquires excess reserves resulting from a transfer of a deposit from another bank. Because some banks may continuously maintain excess reserves, and other banks may utilize excess reserves only after a considerable time lag, the process may continue for some time. Moreover, expansion of deposits may never reach its theoretical limit because of the indefinite retention of excess reserves by some commercial banks. There is, in fact, a tendency for excess reserves to build up as interest rates decline, because the return from using the funds is less. This does not necessarily mean that individual banks are "wasting money," since the amount of excess reserves in an individual bank may be so small that it is not worth the expense incurred in loaning or investing the funds. The profit motive, however, tends to keep the volume of excess reserves at a low level.

Not only does a multiple expansion process result when banks gain excess reserves, but also a multiple contraction occurs when excess reserves are removed from the banking system. Similar to the expansion process, an *individual bank* can eliminate a reserve deficiency by reducing loans and/or investments by a like amount. A $1,000 security sale by an individual bank will reduce its reserve deficiency by $1,000, but total required reserves will decline by only $150 as a result of the $1,000 reduction in demand deposits. Hence, if a $1,000 reserve deficiency previously existed, an $850 reserve deficiency would then exist, even though it was transferred to another bank. The process of contraction through the *banking system* would have to continue until deposits were reduced by $6,667 before the reserve deficiency would be eliminated, assuming the same 15 percent reserve requirement ratio as before. It is clear that the Federal Reserve System can exert a powerful force for either monetary expansion or monetary contraction depending on whether it is increasing or decreasing the reserves of the commercial banking system.

At this point it is useful to clear up a common misconception concerning the monetary process. Book writers, including this one, have a common proclivity for discussing the process of monetary expansion by referring to induced loan expansion following an increase in reserves. There is nothing wrong with this exercise, but unfortunately it suggests to the reader that loan expansion is the only way the money supply increases, and that is wrong. The same effect would be exerted on the money supply if commercial banks were induced to expand investments. Payment for securities purchased would typically be made to municipal or government bond dealers, and deposits by the dealers would be made in either the purchasing bank or some other bank. The important point to make is that the multiple monetary expansion process would be similar regardless of whether loan or investment expansion occurred.

This point may appear obvious, but it is frequently overlooked. The error of assuming that monetary change is possible only through loan change is the source of several more important analytical errors. For example, observers frequently argue that if the Federal Reserve provides new reserves and loan demand is weakening, then there will be no induced increase in the money supply. But since excess reserves earn no interest, bankers will clearly be induced to purchase investments which do yield a return. Similarly, it is often argued that during a period of inflation when loan demand is high and rising, a tighter monetary policy leading to slower reserve creation or even reserve contraction will not reduce monetary growth. But such an argument ignores the obvious fact that banks will be forced to liquidate investment holdings even if they feel constrained to continue increasing loans in response to customer loan demand.

In fact, it follows that critical changes in monetary policy over the business cycle almost always induce significant changes in monetary growth through induced investment changes rather than loan changes. It is indeed true that during a recession when the Federal Reserve is attempting to create monetary ease and induce economic expansion, loan demand is typically weakening. But banks are encouraged to increase their investment portfolio holdings and monetary growth increases. As will be argued subsequently, this rise in the money supply performs a significant role in inducing the subsequent economic expansion. Similarly, during an overheated phase of the economy, loan demand is indeed high and rising and bankers have an obligation to meet legitimate customer loan demand even if the loan/deposit ratio is uncomfortably high. But bankers are forced by a tighter monetary policy at that time to reduce security holdings, which of course reduces deposits and also further raises the loan/deposit ratio for the System. As will also be argued subsequently, the reduced rate of monetary growth resulting essentially from less reserve creation and commercial bank liquidation of security holdings plays a very significant role in slowing economic activity, and frequently results in a recession.

It is sometimes argued that more money in a recession is like "pushing on a string." This argument implicitly admits that the money supply can be increased at such a time by greater reserve creation and addition to bank holdings of securities, but contends that the money will not be spent. This contention is in a form subject to empirical testing. Is there evidence in the past that monetary creation at any point of the business cycle, including recession or depression, did not in fact lead, after a reasonably short lag, to a resumption of economic growth? The empirically derived answer is clearly no, as will become evident by subsequent evidence. Similarly, reduced monetary growth occurring at a time of rising loan demand has always resulted in slower economic activity, frequently labeled a recession.

The willingness of many to assume an easier monetary policy during recession or depression will not lead to increased spending, and hence income creation may well stem from two sophisticated arguments offered by Lord Keynes in the *General Theory*. He argued that under two possible circumstances that might exist during depression, more money would not lead to increased spending. (1) In the event that more money lowered interest rates but investment expenditures were not elastic or sensitive to interest rate change, then more money did not mean more spending. This would be true if that condition was ever obtained and if an easier money policy had no direct stimulating effect on consumer spending. But the evidence suggests that it does have a direct effect on consumer spending, and this increase in turn generates higher investment outlays, not vice versa. (2) If there is an infinite demand for liquidity, more money would not reduce interest rates, and hence would not increase investment outlays. Again this possibility is an intellectual curiosity, but there is no evidence that this condition ever existed in fact. Although Keynes considered these two circumstances as exceptions to the general usefulness of monetary policy for influencing the economy, many of his followers took a much more extreme view and argued that, in general, monetary policy was of limited importance and policy-making attention should be focused on fiscal policy, a supposedly much more potent tool. The evidence suggests the contrary. Instead of monetary expansion being analogous to "pushing on a string," it appears to be more nearly analogous to "pushing on a ramrod"!

ANALYSIS OF CHANGES IN SOURCES AND USES OF RESERVE FUNDS

But back to our main theme, which may be less interesting but is highly relevant to the arguments presented in this book. The writer has the uncomfortable feeling that the content of this chapter is both tedious and complicated for some, while too elementary for others. There appears to be no easy solution to this dilemma. For those who are confused and/or bored, it may be worthwhile to be reminded that the ultimate objective is to forge a method of analysis which will enable one to use monetary change as a useful guide for improving economic judgments and investment timing decisions. It will, hopefully, be worth the time and effort to proceed. Learning is usually a painful process even though ultimately worth the effort. If you have survived so far, read on!

Since changes in deposits result from changes in bank reserves, an understanding of monetary change must be predicated on an analysis of the factors which change bank reserves. Since by far the largest component of the money supply is demand deposits—77 percent of the total—controlling the money stock is essentially a matter of controlling the volume of deposits. As indicated previously, deposit increases can take place only if banks have excess reserves, and monetary contraction must result if reserves decline and a reserve deficiency develops. It is by influencing the volume of bank reserves that the Federal Reserve exerts control over the stock of money.

In analyzing factors influencing the change in bank reserves, it is useful to think in terms of *sources* of potential reserve funds and *uses* of those funds. If all potential reserve funds were actually used as bank reserves, this approach would not be necessary, but such is not the case. Unfortunately, there are also nonreserve uses of potential reserve funds. A simple equation will serve to illuminate this reserve relation: sources of potential reserve funds = nonreserve uses + bank reserves (reserve uses). Therefore, any net increase in potential reserve funds will be accompanied by a similar increase in the sum of nonreserve and reserve uses, and, conversely, a decrease in potential reserve funds will be accompanied by a decline in the sum of nonreserve uses and reserves. Because of our interest in factors influencing deposits, we are primarily interested in changes in bank reserves, but to understand these changes we must analyze changes in both the sources of potential reserve funds and nonreserve uses.

Data on the total sources and uses of reserve funds are available each week in a Federal Reserve Board release, number XF, *Factors Affecting Member Bank Reserves*. An abbreviated and slightly rearranged table follows, giving average weekly data for the week ending August 5, 1970. Observe that sources and uses are equal, and that changes in sources and uses are also the same except for rounding errors.

As a result of a 1959 change in banking laws, banks are now allowed to count some of their cash in vault as reserves. Therefore, on the above date it was estimated that member banks had $5,074 million of vault cash that could be counted as reserves, making a total of $28,091 million. Each commercial bank must keep a specified percentage of its deposits with Federal Reserve banks, and these funds become required reserves. On the above date, members had *required reserves* of $27,960 million. Therefore, *excess reserves* amounted to $131 million.

As indicated in Table 4, there are four basic sources of potential reserve funds for commercial banks—Federal Reserve credit, the gold stock, special drawing rights certificate account, and Treasury currency outstanding. Funds derived from

Se e p. 37

TABLE 4

**Sources and Uses of Potential Commercial Bank Reserves,
Millions of Dollars
(week ending August 5, 1970)**

Sources		Change From	
		Week Ago	Year Ago
Reserve bank credit	$63,669	+210	+3,067
Gold stock	11,367		+1,000
Special drawing rights certificate account	400		+ 400
Treasury currency outstanding	6,998	+ 5	+ 259
Total	$82,435	+215	+4,727
Uses			
Currency in circulation	$54,587	+ 99	+3,467
Treasury cash holdings	461	+ 1	− 202
Treasury deposits with Federal Reserve banks	1,054	− 5	+ 187
Foreign deposits with Federal Reserve banks	190	+ 17	+ 37
Other deposits with Federal Reserve banks	790	+ 32	+ 314
Other Federal Reserve accounts (net)	2,337	+120	+ 219
Total nonreserve uses	$59,417	+262	+4,020
Total member bank reserves with Federal Reserve	$23,017	− 48	+ 704
Total uses of potential reserves	$82,434	+214	+4,724

Source: Board of Governors, Federal Reserve System.

these sources may actually be used as reserves, or they may be utilized for nonreserve purposes. Nonreserve uses of potential reserve funds include usage in the form of currency in circulation, Treasury cash holdings, Treasury deposits with the Federal Reserve, foreign and other deposits with the Federal Reserve, and other Federal Reserve accounts.

Reserve bank credit (Table 4), one source of potential reserves, can be increased through purchases by the Federal Reserve Open Market Committee of U.S. government securities or acceptances, through an increase in borrowings by commercial banks from Federal Reserve banks, or through an increase in float or uncollected balances of checks outstanding. The

Federal Reserve Open Market Committee has direct and complete control over the timing and the amount of securities and acceptances bought or sold. The System can affect borrowings by commercial banks from the Federal Reserve banks by variations in the discount rate relative to open market rates and by direct restraints on borrowings at the discount window. It cannot directly affect float, which varies with the long-term growth and improvement of the banking and transportation system and with short-run seasonal fluctuations. Therefore, the most important methods available to the Federal Reserve for affecting sources of potential reserve funds are open market purchases and sales, variation in the discount rate, and direct restraints on borrowing by banks. An increase in either of these sources of potential reserve funds will increase reserves of commercial banks unless a decrease in other source factors or an offsetting increase in nonreserve uses occurs.

To clarify the effect of changes in the sources of potential reserve funds, T-account analysis is again helpful. Let us consider first the major variable used for executing monetary policy—open market operations. This variable may be used both for offsetting undesirable short-run seasonal or random influences, and for executing the broader purposes of monetary policy. When the Federal Reserve System, through the New York Federal Reserve Bank, buys a U.S. government security from a government security dealer, it makes payment by a check issued on itself. The dealer then deposits the check and it is presented for payment at the regional Federal Reserve bank. Let us assume a purchase of $1 billion was made in the manner indicated.

It is therefore clear that a Federal Reserve open market purchase of $1 billion from a government dealer results in a $1 billion increase in bank reserves and an initial increase of $1 billion in deposits. Assuming an average required reserve ratio

TABLE 5

Partial Balance Sheet

Federal Reserve Bank

U.S. government securities + $1 billion	Member bank reserve deposit + $1 billion

Commercial Bank

Reserves with Federal Reserve bank + $1 billion	Customer deposit + $1 billion

of 15 percent, $850,000 excess reserves are created, subject to the ultimate multiple expansion previously described. If the expansion process goes to the theoretical limit, there is an ultimate increase of $6.67 billion in deposits. A purchase by the Federal Reserve money desk in New York of a bankers acceptance or federal agency obligation has the same effect. If, instead of a purchase of government securities or bankers acceptance or federal agency obligation a sale is made, reserves are reduced by $1 billion, and the multiple contraction process at the limit reduces the money stock by $6.67 billion.

If an increase in Federal Reserve credit occurs as a result of an increase in borrowing by commercial banks from a Federal Reserve bank, reserves go up by the amount of borrowing, but there is no initial increase in the stock of money. Nonetheless, these newly acquired reserves can also be expanded into a $6.67 billion increase in deposits, assuming that $1 billion was borrowed. Banks that find themselves in a deficit reserve position may do one of three things: (1) liquidate loans or investments; (2) borrow reserves or "Fed funds" from other banks; or (3) borrow from the Federal Reserve. Decision between the last two choices depends partly on the two rates of interest. The first alternative is probably selected if the deficit position is expected to be long lasting, whereas the latter two usually apply when a temporary deficit is expected. An increase in total reserves within the banking system occurs only when the commercial bank decides to relieve its reserve deficit by borrowing from the regional Federal Reserve bank.

The third and final way in which total Federal Reserve credit outstanding rises is an increase in float. Float occurs when one bank's reserve account with the Federal Reserve is credited for checks sent for collection prior to the debiting of the reserve account of the bank against which the checks were drawn. Many of the checks sent to the Federal Reserve for collection result in an immediate crediting and debiting of the two commercial banks involved in the transaction. However, nearly all checks are credited to the account of the depositing bank no later than two days after they are received at the Federal Reserve bank, even though some of the checks may not yet have been collected. In other words, one bank's reserve account is increased prior to the compensating decrease in another bank's reserve accounts, and hence float arises. The reserve credit given for checks not yet collected is labeled "float."

As float arises, total member bank reserves also rise by the same amount. Let us assume that bank A receives a $1,000 check (Table 6) written on bank B in a distant town. It credits the account of its depositor, debits "cash items in process of collection," and sends the check to the regional Federal Reserve for collection. The Federal Reserve bank increases its asset account "cash item in process of collection" and initially increases its liability item "deferred availability cash item" prior to increasing bank A's reserve deposit. Up to this point, no float has developed, but if at the end of two days the check is still not collected, the Federal Reserve bank reduces the deferred availability item and increases bank A's reserve account. At that point, float develops and the banking system enjoys an increase in total reserves.

However, when the check is collected from bank B, reserves

TABLE 6

Partial Balance Sheet

Federal Reserve Bank

(2) Uncollected cash item + $1,000	Deferred availability + $1,000
(3)	Deferred availability — $1,000
	Bank A reserve deposit + $1,000

Commercial Bank A

(1) Cash item in process of collection + $1,000	Deposit + $1,000
(4) Cash item — $1,000 reserve with Federal Reserve + $1,000	

of that bank are decreased, and total member bank reserves are then back at the initial level.

The second major source of potential reserve funds is the gold stock. Monetary effects of a change in the gold stock are complex. When either freshly mined gold or gold from abroad is sold to the U.S. Treasury, sources of potential reserve funds are expanded by a like amount. Let us assume that the U.S. Treasury purchases $1,000 worth of gold (Table 7), and payment is made by a check drawn on the Treasury's deposit with a Federal Reserve bank. The recipient of the check deposits it with a commercial bank, and deposits and reserves go up by $1,000. But in the process of paying for the gold, the U.S. Treasury balances with the Federal Reserve bank are reduced by $1,000. The Treasury replenishes those funds by issuing a gold certificate to the Federal Reserve for the amount of the purchase, and its deposit account is increased.

It is therefore clear that total reserves and deposits rise in the first instance by the amount of the $1,000 gold purchase. With a 15 percent reserve requirement, excess reserves rise by $850 which could be expanded 6⅔ times. An outflow of gold has the opposite effect. Buyers of gold make payment by checks on commercial banks, and the checks are sent to the Federal Reserve bank for collection. Therefore,

TABLE 7

Partial Balance Sheet

U.S. Treasury

(1) Gold + $1,000 Deposit with Federal Reserve bank — $1,000	
(4) Deposit with Federal Reserve bank + $1,000	Gold certificates + $1,000

Federal Reserve Bank

	(3) Member bank reserve deposit + $1,000 U.S. Treasury deposit — $1,000
(5) Gold certificates + $1,000	U.S. Treasury deposit + $1,000

Commercial Bank

(2) Reserve with Federal Reserve + $1,000	Deposits + $1,000

commercial bank reserves are decreased by the amount of the gold purchases, and Treasury balances are in the first instance increased. But these funds are used for retiring a like amount of gold certificates held by the Federal Reserve bank.

The gold stock is not normally subject to direct control by the Federal Reserve Board or other government authorities, although gold flows may be and frequently are offset by compensating changes in Federal Reserve credit. Gold flows are usually affected by such factors as the size of the deficit in the U.S. balance of payments and the relative preference of foreign central banks for gold versus dollars. Variations in the gold stock are occasionally important, but on a week-to-week basis they are usually inconsequential. In those periods when gold outflows become a significant factor, the Federal Reserve may alter its open market activities in order to compensate for them unless the resulting altered bank reserves are consistent with current economic policies. An example of offsetting Federal Reserve operations occurred during the 1960 recession, when economic policy was directed at halting the recession and generating recovery. Despite the outflow of $1.5 billion gold in the last half of 1960, total bank reserves rose substantially, due mainly to Federal Reserve open market purchases of U.S. securities. It should be noted that in earlier years the Federal Reserve sometimes attempted to affect gold flows directly by supporting short-term interest rates and trading in foreign currency. These efforts have been directed at deterring short-term capital outflows by discouraging speculative activities and by raising short-term interest rates in the U.S. relative to those available abroad. Since 1968, gold flows have been less important, due perhaps to a growing reluctance of the U.S. Treasury to redeem dollars held by foreigners with gold.

On January 1, 1970, a new international reserve asset came into existence when the International Monetary Fund allocated Special Drawing Right (SDR) equivalents to 104 countries. The initial allocation of SDR's to the U.S. was $867 million. The Secretary of the Treasury may issue SDR certificates (broadly equivalent to gold certificates) to the Federal Reserve banks for the purpose of financing SDR acquisitions or for financing exchange stabilization operations. On August 5, 1970, $400 million of SDR's had been monetized in that way. The Federal Reserve credits a special account of the Treasury with the amount of monetization and debits the Federal Reserve SDR certificate account by a like amount. The SDR certificate account then becomes one of the sources of potential bank reserves similar to the gold certificate account.[3]

A fourth but minor source of potential bank reserves is Treasury currency outstanding. The amount outstanding has increased gradually over time, but short-run changes are small and have minor effects on total bank reserves. Treasury currency consists mostly of coins plus United States notes and

---

[3] See "SDR's in Federal Reserve Operations and Statistics," *Federal Reserve Bulletin*, May, 1970, pp. 421–424.

some prior currency which is now in process of retirement. When the Treasury issues new currency, it is shipped to the Federal Reserve for credit to Treasury deposits. When these resulting deposits are drawn down as the Treasury makes expenditures, an increase in commercial bank reserves will result.

Now let us turn to an analysis of uses of potential reserve funds. One of the most seasonally volatile nonreserve uses is currency in circulation. Although holders of money may draw no sharp distinction between their demand deposits and currency, a transfer in form from deposits to currency has a sharp impact on bank reserves. The public typically acquires cash by "cashing" a check. Suppose a bank customer cashes a $100 check (Table 8) against his account in exchange for currency.

TABLE 8

Partial Balance Sheet

Commercial Bank

(1) Vault cash — $100	Deposits — $100
(2) Vault cash + $100 reserve with Federal Reserve — $100	

Federal Reserve Bank

(3)	Member bank reserve deposit — $100
	Federal Reserve notes outstanding + $100

Commercial bank deposits decline by $100, and the bank's currency holding is decreased by a like amount. But the currency must be replaced by the bank to meet other customer demands, and this is achieved by ordering currency from the regional Federal Reserve bank and making payment by authorizing a reduction in its reserve balance. The public now has the same amount of money as before, but more is in currency and less in demand deposit form. However, bank reserves have been decreased by $100, and excess reserves have declined by $85, since required reserves slipped $15. Unless more reserves were acquired, the banking system would have to liquidate loans and/or investments, and, hence, deposits amounting to $567 ($85 × 6⅔), assuming a 15 percent average required reserve ratio.

When currency is returned to the banking system, the process is reversed. The Federal Reserve takes action frequently to offset the destabilizing influence of currency outflows and inflows. The foregoing analysis, incidentally, provides some insight into the reason for widespread bank failures during the Great Depression when depositors attempted to convert their funds into currency. The resulting reserve deficiency forced sale of investments and the calling of loans, and thereby intensified the depression. Fortunately, there has been no modern parallel to that experience, largely because of deposit insurance.

Another nonreserve use of potential reserve funds of considerable importance is Treasury deposits with the Federal Reserve. The Treasury makes most payments out of funds on deposit with the Federal Reserve, but the bulk of Treasury funds are on deposit with commercial banks in accounts labeled "tax and loan accounts." Transfers are made regularly from the tax and loan accounts with member banks to Treasury deposits with the Federal Reserve, from which most Treasury checks are paid. A transfer of Treasury funds from commercial banks to the Federal Reserve will have an effect similar to the withdrawal of currency from a commercial bank, as indicated in Table 9, which assumes a $1 million transfer. Reserves of commercial banks are reduced by the amount of the transfer to the Federal Reserve bank, and excess reserves decline by $850,000, assuming a 15 percent average required reserve ratio. In the first instance, the money stock is unaffected, however, since treasury demand deposits held with commercial banks are excluded from the money supply. Due to the potentially

TABLE 9
Partial Balance Sheet

Federal Reserve Bank

	Member bank reserve deposits — $1 million U.S. Treasury deposit + $1 million

Commercial Bank

Reserves with F. R. bank — $1 million	U.S. government deposits — $1 million

disturbing influence of Treasury transfers, special attention is given to attempting to keep Treasury balances with the Federal Reserve fairly uniform. In addition, in recent years such fluctuations have been reduced substantially by daily adjustments in the tax and loan balances at large commercial banks. The pulling down of Treasury balances with the Federal Reserve resulting from Treasury expenditures in excess of new deposits with the Federal Reserve bank decreases nonreserve uses and tends to increase commercial bank reserves.

Additional nonreserve uses of potential reserve funds which are of minor importance are Treasury cash holdings, foreign and other deposits in Federal Reserve banks, and other Federal Reserve accounts. The Treasury holds some cash in its own vaults, and changes in these holdings affect member bank reserves in the same manner as changes in the Treasury's deposit account with the Federal Reserve. Foreign central banks, international institutions, and some nonmember banks keep funds on deposit in Federal Reserve banks. These funds usually build up out of funds transferred from member banks and result in a decrease in member bank reserves. When a reverse flow occurs, member bank balances are augmented. Other Federal Reserve accounts represent a combination of the balance sheet items not already considered as separate factors affecting reserves. When this residual dollar figure increases, usually in response to net current earnings of the reserve banks, bank reserves are reduced. When this factor declines, bank reserves rise.

To recapitulate briefly, the ability of commercial banks to expand loans and investments, deposits, and, hence, the money stock (when the required reserve ratio is fixed) depends on total reserves and their distribution between required and excess reserves. Potential bank reserves are provided by Federal Reserve credit, the gold stock, the Special Drawing Right certificate account, and Treasury currency outstanding. These may be used as reserves of commercial banks, or they may go into nonreserve uses. The following simple equations summarize the pertinent relations which determine the ability of commercial banks to expand the stock of money.

1. Sources of potential reserve funds = nonreserves uses + member bank reserves with the Federal Reserve banks.
2. Member bank reserves = reserves with the Federal Reserve banks + cash allowed as reserves.
3. Member bank reserves — required reserves = excess reserves.

Unless commercial banks have either excess reserves or access to them through the discount window, they are unable to further expand the stock of money. For the banking system as a whole, each dollar of excess reserves may be expanded 6⅔ times assuming an average reserve requirement of 15 percent. The expansion of deposits comes about through an increase in total loans and/or investments. With each $1.00 of excess reserves, $6.67 of loans and/or investments may be made before the resulting new deposits will convert the $1.00 of excess reserves into required reserves.

One additional factor should be recognized at this point. The Federal Reserve has the power to increase or decrease the required ratio within limits set by law. By raising the average required reserve ratio, required reserves can be increased, thereby decreasing the amount of excess reserves so long as total reserves are unchanged. A reduction in the average required reserve ratio will increase the supply of excess reserves.

Manipulation of the required reserve ratio can, therefore, increase or decrease excess reserves without affecting either the total of potential reserve funds or their uses. Furthermore, the lower the average reserve ratio, the larger the possible multiple expansion of each dollar of excess reserves. As indicated previously, the potential multiple expansion of excess reserves varies directly with the reciprocal of the required reserve ratio, i.e., potential multiple expansion = 1 ÷ the average required reserve ratio.

Since the Federal Reserve System has the power to increase or decrease the total sources of potential reserve funds, and also the power to change the average required ratio, it therefore has the power to determine the stock of money. The simple, largely correct, and most relevant observation is that monetary policy as set by the Federal Reserve Board can determine the growth rate of the stock of money, even though the Federal Reserve does not directly control all the factors affecting reserves.

ANOTHER WAY OF VIEWING
THESE RELATIONS

Financial analysts are accustomed to viewing financial data in a sources and uses context similar to the explanation offered above. But economists are accustomed to thinking in demand and supply terms. By a simple rearrangement of the accounts discussed above, it is possible to analyze the monetary expansion and contraction forces in terms of the supply of and demand for the monetary base.[4] Viewing the process in this manner has the advantage of repetition in a different form

---

[4] See Leonall C. Andersen and Jerry L. Jordan, "The Monetary Base—Explanation and Analytical Use," *Federal Reserve Bank of St. Louis Review,* August, 1968, pp. 7–11, for an excellent discussion. Also David Fand, "Some Issues in Monetary Economics," *Federal Reserve Bank of St. Louis Review,* January, 1970, especially pp. 12–16.

which should add to understanding, but it is also possible to develop the monetary base concept which is made available weekly and provides another useful series for analyzing current monetary policy.

The monetary base has received attention of late because (1) there is a large body of monetary theory which uses the monetary base as an important link between monetary actions by the Federal Reserve System and their ultimate effect on economic activity and financial markets; (2) among all the variables cited as alternative measures of monetary actions by the Fed, the monetary authorities have the most complete control over the monetary base, i.e., the base reflects the actions of the Federal Reserve more directly than the other measures do.

As explained by the Federal Reserve Bank of St. Louis, three concepts are used in computing the monetary base:

1. The *source base* is derived from the accounts described above, but the arrangement is somewhat different. It is calculated as shown in Table 10. The source base may be measured by summing the monetary liabilities of the Federal Reserve and Treasury. These liabilities are called "uses of base" and consist of member bank deposits with the Federal Reserve banks and currency held by the banks and nonbank holders. Uses are again equal to sources, or the quantity supplied equals the quantity demanded. For analytical purposes it is important to distinguish between the source base as a magnitude supplied by monetary authorities and the demand for the base by other sectors of the economy (see Table 10).

2. Reserve adjustments must be made in order to maintain comparability in the source base over time. Changes in laws and regulations and changes in the distribution of deposits among banks which have different reserve requirements make the adjustment necessary. " 'Reserve adjustments' allow for the effects of changes in reserve requirements on member bank

TABLE 10

Calculation of the Source Base, Millions of Dollars
(week ending August 5, 1970)

Sources of Base

Federal Reserve bank credit	63,669
Gold stock	11,367
Special Drawing Rights certificate account	400
Treasury currency outstanding	6,998
Minus	
Treasury deposits with Federal Reserve banks	1,054
Treasury cash holdings	461
Foreign deposits with Federal Reserve banks	190
Other deposits with Federal Reserve banks	790
Other Federal Reserve accounts	2,337
	77,602

Uses of Base

Member bank deposits at Federal Reserve bank	23,017
Currency held in banks	5,074
Currency held by public	49,513
	77,604

deposits, and for changes in the proportion of deposits subject to different reserve requirements (reserve city member banks versus country member banks versus nonmember banks), demand deposits versus time deposits, and recently the over and under $5 million reserve requirement differentials on both demand and time deposits."[5]

3. The sum of the "source base" and "reserve adjustments" is defined as the monetary base.

The source base is by far the most important part of the supply of the monetary base. Federal Reserve credit, the major component of the monetary base, is directly under the control of the Federal Reserve. Studies by Karl Brunner demonstrate that improvements in Federal Reserve credit dominate improvements in other sources of the source base and hence

---

[5] Leonall C. Andersen and Jerry L. Jordan, "The Monetary Base—Explanation and Analytical Use," *Federal Reserve Bank of St. Louis Review,* August, 1968, p. 8.

determine most of the improvements of the monetary base.[6] Leonall Andersen has also demonstrated that Federal Reserve open market operations are able to offset, to a high degree, seasonal and irregular improvements in other components of the source base.[7] It follows that the Federal Reserve can, if it so chooses, achieve a desired level of the monetary base and hence the money supply.

The supply of the monetary base, then, is substantially under the complete control of the Federal Reserve. But the demand for the monetary base emanates from the demand of commercial banks for excess reserves and required reserves and the demand of the nonbank public for currency.

Data on the monetary base are reported weekly and they are another useful way of analyzing Federal Reserve policy. Their importance arises from: (1) being under the direct control of the Federal Reserve System; (2) the ability to be changed by monetary managers in a predictable manner; and (3) the base and other monetary variables having an important influence on output, employment, prices, and financial markets.

[6] Karl Brunner, "The Role of Money and Monetary Policy," *Federal Reserve Bank of St. Louis Review,* July, 1968.

[7] Leonall C. Andersen, "Federal Reserve Defensive Operations and Short Run Control of the Money Stock," *Journal of Political Economy,* April, 1968.

4

Detecting
and Measuring
Monetary Change

At this point, the reader is aware that the author's objective is to develop an understanding of a method of analysis which will enable the careful analyst to use monetary change as a guide to improving economic judgments and investment timing decisions. Up to the present, it has been demonstrated that (1) monetary change has a leading and fairly consistent relation to subsequent changes in financial markets and economic activity; (2) a simple explanation utilizing money as the causal variable rationalizes the foregoing relationships; (3) the process of monetary change can be useful if the analyst understands (*a*) the elementary structure of the banking system, (*b*) the process of multiple expansion and contraction of money, and (*c*) the analysis of sources and uses of potential reserve funds and the monetary base concept. Now that we understand what factors cause money to vary, there remains the important

68

problem of detecting and measuring monetary change. Unfortunately, there is not unanimous agreement as to how this task is best performed. Perhaps the most obvious approach is to rely on the statements of Federal Reserve officials concerning current monetary policy. But while these statements may occasionally provide a useful explanation of current policy, they cannot be a substitute for analysis. Federal Reserve officials are generally reluctant to keep the market informed as to their present and planned actions, although they have been less secretive of late. Hopefully, this trend will continue. There is good reason for top Federal Reserve officials to avoid an explicit and detailed report of current and expected policy because of the effects on financial markets and the potential gain to traders of executing orders ahead of Federal Reserve action. There appears to be no reason for the Federal Reserve to keep the public in the dark concerning the general thrust of their policy in the past as well as their expected thrust into the future. If monetary policy is as important as contended in this book, the provision of information concerning past and planned action by the Federal Reserve would be likely to exert a stabilizing impact on expectations of market participants. Markets can adjust smoothly and efficiently to a changed policy thrust if they remain informed of intent and implementation. Sudden surprises lead to at least temporary disorder and confusion.

The Full Employment Act of 1946 established machinery for public review of economic policy as formulated by the President and his top economic officials including the Council of Economic Advisers, the Treasury, and the Bureau of the Budget. In other words, spending and taxing decisions and plans are annually reviewed before the Joint Economic Committee, and ultimately by other responsible committees of Congress. Although Federal Reserve officials frequently testify before congressional committees, their participation is not an integral part of the procedures established by the Full Employment Act, and their testimony has, until recently, been quite general, without the specifics necessary to keep the markets well informed as to the intent and basic thrust of policy. In other words, the public has been well informed concerning planned fiscal policy, but kept largely in the dark concerning monetary policy. If the thesis of this book is correct to the effect that monetary change is a much more important variable for influencing subsequent economic activity than is fiscal policy, then the formal procedures established by the Employment Act of 1946 left out the star actor. The need for coordination of monetary and fiscal policy within the government has been achieved by establishing an informal group of leading economic policy makers who maintain close contact with the President. This group includes the chairman of the Federal Reserve Board, the secretary of the Treasury, the director of the Office of Management and Budget, and the chairman of the Council of Economic Advisers. Although this group undoubtedly provides close internal coordination, the public does not have the benefit of being informed in a formal way concerning monetary policy.

It has been argued by the author and others that the Federal Reserve Board should be required to present its plan for the forthcoming year to the Joint Economic Committee so the public could be informed as to the basic intent and thrust of monetary policy.[1] At the request of Senator William Proxmire in May 1968, the Federal Reserve now testifies before the Joint Economic Committee of Congress quarterly.[2] Until recently

---

[1] See Beryl W. Sprinkel, "Proposal for a Federal Reserve Annual Monetary Plan," *Compendium on Monetary Policy Guidelines and Federal Reserve Structure, Committee on Banking and Currency, House of Representatives,* December, 1968, pp. 539–42.

[2] "Standards for Guiding Monetary Action," *Report of the Joint Economic Committee, Congress of the United States* (Washington, D.C.: U.S. Government Printing Office, July, 1968), p. 20.

this testimony was quite general and provided little insight into Federal Reserve policy objectives, or what variables under its influence it considers of importance.

There is growing evidence that policies and practices at the Federal Reserve are changing, and for the better. Dr. Arthur F. Burns, the current chairman of the Federal Reserve Board, informed the Joint Economic Committee in March 1970 that he believed the Federal Reserve should promote growth in the money supply at most times, including 1970, at an annual rate ranging between 2 percent to 6 percent.[3] In testimony before the Senate Banking Committee, he laid out, in clearer fashion than ever before, the economic problems as the Board perceived them, and considerable detail concerning what the Federal Reserve objectives and policy thrust were likely to be in the months ahead.[4] Hopefully, this trend toward increased candor will continue.

In addition to testimony of Federal Reserve officials before Congressional committees, speeches by members of the Board of Governors are available shortly after delivery, and they occasionally provide useful insights into present and proposed policies. Although "Fed listening" is a useful tool for anyone interested in following monetary policy developments for purposes of projecting economic or financial market changes, "Fed watching" is even more important. The prudent analyst of money must be more interested in what monetary authorities are doing than in what they say they are trying to do, for, unfortunately, there has not always been a close relation between monetary intent and results. Let us turn to a consideration of how to best monitor Federal Reserve actions.

---

[3] Arthur F. Burns, letter to the Joint Economic Committee, Congress of the United States, March 22, 1970.

[4] Arthur F. Burns, testimony before the Joint Economic Committee, Congress of the United States, February 18, 1970 (Washington, D.C.: U.S. Government Printing Office).

MONEY STOCK PROBABLY THE BEST
MEASURE OF MONETARY CHANGE

Since banking data are published promptly and seldom require extensive revision, there is no shortage of facts. The problem is one of deciding which facts are most relevant. The most direct, and in many ways the most useful, means of measuring a monetary policy change is that of observing changes in the stock of money. Data on the daily average stock of money are available weekly in a Federal Reserve Board release, *Demand Deposits, Currency and Related Items,* which reflects changes brought about by monetary policy action, both planned and unplanned, as well as changes resulting from other forces. Also, the St. Louis Federal Reserve Bank publishes a weekly release on the money supply in written and chart form entitled "U.S. Financial Data" which is invaluable to the "Fed watcher" (Chart 6). Money stock data available weekly are distorted by serious random influences not readily removable. Nonetheless, weekly data sometimes give a useful clue to most recent changes. Weekly data are available with a lag of only eight days.

But raw average money stock data alone will not provide the proper tool. To begin with, the usual seasonal influence must be removed from the data so the analyst can determine whether an apparent change is real or merely seasonal in nature. Fortunately, money stock data are reported in both raw and seasonally adjusted form.

Further adjustment is necessary if the data are to be of maximum usefulness. In addition to the seasonal and random influences which affect the magnitude of monetary change, there are also a long-term or secular growth trend and a cyclical trend. The cyclical changes in the monetary series are most useful for our purposes. Usually, the stock of money grows in

CHART 6

MONEY STOCK
Averages of Daily Figures
Seasonally Adjusted

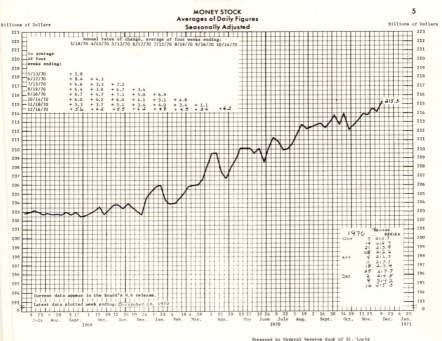

Prepared by Federal Reserve Bank of St. Louis

periods both of business expansion and contraction. Although the money stock has inevitably declined in deep depressions, it has frequently continued to rise in mild recessions, although not always. For example, there was a moderate absolute decline in the stock of money from mid-1959 to mid-1960 prior to the mild 1960–61 recession. However, the money stock began expanding in the first month of business contraction, somewhat sooner with respect to the upper turning point of the business cycle than is typically the case. Prior to the 1969–70 recession, monetary growth declined, but the stock of money did not decrease.

Even though the money stock may rise during recessions, this does not mean there is no relation between monetary change and the business cycle. It may merely mean the secular upward trend is stronger than the cyclical trend, so that the latter is not readily apparent in the seasonally adjusted data. Therefore, a method of removing the long-term trend must be adopted.

The two most common ways of eliminating a secular trend from the cyclical pattern in time series data are to express the data in terms of deviations from trend or to compute the rate of change in the data. Although rates of change often yield a rather erratic or choppy series, they do not require a decision about the kind of trend to fit or the period to cover. Furthermore, the observations for any particular period do not depend on distant observations for other periods that affect fitted trends. Also, the series can be extended backward or forward without either recomputing or extrapolating trends. The trend adjustment chosen in this book is the computation of annual rates of change in the stock of money.[5] An economic factor conditioning the choice is that monetary authorities may readily alter the secular trend in the stock of money as conditions change. It is therefore desirable to allow for a trend that can shift drastically over time, and rate-of-change computations do this.

One final adjustment to the data appears warranted if the resulting series is to be operational, provided the reader is not convinced that all meaning has already been adjusted out of the raw monetary data. Ideally, it would be desirable to have a

_____

[5] See Milton Friedman, "The Supply of Money and Change in Prices and Output," *The Relationship of Prices to Economic Stability and Growth, Compendium,* U.S. Congress Joint Economic Committee Document No. 23734, March 31, 1958 (Washington, D.C.: U.S. Government Printing Office, 1958), pp. 241–56; "The Lag in Effect of Monetary Policy," *Journal of Political Economy,* October, 1961, especially pp. 453–54; Clark Warburton, "The Volume of Money and the Price Levels between World Wars," *Journal of Political Economy,* June, 1945, pp. 153–54.

rate-of-change series which is both smooth and highly sensitive to recent changes in the money stock. Unfortunately, we cannot have both. In the real world of practical data manipulation, the analyst is frequently faced with unpleasant choices between competing desires that must be compromised. Such is the present case. The analyst can have a highly sensitive but erratic series by computing the annual rate of growth each month, that is, computing the percentage change from the preceding month and annualizing by multiplying the resultant percentage by 12.

At the other extreme, an annualized percentage change from the same month a year ago will yield a relatively smooth curve, but one that is rather insensitive to recent changes. The resulting percentage change data will be influenced not only by the recent change but also by the level existing one year ago. A reasonable compromise results from computing a current annualized rate of change for each month but averaging the most recent six months' rates. The resulting series removes most short-run erratic movements but retains moderate sensitivity to average recent developments. For those reasons, the six-month moving average is the series used in subsequent charts reflecting monetary growth. Nonetheless, an analyst should not become a slave to the particular form of arithmetical computation adopted. Hence, the most sensitive series also should be computed and analyzed in detecting most recent fluctuations in monetary growth.[6]

In detecting and measuring monetary change, the ultimate answer to what is happening to the nation's liquidity is provided by measuring the rate of monetary change in the manner indicated above. This technique has the advantage of being simple, direct, and timely, and for most purposes provides both a necessary and sufficient measure.

---

[6] See Appendix for further elaboration.

MEASURING CHANGES IN RESERVES, MONETARY BASE, FEDERAL RESERVE CREDIT, AND BANK CREDIT PROXY

A careful current analysis of sources and uses of potential reserves can frequently provide useful supplementary information. Analysis of changes in the individual items making up the sources and uses of potential reserve funds is difficult because of short-run seasonal and random fluctuations. For example, a significant increase in Federal Reserve purchases of U.S. government securities in the last half of the year may or may not indicate an expansive monetary policy. Substantial seasonal increases of money in circulation require offsetting action by the Federal Reserve if there is to be no contraction in deposits. Gold flows into or out of the nation may also require offsetting action by the monetary authority. Since it is extremely difficult for the human mind to evaluate correctly the impact of several simultaneously changing variables, it is much more useful to concentrate attention on relevant monetary aggregates.

Bank reserves of all member banks reflect the net effect on reserves of all changes in the sources and nonreserve uses of potential reserve funds. As pointed out previously, changes in total bank reserves are the most important factor determining the ability of banks to change loans and investment totals and, hence, the stock of money.

However, if changes in total bank reserves are to provide useful information, this series also must be substantially adjusted. The usual seasonal movement must be removed from the series so the analyst can determine when an apparent change is of basic significance or merely seasonal in nature. Prior to removing the seasonal influences, however, a more basic adjustment is necessary. As indicated previously, the

Federal Reserve can increase excess reserves either by increasing total reserves or by reducing the required reserve ratio, thereby reducing required reserves. Therefore, if the total reserve series is to properly reflect the ability of the banking system to expand bank credit and, hence, the stock of money, the historical series must be adjusted for changes in required reserves. Although the Federal Reserve frequently adjusts total reserves by increasing the total sources of potential reserves created, changes in the required reserve ratio are infrequent; hence, the adjustment problem posed is minor. Fortunately, the reserve data are reported in fully adjusted form on a weekly basis by the St. Louis Federal Reserve Bank in its release entitled *U.S. Financial Data* (Chart 7).

The relation between reserves of member banks and the money supply is not perfect. A shift between private deposits and U.S. Treasury deposits in commercial banks results in a change in the money supply, but not in total reserves. Changes in excess reserves, which are under the control of commercial banks, also cause divergencies between total reserves and the stock of money.

Movements of deposits between classes of banks which have a different required reserve ratio behind demand deposits may also cause a lack of correspondence between reserve changes and money stock changes. For example, reserve city banks have a required reserve ratio on deposits over $5 million of 17½ percent, whereas country banks are required to keep only 13 percent reserves on deposits over $5 million. A deposit shift between banks with different reserve requirements causes a change in the average required reserve ratio, and hence affects the amount of potential deposits based on a given amount of reserves.

The movement of funds from time deposits to demand deposits or vice versa has a similar effect, since the required reserve ratio is considerably less for time deposits, and the shift in effect changes the average required reserve ratio. Time deposits on the average grew faster than demand deposits over a long period of time, but the relative shift was so gradual that little distortion between reserves and total deposit growth resulted. However, on two occasions in recent years the shift was substantial, and the resulting distortion was considerable.

CHART 7

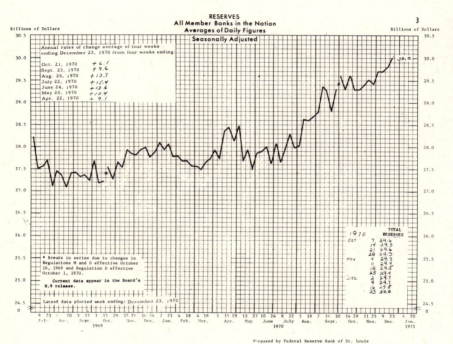

Prepared by Federal Reserve Bank of St. Louis

During 1966, and again in 1969 extending into 1970, rapidly rising market interest rates, combined with legally imposed ceiling rates that commercial banks were permitted to pay for time money, resulted in a substantial outflow of time money from commercial banks. Investors became acutely aware of the fact that much larger returns could be realized by purchasing

Treasury bills and commercial paper and there was erosion in both savings accounts and certificates of deposit. Although monetary policy tightened during each of those periods, as evidenced by reduced growth in bank reserves, the bind on the monetary system was even more severe than reflected by the reserve trend, since many of the time deposits shifted to demand deposits, which have a higher reserve requirement. Hence, a given amount of reserves was capable of supporting fewer deposits than previously.

Changes in demand deposits of nonmember banks cause a change in the stock of money without a change in reserves. Although demand deposits of nonmember banks are included in the money stock, changes in these deposits may occur without a change in member bank reserves, since legal reserves of nonmember banks are not required to be in the same form as those of member banks.

In addition, a change in interbank balances results in a distortion between reserve changes and changes in the money stock. When a country member bank transfers deposits from its account with the Federal Reserve Bank to its city correspondent bank, the reserve requirement against those funds rises to 17½ percent. For the banking system as a whole, excess reserves decline and monetary contraction results, even though total reserves are unchanged.

Finally, movements of currency into and out of banks affect both reserves and money, but not in equal proportions. As pointed out in the analysis of sources and uses of potential reserve funds, a movement of currency into banks adds to bank reserves. Based on these newly acquired reserves, the banking system can expand credit and deposits. But the deposit expansion is partially offset by a contraction in the currency component of the money supply. Thus, the net expansion in the stock of money is less than if the increase in reserves comes from other sources. An outflow of currency produces a reduction in reserves, but causes a smaller initial contraction of the money stock than if the reserve reduction is induced by another factor, since the resulting contraction is partially offset by the increase in the currency component of money. Shifts in the composition of the stock of money between currency and deposits tend to be of very modest proportions in most cases, and only in periods of "bank panics" similar to the early 1930's, is this factor of great importance. Existence of deposit insurance substantially reduces the risk of such an occurrence.

Despite the above qualifications concerning the potential imperfections in the relation between bank reserves and the stock of money, the actual distortions are generally of small magnitude and usually can be ignored. It is nonetheless important that the analyst be aware of these potential distortions so he may avoid being a victim of the system of analysis on those few occasions when one of the above disturbances develops.

The monetary base previously discussed is adjusted for some of the factors that influence monetary change. The St. Louis Federal Reserve Bank data are reported in seasonally adjusted form, as are member bank reserve data. Similarly, each series is adjusted for changes in reserve requirements over time. Furthermore, the reserve base data are previously adjusted for changes in the proportion of deposits subject to different reserve requirements (reserve city member banks versus country member banks versus nonmember banks, demand deposits versus time deposits, and the over and under $5 million reserve requirement differentials on both demand and time deposits). The method of computation also adjusts for changes in Treasury deposits at the Federal Reserve, Treasury cash holdings, other deposits, and other Federal Reserve accounts. Nonetheless, changes in currency held by the public can, in the short run, lead to a variation between the trend of the monetary base and the money supply. Also, changes in the amount of excess reserves maintained by the commercial banking system can lead to a disparity.

Since changes in Federal Reserve credit tend to dominate changes in the monetary base, this series is frequently useful in detecting the thrust of monetary policy. This series is sometimes available in the St. Louis Federal Reserve Bank report and is presented in seasonally adjusted form. Short-run changes in float, discounts, and advances influence Federal Reserve credit totals, but change in holdings of securities by the Federal Reserve System is by far the most important factor, both in terms of frequency of use and magnitude of effect.

Another measure of monetary policy change is provided by the "bank credit proxy." This series was developed by the staff of the Federal Reserve Board for the purpose of providing a prompt estimate of recent changes in total bank credit. Unfortunately, data on total bank credit at all commercial banks are available only for the last Wednesday of a month. The bank credit proxy is available on a daily average basis for each week. The bank credit proxy utilizes total deposit liabilities of member banks to approximate total loans and investments (or bank credit) which appear on the other side of the banking system's combined balance sheet. Unfortunately, total deposits are not a perfect substitute for total loans and investments, since there are many other factors, sometimes volatile, that appear on both sides of the balance sheet. The proxy does not pick up changes in bank credit due to changes in nondeposit liabilities, bank capital, the banks' cash position, or the percentage of total bank credit supplied by nonmember banks. These shortcomings must be considered when using the bank credit proxy in analyzing Federal Reserve policy.

Although the bank credit proxy always has drawbacks as a measure of Federal Reserve policy, it was particularly troublesome in 1969 and 1970. Regulation Q, which set ceiling

CHART 8

MEMBER BANK DEPOSITS SUBJECT TO RESERVE REQUIREMENTS
(CREDIT PROXY)

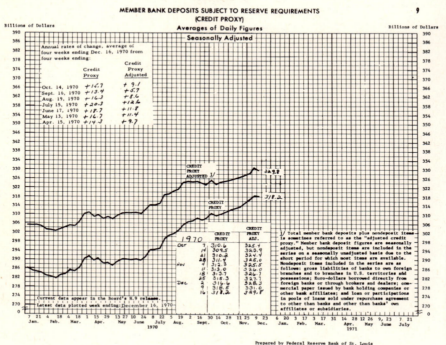

Prepared by Federal Reserve Bank of St. Louis

rates that banks were permitted to pay on time and savings deposits, prevented banks from paying rates competitive with the rising returns available on such assets as Treasury bills, commercial paper, corporate bonds, etc. Considerable time money flowed from banks and resulted in a conversion of time deposits into demand deposits. Since reserve requirements for demand deposits were higher than for time deposits, excess reserves were reduced. Thus, a given growth of total reserves tended to be associated with a smaller rate of growth in total deposits and a faster growth in demand deposits and the money supply than would have been the case had the interest rate ceilings not been effective. Clearly, the decline in the bank credit proxy in much of 1969 overstated the severity of monetary restraint.

Banks reacted to the interest rate ceilings by creating nondeposit liabilities, i.e., liabilities subject to neither reserve requirements nor interest rate ceilings. Many larger banks borrowed in the Eurodollar market, sold assets under repurchase agreements, and sold commercial paper in the short-term money market. These adjustments made possible an expansion in bank credit. Thus, change in the bank credit proxy was a poor indicator of the direction and magnitude of change in total bank credit. A reversal in these trends in 1970, which followed the elimination of Regulation Q ceilings on short-term CD's, resulted in a rapid growth in time money, and hence a rapid growth in the bank credit proxy.

Following the 1969 experience, monetary authorities adjusted the bank credit proxy to take into account Eurodollar borrowings, other major nondeposit sources of funds, such as sale of assets under repurchase agreements, and sale of commercial paper. Chart 8, reported regularly by the St. Louis Federal Reserve Bank, displays trends in both the bank credit proxy and adjusted credit proxy.

Frequently, Federal Reserve credit, the monetary base, bank reserves, and the quantity of money portray similar trends, and hence give unambiguous indication of the basic thrust of monetary policy (Chart 9). But such happy circumstances do not always occur. When contrary indications develop, careful analysis of sources and uses of potential reserve funds usually resolves any existing doubts. Although the Federal Reserve does not have direct control over the money supply, but rather affects this series through other variables, the monetary analyst is interested in monetary results as reflected in the money supply; changes in this variable are closely related to subsequent economic and financial market changes. Let us now turn to an ever popular monetary indicator which

CHART 9

Member Bank Reserves, Federal Reserve Credit, Monetary Base, and Stock of Money

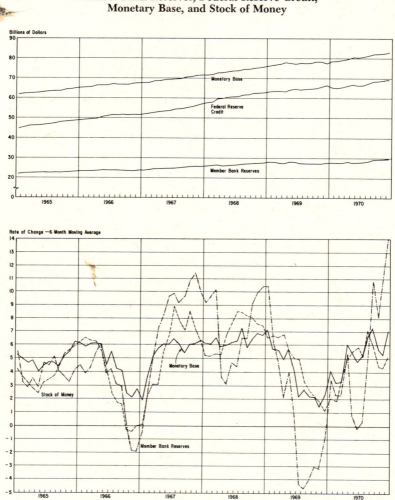

Sources: Federal Reserve Bank of St. Louis; Federal Reserve Board. Data prepared by Harris Trust and Savings Bank.

has very limited reliability and usefulness. The free reserve indicator is discussed on the assumption that it is just as important to know which indicator to avoid as to know which indicators to use.

FREE RESERVES—THE CONVENTIONAL BUT UNRELIABLE MEASURE

The most frequently used, but least reliable, measure of monetary policy as it affects monetary expansion, is free reserves (Chart 10).[7] Free reserves or net borrowed reserves are defined as excess reserves minus borrowings of commercial banks from the Federal Reserve System. It is the free reserve concept which is most regularly referred to by bankers, financial writers, and until recently, representatives of the Federal Reserve. Unfortunately, most casual observers believe that free reserves mean the reserves that banks have free to loan or invest. But the term "free reserves" bears scant relation to that concept. The reason for the heavy reliance on free reserves as a measure of monetary policy is difficult to understand, in view of its many important limitations. Its popularity may be due to familiarity and its availability in the financial press each Friday morning. Perhaps the basic explanation for its persistent popularity is lack of widespread understanding of the severe weakness of free reserves or net borrowed reserves as a measure of monetary change. Free reserves fluctuate with the business cycle from sizable negative magnitudes in the last part of a business expansion to sizable positive sums during recession periods. The cyclical swing is due to changes in both excess reserves and borrowings, but primarily in borrowings. Excess reserves tend

---

[7] For an excellent definitive theoretical and statistical discussion of the relation between free reserves and the stock of money see A. James Meigs, *Free Reserves and the Money Supply* (Chicago: University of Chicago Press, 1962).

CHART 10

Reserve Position

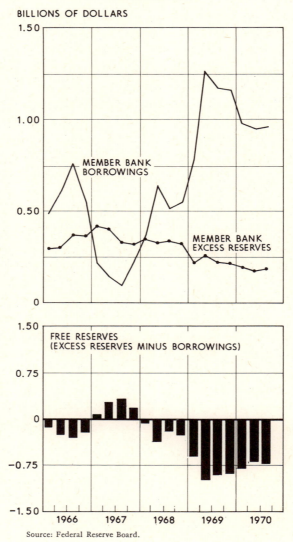

BILLIONS OF DOLLARS

MEMBER BANK BORROWINGS

MEMBER BANK EXCESS RESERVES

FREE RESERVES (EXCESS RESERVES MINUS BORROWINGS)

Source: Federal Reserve Board.

to increase in recession periods when lower interest rates reduce the incentive for banks to keep all their excess funds fully loaned or invested. During periods of rising economic activity and higher interest rates, excess reserves are kept near the operating minimum. On the other hand, borrowings from Federal Reserve banks decrease sharply during recession periods, since the opportunities for borrowing and loaning the funds at a higher rate are substantially reduced. As economic activity improves, credit demands increase, interest rates rise relative to the discount rate, borrowing again becomes profitable, and the volume of borrowing sharply increases. Even though it is profitable, an individual bank probably would not borrow from the Federal Reserve bank for long periods of time because of fear that the Federal Reserve would exercise its "right" to deny credit. However, the elimination of an overinvested position by sales of securities and repayment to the Federal Reserve through an individual bank would merely transfer the deficit reserve position to another bank, which would have an incentive to borrow from the Federal Reserve. Therefore, it is possible for the banking system to build up its indebtedness to the Federal Reserve System as it becomes more profitable to do so, even though no single bank is motivated only by the profit incentive.

But why are free reserve changes a misleading guide to understanding monetary policy? Of prime importance is the fact that free reserves are not closely correlated with bank reserves, the monetary base, or the stock of money and, hence, usually do not provide a proper clue to understanding monetary policy changes. The reason for the poor relations is that any given level of free reserves is consistent with monetary expansion, stability, or contraction. Free reserves concentrate attention on only two of the many factors affecting the ability of the banking system to either expand or contract credit and the stock of money. Borrowing from the Federal

Reserve is one of the sources of potential reserve funds; thus, an increase in borrowings tends to raise total bank reserves, but an increase in borrowings tends to reduce free reserves and suggests monetary restriction. Conversely, a reduction in borrowings from the Federal Reserve tends to reduce the reserves in the banking system and exerts a restrictive effect on monetary expansion; yet free reserves are increased, thereby suggesting an expansive monetary trend. Also, an increase in excess reserves increases free reserves, but reduces the amount of deposits that a given level of total reserves supports. Many factors other than free reserves affect the ability of banks to expand and contract deposits, and the single series that reflects most of them is total reserves of member banks.

Meigs[8] persuasively argues that the most fruitful hypothesis concerning free reserves is that banks seek to maintain certain desired ratios of excess reserves and borrowings (or free reserves) to total deposits. He demonstrates that these desired ratios depend on the market rate of interest and the discount rate, since these are the major factors influencing profitability of loan and investment decisions. The higher the market rates of interest, the lower will be the banking system's desired level of free reserves. The higher the market interest rates relative to the discount rate, the higher will be the banking system's desired level of borrowing from Federal Reserve banks. Higher market rates of interest tend to lower desired excess reserves, since the costs of maintaining idle funds increase. As interest rates and the amount of reserves change, the actual ratios depart from the desired ratios. In trying to adjust the actual reserve ratios to the desired ratios, banks increase or decrease loans and investments, thus causing deposits to change.

There tends to be a considerable lag between an apparent change in monetary policy as measured by free reserves and the

---

[8] *Ibid*, especially Chapters 1, 4 and 6.

reflection of a change in the rate of growth of the stock of money. Although the length of the lag can be determined in hindsight, it can be determined when it is happening only by focusing attention on total reserves of banks or closely related variables. The slippage between changing free reserves and changing monetary growth arises because of institutional and market factors, namely, the existence of a discount mechanism whereby banks can, at their own initiative, borrow additional reserve funds or pay off debts to the Federal Reserve, and also the ability of banks independently to vary the volume of excess reserves.

During a business expansion, interest rates usually rise relative to the discount rate as demands for credit by private borrowers increase. Under such conditions, the Federal Reserve Board, when operating a flexible monetary policy, usually restricts the volume of reserve funds through open market sales of securities. Banks increase their borrowings from the Federal Reserve as interest rates rise relative to the discount rate. Since banks are in business for profit, they are inclined to concentrate their borrowings from the Federal Reserve at a time when it is advantageous from a profit point of view. Also, excess reserves decline in such periods, since banks tend to keep their funds fully invested when it is costly in terms of foregone returns to maintain a high level of excess reserves for which they receive no interest.

When monetary policy is eased, presumably when the economy begins a descent into a recession, the Federal Reserve System may provide additional reserves, but at the same time, the demand for money declines, and interest rates usually drop relative to the discount rate. The typical reaction of the banking system is first to pay off debt to the Federal Reserve, since borrowing is less profitable, and then to restore liquidity that was reduced during the boom phase. Since the demand for money is reduced and interest rates typically decline relative to the discount rate, it becomes less profitable to borrow from the Federal Reserve; borrowing is reduced, thereby reducing total reserves. Further, there is a tendency in the banking system to allow excess reserves to rise as a result of the reduced profitability of investing marginal funds.

These adjustments mean that even though the Federal Reserve may be providing additional funds to the banking system, member bank reserves may be growing less rapidly, or even declining. Hence, we find the anomalous situation wherein an increase in the amount of reserve funds provided directly by the Federal Reserve System does not lead to an immediate increase in member bank reserves, bank assets, and thus the money stock. The length of the time lag prior to an increase in the stock of money will depend on how vigorously the Federal Reserve pursues its easy money policy and how rapidly commercial banks pay off debt and raise excess reserves. Eventually, the liquidity needs of the banking system will be met, outstanding loans from Federal Reserve banks will approach zero, and excess reserves will be sufficiently high to impel the lending or investment of additional funds. Since a period of declining business activity is characterized by a declining loan trend, investments must rise more rapidly than loans are declining before the total money stock increases. Although, as previously noted, book writers are fond of pointing out that expansion and contraction in bank loans bring change in the money stock, it is worthwhile to note again that it is usually change in bank investments that accounts for both the upper and lower turning points in the money stock growth rate series.

Past cycles reveal several examples of the possible misleading indications given by changes in free reserves when unsupported by comparisons with total reserves, the monetary base, and the stock of money. In early 1960, free reserves increased substantially several months in advance of the May business cycle peak. However, at the same time, member bank reserves were declining sharply, along with the stock of money. The free reserve improvement occurred primarily because of a reduction in outstanding loans from the Federal Reserve System. Thus, commercial bank debt reduction lowered the reserves available to the banking system, and the member bank reserve figure indicated that this reduction was not initially offset by other factors which provided reserve funds. It was not until the second quarter of 1960 that total reserves began to rise rapidly, and shortly thereafter monetary expansion began. This expansion continued throughout the 1960 period of rapid gold outflow, even though an outflow of gold tends to reduce bank reserves and the stock of money. Monetary expansion continued only because the Federal Reserve more than offset the adverse monetary effects of the gold outflow, as evidenced by a continued rise in member bank reserves.

During 1961, free reserves held steady near the $500 million level. However, during the year both monetary expansion and contraction occurred. Total reserves began a modest contraction during the first quarter and declined until August, when a sharp rise began. It is not surprising that changes in the stock of money during 1961 displayed the same pattern, after allowing for a slight lag. Monetary growth ceased in the first quarter of 1961 and declined slightly until September, when a sharp expansion began and lasted throughout the balance of the year. The same pattern occurred in 1962. In the latter part of 1963 the rate of growth of the money stock rose despite a decline in free reserves.

During the late 1960's and 1970 there were numerous examples of conflicting signs from free reserves versus monetary aggregates. The years of 1967 and 1968 recorded massive increases in monetary aggregates, but in 1968 free reserves shifted to a negative position as borrowings from the Federal

Reserve rose sharply, thereby supplying additional reserves to the banking system. In 1969 both the aggregates and free reserves suggested a tighter monetary policy. During June and July, 1970, another interesting countermovement occurred. Following the Penn Central bankruptcy there was increasing concern that many companies with outstanding commercial paper would have difficulty in renewing maturities and, in fact, some did. In addition to eliminating ceilings on large, short-term certificates, the Federal Reserve encouraged banks to borrow to accommodate corporate credit demands emanating from corporations abruptly leaving the commercial paper market. Many banks did so, bank borrowings rose, and free reserves declined sharply. But monetary aggregates indicated that an expansive monetary policy was still being pursued.

It is clear from the above analysis and examples that early changes in the supply of reserves made available by the Federal Reserve System in the beginning of either a recession or an expansion phase of a business cycle will be offset temporarily by action taken by the banking system. Hence, even though free reserves may change, there will be no immediate effect on monetary growth. To the extent that the Federal Reserve Board takes aggressive offsetting action in the beginning phase of a policy change, the time required for effecting a change in the money stock will be reduced. So long as the Federal Reserve limits early changes to modest amounts, which appears to have been typical of past policy, a considerable slippage will remain. On other occasions, when there is no financial incentive for varying free reserves, a change in reserves provided by the Federal Reserve may result in a prompt change in monetary growth. In summary, changes in free reserves confirm the popular assumption that bankers are good managers of money, i.e., they adjust money positions to changing pecuniary incentives. Free reserve changes are usually closely related to changes in short-term interest rates and are therefore a good, but unnecessary, proxy for the Treasury bill rate. In no way do fluctuations in free reserves add to useful knowledge concerning Federal Reserve policies.

CONCLUSIONS

The statement that the Federal Reserve can determine the rate of growth of the stock of money appears to be approximately correct, since the Federal Reserve can determine Federal Reserve credit, the monetary base, and ultimately, member bank reserves. It should be recognized, however, that during the beginning phase of a policy change some slippage is introduced as a result of the reaction of the private banking system, unless the Federal Reserve moves aggressively to offset commercial bank action. Some analysts have argued that Federal Reserve action alone cannot increase the stock of money, since the final step can be accomplished only if the banking system utilizes the reserves made available. Even though this statement is technically correct, it must be recognized that the profit incentive provides considerable assurance that additional reserve funds will be utilized for either loans or investments, and therefore the stock of money will respond.

A monetary analyst often can predict changes in the money stock by a careful analysis of current Federal Reserve policy, since the facts relating to Federal Reserve policy are made available weekly. Therefore, even though the Federal Reserve does not have direct control over all the factors which affect reserves of banks, it does have the power to create or destroy sufficient sources of potential reserve funds to bring about any effect it may desire on total reserves of member banks, especially over a period of a few weeks.

For example, through the sale of government securities held on June 24, 1970, the Federal Reserve could reduce sources of reserve funds by about $57.0 billion, which would tend to reduce total reserves by a like amount. If reserve requirements were raised to the statutory maximum of 22 percent for reserve city banks and 14 percent for country banks, required reserves would be increased from the approximately $27.2 billion in effect on June 24, 1970 to $32.3 billion, a rise of about $5.1 billion. Required reserves for reserve city banks would rise from $17.0 billion to $21.4 billion, while country bank required reserves would increase from $10.1 billion to $10.9 billion. In other words, open market sales of government securities plus an increase in required reserve ratios to the statutory maximum would be capable of creating a combined reserve deficit of about $62.1 billion. There is no practical limit to the amount of reserves the Fed can create.

It is therefore clear that the Federal Reserve has sufficient power to offset any extraneous influence on the reserves of the banking system that it considers undesirable. It should be kept in mind that for each $1.00 of excess reserves created by the Federal Reserve System, the commercial banking system can bring about a $6\frac{2}{3}$-fold increase in assets and deposits with present average reserve requirements. If the required reserve ratios were lowered to the statutory minimum, the expansion ratio would be about 11 to 1, whereas with maximum required reserve ratios, the expansion ratio would be only $5\frac{1}{4}$ to 1. Conversely, for each $1.00 of reserves destroyed, commercial banks are forced to bring about a $6\frac{2}{3}$-fold decrease in the money stock with present average reserve requirements, an 11-fold decrease with minimum reserve requirements, and a $5\frac{1}{4}$-fold decrease with maximum reserve ratios. Therefore, the Federal Reserve has sufficient power to bring about any change it deems desirable in the total stock of money.

The monetary analyst can best detect and measure the effects of monetary policy action by reviewing policy statements of Federal Reserve officials, and by observing current changes in the stock of money, member bank reserves, the monetary base, and Federal Reserve credit. The bank credit proxy should also be examined, since it receives close scrutiny by policy makers. Free reserves should be ignored for this purpose. Statements by officials will sometimes provide a clue as to what their policy is attempting to accomplish, but careful analysis of change in the stock of money will provide the best guide as to the actual net effect of monetary actions. Analysis of current monetary policy actions must always be made in the context of current economic trends. Perhaps the most pertinent question the analyst should ask is "What monetary action would I take in present circumstances if I were the Federal Reserve Board and had its view on the effect of monetary policy as evidenced in past writing and performance?" If the above approaches are applied constantly, an observer will always be well informed on current monetary developments and will frequently be in a position to predict major changes in monetary trends with considerable accuracy.

CASE STUDY 1970

Detecting a change in monetary policy in 1970 involved an interesting combination of game playing, listening, and watching. The basic thrust of President Nixon's economic policy to cool an intense inflation without creating a protracted recession was clear throughout 1969. It was clear from statements of objectives by the President and his major economic policy makers, as well as by policies pursued. Fiscal policy in 1969 remained firm, and monetary policy became increasingly restrictive as the year transpired.

By late summer and fall, most monetarists were convinced that the restrictive monetary policy dating from the third quarter of 1968 had been sufficiently severe to induce either a recession or significant slowdown in the economy. As the fall passed and winter set in, economic indicators confirmed that at least a slowdown was under way.

However, inflationary psychology was rampant. Surveys of plant and equipment plans (a lagging indicator) suggested further sharp increases in 1970. Statements by policy makers continued to emphasize inflation concerns while minimizing the recession threat. Unemployment, which had decreased to 3.3 percent in late 1968, did not begin a significant rise until September 1969, and that proved to be a false start not exceeded until February 1970. Prices continued to rise rapidly in the first several months following the slowdown, typical of such periods in the past.

In the meantime, a random influence caused a sharp spurt in the money supply in late December 1969, but interest rates continued to reflect the serious inflationary psychology that permeated the economy. In January the money supply dropped to prior levels and unemployment continued to rise. There was increasing talk about the possibility of recession, including the political and economic costs that would result if it actually developed. Not surprisingly, the Secretary of Labor, George P. Shultz, was the first administration official who began to publicly call for an easing of monetary policy to cushion the deteriorating economy. This move was understandable, both because of his concern for the labor markets and his known agreement with the monetarist position. Monetarists were joined by economists of other persuasions in calling for a less restrictive monetary policy.

On January 31, 1970, President Nixon swore in Dr. Arthur F. Burns as the new chairman of the Federal Reserve Board. Dr. Burns had quite properly carefully avoided any recent public statement concerning either the economy or monetary policy. Furthermore, it was well known that he was not of Keynesian persuasion and that he leaned toward the monetarist camp. But he had only one vote, and a prior majority of the Board had voted for a continued tight monetary policy, according to the latest published report.

It was at that point that careful perusal of monetary aggregates such as the money supply, monetary base, Federal Reserve credit, and bank reserves became indispensable. By late February 1970 these aggregates began to suggest to a perceptive observer that a change was in the wind, but as usual the evidence was inconclusive because it was short-lived and might not have represented a trend. On February 18, 1970, Dr. Burns testified before the Joint Economic Committee and strongly suggested that a change was under way because of the growing concern about the deteriorating business climate. Furthermore, there was beginning evidence among wholesale price series that inflation was ebbing. Within several weeks after Burns' testimony, monetary aggregates confirmed in no uncertain terms that a change had indeed transpired. Despite the interruption of the Cambodian invasion and the Penn Central bankruptcy, which seriously disturbed investors and financial markets, monetary aggregates, on the average, continued to reflect an expansive monetary policy.

In summary, the monetary analyst must focus his attention on changes in monetary policy, for it is these changes that have implications for subsequent trends in financial markets, inflation, and economic activity. To perform this task effectively, the observer must be well informed concerning recent trends in the economy; he must understand the policy objectives of responsible authorities; he must attempt to place himself in the policy maker's role and ask how he would react; he must keep his ear carefully attuned to the nuances that become evident in policy makers' public utterances; but most of all, he must meticulously follow the monetary aggregates in order to make certain that public utterances are being confirmed by appropriate action. The job of detecting a policy shift shortly after it occurs is not impossible, but must be approached with the attitude of a super sleuth armed with competing theories, ever ready to look for confirming or contradictory facts either in the form of public statements or hard statistical evidence. The task is indeed challenging, but well worth the effort if one wishes to avoid costly surprises in financial markets and economic trends.

CHAPTER 5

Money and Business Fluctuations

Business forecasting is a hazardous art, frequently practiced but seldom mastered. The name of the game is to anticipate change before it occurs in order to avoid costly surprises, especially at turning points of the business cycle. There is no way for mere humans to penetrate perfectly the mist of the unknown future. But there are ways of reducing the degree of uncertainty and range of error. The rewards are great if an estimate of the future is essentially correct, believed, and acted upon ahead of other market participants. Of course, the costs of being wrong are equally large, and, upon more than one occasion, have shortened the employment tenure of a practicing economist.

The conventional business forecast presents a detailed analysis of individual GNP components, adds the separate estimates, and hence derives a total GNP estimate for the period ahead. One of the major advantages of using a GNP framework is that the system forces internal consistency. In other words, double counting is avoided and all components of the economy are included. But there are an infinite number of estimates that are internally consistent, and only one is right! Each time an economist presents a carefully reasoned projection, this fact should be remembered. Although bad logic is unlikely to improve a forecast, good logic does not insure success.

There is an understandable tendency for all forecasters to project the known into the unknown, or to extend recent trends in economic variables into the future. In fact, the extrapolation technique often works quite well. It works well except at the point in time when a business forecast is really needed and would prove useful and profitable, i.e., turning points in the business cycle. It is at turning points of business cycles that forecasters have had their greatest difficulty.[1] This fact is of course not surprising, but it does point up the critical need for utilizing a theory of business fluctuations that has been carefully tested in the past and found useful in anticipating turning points in advance of the fact. Not only will the use of such a theory increase the probability that one will be right most of the time, but also it will also give one confidence to act upon his judgment in the face of imperfect knowledge. Forecasting the future always deals with uncertainties, and the objective must be to reduce them as much as possible. Nonetheless, implementation must be carried out only in prudent measures—some "scat" room must be left in the event that the most probable pattern of events does not transpire as expected. It is important to remember that the future can never be known with certainty. However, the present state of theory and empirical testing can provide considerable guidance. Recognition of the inevitable risks does not leave us in abysmal ignorance.

The two available theories are those previously described

---

[1] Victor Zarnowitz, *An Appraisal of Short-Term Economic Forecasts,* National Bureau of Economic Research (New York: Columbia University Press, 1967).

briefly in Chapter 1, i.e., the quantity theory of the monetarist and the income-expenditure theory of the fiscalist. Each theory endeavors to explain and predict expenditure or income change. The monetarist places change in the money supply in the star role, while the fiscalist emphasizes changes in investment and the full employment budget. It is the thesis of this book that monetarists have enjoyed the better of the argument, primarily because the quantity theory has yielded much better predictions. Let us now examine the argument and evidence in more detail.

The quantity theory is not a new theory, but the monetarist was sent into nearly total eclipse with the development of the Keynesian income-expenditure theory in the mid 1930's. Only recently, as the new economics proved inadequate to the task of achieving economic stability as well as predictive accuracy, has professional and public attention shifted toward the monetarist explanation.

For over a century and a half, some economists have contended that the amount of money in an economic system is an important determinant of total spending, income creation, and the general price level. Since many prices, including wages, are inflexible downward in the short run, it appears plausible that monetary change may affect short-run employment and production trends if it affects total spending. Perhaps the most effective means of approaching an understanding of the quantity theory is by using the "equation of exchange" developed by Irving Fisher during the early part of the twentieth century.[2]

The equation of exchange separates the relevant factors of the economy into four broad categories defined as follows:

M = average quantity of money during a given period.
V = average turnover of money during a given period.

---

[2] Irving Fisher and Harry Gunnison Brown, *The Purchasing Power of Money* (New York: MacMillan Company, 1926).

$P =$ average price level of goods and services sold during a given period.

$T =$ volume of transactions during a given period.

If we multiply M, the money stock, times V, the average turnover, we have MV, which is the amount of money spent on transactions during the period under consideration. Likewise we can multiply P, the average price level, times T, the unit measurement of volume of transactions, and secure a total PT, which represents the amount of money sellers received for their sales during the period under consideration. Since the amount of money spent in any period must be equal to the amount of money received, it therefore follows that $MV = PT$. This equation is labeled the equation of exchange. It is clear that the equation of exchange is a truism, correct by definition, and hence is not the quantity theory of money. The above equation does not have the basic essential of any useful theory—namely, the capacity for being disproved. Nonetheless, the equation of exchange, $MV = PT$, does serve a useful role by establishing the major categories with which the quantity theory is concerned.

It is possible to make a useful reformulation of the equation of exchange by substituting X (total real output during a given period) for T. There exists no adequate measure of T, but real output is measured and reported each quarter in the real gross national product series, which represents the real value of finally produced goods and services after adjustment for price changes. In the reformulation of the equation of exchange, $MV = PX$, the definition of M remains the same, but V is now defined as the average turnover of money spent on final production during a given period, and P becomes the average price level of finally produced goods and services during a given period. This price series is quantified in the series usually referred to as the GNP price deflator. It is clear that $MV = PX$, since MV now represents the amount of money spent on current production during a given period, and PX represents the amount of money received from the sale of current production of goods and services during the same period.

To convert the "equation of exchange" into the quantity theory, an assumption must be made concerning independency and dependency of the variables contained in the equation. In other words, the equation of exchange says nothing about which variable provides the motivating force. All it says is that a change in any one variable will be affected by sufficient change in one or more of the other three variables so that MV remains equal to PX. All versions of the quantity theory consider M, the quantity of money, to be the independent variable, even though, as explained previously, it can be determined by the monetary authority, i.e., the Federal Reserve System. Theorists argue that V, velocity, is determined by both long-term and cyclical factors. It is in this area that much of the debate over the effects of a changing stock of money is centered. Some contend that changes in velocity automatically offset changes in the money stock; therefore, a changing stock of money does not affect prices, output, and hence employment. It is not essential to assume that V is constant in order to derive a useful theory. It is only necessary that we establish that changes in V do not consistently offset changes in M, so that changes in the money stock do affect total spending.

Monetarists argue that the price level is a dependent variable determined by the volume of total spending and the level of output. Potential total output is determined by such long-range factors as the amount of labor and capital available, as well as the productivity of the factors of production. It is clear that actual output is determined also by total spending. After full employment is attained, it is impossible to raise output further except by increasing the amount of either capital or labor or raising productivity. However, output can be increased when the economy is functioning at less than full employment by increasing total spending. Earlier classical economists once argued that there would be a tendency for an economic system to maintain full employment at all levels of demand, but it is clear that in the real contemporary world, price and wage rigidities tend to lead to reduced employment when total demand weakens.

From the above analysis, an economist would predict that a decline in total spending would lead to both lower output and increased unemployment. Furthermore, if we momentarily assume that velocity changes do not compensate for changes in the money stock (this assumption is to be considered later), a monetarist would predict that a decline in the rate of monetary growth would shortly result in an economic slowdown due to the adverse effect on total spending. A monetarist would also argue, conversely, that a rise in the rate of monetary growth would shortly increase total spending and, hence, would result in an expansion in economic activity.

The argument can be made in a somewhat different and perhaps more meaningful fashion. Economic units, including individuals and businesses, attempt to diversify their holdings of assets between non-monetary assets such as real estate, and monetary assets such as demand deposits and currency. Their willingness to hold money depends on its cost, i.e., the sacrificed return from not holding other assets and the demand for money for exchange purposes. At any point in time with a given stock of money, economic units either have an optimum distribution of nonmonetary to monetary assets and projected expenditures or are attempting to achieve such an optimum. If the stock of money is rapidly increased relative to other assets and projected income, economic units find they have an excess of money. They therefore increase their spending on assets and goods, and this action has the effect of bidding up prices if the economy is at or near full employment, but primarily raises output if unemployment exists. This increased spending continues until incomes are raised to such a level that the increased value of assets and expected income balances the higher stock of money. Conversely, if the money stock is sharply decreased relative to nonmonetary assets and income, economic units attempt to restore liquidity by rearranging assets and conserving cash. Therefore, total spending declines and exerts downward pressure on prices and production to the point where the lower money stock is in balance with the reduced level of income. Although economic units cannot actually increase or decrease the money stock through their own actions, they can bring about changes in asset distribution and total spending and, hence, changes in prices and employment.

Monetarists contend that changes in the money supply directly affect both consumption and investment spending. The new economists following the Keynesian tradition emphasize the argument that more money in the economic system does not affect consumption outlays directly but has its major impact on investment spending through the tendency for more money to reduce interest rates. Similarly, they emphasize that a change in fiscal policy, for example a tax cut, increases disposable income and hence consumer outlays. The monetarist would deny that a tax cut per se would increase spending unless it were accompanied by an increase in the quantity of money.

As will be described later in more detail, there is also a significant difference in the two theories concerning the factors affecting interest rates. New economists believe that an easier monetary policy can permanently lower interest rates, since they say that interest rates are essentially determined by the liquidity preference schedule for money and the stock of money. Hence, they argue that an easier money policy can induce greater investment and ultimately more economic growth by reducing interest rates. The inflationary impact, they contend, can be offset with a tight fiscal policy and wage-price guidelines.

Monetarists, on the other hand, differentiate sharply between the real rate of interest (money rate adjusted for inflation) and the market rate of interest. They argue that the real rate of interest is determined by basic real variables in the economy, including the long-run supply of savings and the real productivity of capital. An easier monetary policy may temporarily reduce the market rate of interest, but the longer run effect may be the opposite, since more money results in higher prices (after full employment) and a rising price level causes higher interest rates. Instead of more money causing lower market rates, an easier monetary policy, monetarists contend, brings higher interest rates. In other words, monetarists argue that market rates of interest include the real rate of interest plus the expected rate of inflation. Rather than looking upon monetary and fiscal policies as substitutes, they believe that these two policies are better viewed as complements.

BUT WHAT ARE THE FACTS?

Neat explanations or rationales are empty intellectual exercises unless they can be verified in the real world. The science of economics may be elegant and challenging to the intellect, but unless it has some relation to the world in which we live and work, it can have little effect on decisions, either private or public. Therefore, it behooves an economist to test the validity of theoretical contentions if they are to be of practical significance. The income-expenditure theory and the monetarist theory are equally logical. But since they frequently yield contrary predictions they cannot be equally right!

In the early post World War II years, only one economist, who was largely ignored at the time, was busily engaged in documenting the relation between monetary change and the business cycle. Clark Warburton, an economist with the Federal Deposit Insurance Corporation, published many empirically oriented articles contending that short-run economic cycles were largely induced by changes in the money supply.[3] But no one was listening, reading, and believing. No one, that is, except a few non-Keynesians whose intellectual roots can usually be traced back to Irving Fisher. The author had the good fortune to come under the influence of a former student and co-author with Fisher, Harry Gunnison Brown[4] of the University of Missouri, who was much impressed with Warburton's works and passed them on to his students. When Milton Friedman and Anna Schwartz published their monetary classic in 1963, they included the following passage concerning Warburton in the preface: ". . . time and again, as we came to some conclusion that seemed to us novel and original, we found he (Warburton) had been there before."[5] In more recent times there has been voluminous research work compiled and the answer rings loud and clear—money calls the tune.

Chart 11 displays changes in the rate of monetary growth from 1920, and a gross national product velocity of money, i.e., current GNP ÷ average stock of money. The time periods from peaks to troughs of business cycles are shaded. (National Bureau of Economic Research datings are used.) The money supply plotted is a six-month moving average annual rate of expansion, which yields reasonable smoothness without rendering the series insensitive to short-run changes. Table 11 relates business cycle turning points since 1919 to turning points in the rate of monetary growth. On the average, monetary growth turned down 15.8 months before recessions, and rose 8.1 months before recoveries.

[3] See Clark Warburton, "The Misplaced Emphasis in Contemporary Business Fluctuation Theory," *Journal of Business,* Vol. XIX (1946), pp. 199–220.

[4] Irving Fisher, Harry Gunnison Brown, *The Purchasing Power of Money* (New York: MacMillan Company, 1926).

[5] Milton Friedman and Anna Schwartz, *A Monetary History of the United States 1867–1960* (Princeton, N.J.: Princeton University Press, 1963), p. XXII.

CHART 11

Money, Velocity, and Business

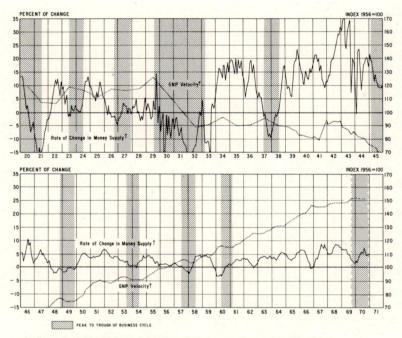

PEAK TO TROUGH OF BUSINESS CYCLE

* All commercial banks demand deposits adj. + currency (seasonally adjusted).
† Annual rate of monthly change, 6-month moving average.
‡ Annual data before 1939; quarterly since 1939.
Jagged area represents a significant slowdown in business activity.
Source: Dept. of Commerce, Fed. Res. Bd., Nat'l. Bureau of Econ. Research, Inc.

What can we make of all these facts? First let us consider whether the money supply series is a useful statistical indicator of revivals and recessions. The National Bureau of Economic Research has established a set of useful criteria for making such a determination.[6] (1) The indicator should have a record of

---

[6] Geoffrey H. Moore, *Statistical Indicators of Cyclical Revivals and Recessions* (Occasional Paper No. 31), (New York: National Bureau of Economic Research, Inc., 1950), p. 20.

TABLE 11

**Lead of Monetary* Growth-Rate Turning Points before
Business Cycle Turning Points**

(lead before downturns)

Monetary Growth-Rate Peaks†	Business Cycle Peaks	Months Series Lead	
December 1918	January 1920	13	
September 1922	May 1923	8	
November 1924	October 1926	23	
December 1928 (April 1928)	June 1929	6	(14)
July 1936 (June 1935)	May 1937	10	(23)
December 1951	July 1953	19	
February 1955	July 1957	29	
November 1958	May 1960	18	
July 1968 (July 1967)	November 1969^E	16	(28)
	Range	29–6	
	Average	15.8	(19.4)

(lead before upturns)

Monetary Growth-Rate Troughs†	Business Cycle Troughs	Months Series Lead	
June 1921	July 1921	1	
August 1923	July 1924	11	
December 1926	November 1927	11	
March 1932	March 1933	12	
December 1937	June 1938	6	
February 1949 (July 1948)	October 1949	8	(15)
November 1953 (March 1954)	August 1954	9	(5)
January 1958	April 1958	3	
May 1960	February 1961	9	
December 1969 (February 1970)	November 1970^E	11	(9)
	Range	12–1	(15–1)
	Average	8.1	(8.2)

* Money = Demand deposits and currency.
† Computed on a 6-month moving average.
Source: Federal Reserve, U.S. Department of Commerce, Harris Trust and Savings Bank.

a half-century or longer, thus showing its relation to business cycles under many different conditions. (2) The indicator should lead the month of revival by an invariable interval, and the same should be true for recessions. (3) The indicator should have no erratic movements which serve to mislead the analyst, but should have a smooth movement from peak to trough to peak. (4) Cyclical movements of the indicator should be pronounced, so that they can be readily recognized, and should give an indication of the relative amplitude of impending business changes. (5) The indicator should be so related to general business activity that it establishes as much confidence as possible that its future behavior with regard to business cycles will be like its past behavior.

It must be recognized, of course, that in the real world we can never hope to find an ideal indicator, but to the extent that the real world indicators vary from the above criteria, they will be of less value to the forecaster. The evidence displayed in Chart 11 and Table 11 agrees fairly well with the above criteria. There is a long period of evidence; the series leads both recessions and recoveries, although not by an invariable interval; there are few erratic movements; cyclical movements are pronounced; and the indicator instills confidence, since it is consistent with a well-known and long-lived economic theory. Following are the four important conclusions that can be derived from these data:[7]

1. All business declines since 1918[8] were preceded by a reduction in the rate of monetary growth. As indicated in Table 11, which presents data covering the last 52 years, the average lead excluding the 1945 and 1949 downturns[9] was

---

[7] Much of the following material in this section appeared in Beryl W. Sprinkel, "Monetary Growth as a Cyclical Predictor," *Journal of Finance*, September, 1959, pp. 333–46.

[8] Other data indicate the same relations existed prior to 1918.

[9] Although 1945 is designated by the National Bureau of Economic Research as a period of cyclical downturn, this cycle was omitted in the above computations because of the nature of the adjustment, which involved primarily a reallocation of resources from production of war goods to production of civilian goods. The rate of monetary growth declined throughout the early postwar period as well as the later years of the war, and it was not until 1949 that a recession developed. Excessive war-created liquidity apparently prevented the usual relationship between a declining monetary growth rate and the business cycle from becoming evident during this period.

15.8 months. The lead prior to business downturns varied from 6 to 29 months. The long 29-month lead occurred prior to the 1957 recession, when the rate of decline in monetary growth was unusually small. The short 6-month lead occurred before the 1929 downturn and could alternatively be designated as a 14-month lead. Choosing peaks and troughs of the monetary growth rate, even in hindsight, is sometimes difficult.

2. Recoveries since 1918 were consistently preceded by a rise in the rate of monetary growth. As indicated in Table 11, the average lead was 8.1 months. The lead prior to recoveries varied from 1 to 12 months with most leads ranging between 8 and 12 months.

The average lag between a change in the monetary growth rate and the subsequent business change was less prior to recovery than it was before the recession phase of the business cycle.

3. Typically, the index of GNP velocity of money, which measures the average number of times the money stock is spent on GNP, tends to rise during much of the period when the rate of monetary growth is declining, and tends to decline for a shorter period when monetary growth rises. Indeed, changes in the trend of velocity are approximately coincident with the peaks and troughs of business cycles. This is well known, as a result of earlier research.[10] It appears, therefore, that those who contend that countercyclical changes in the money stock are not fully offset by changes in velocity are correct. On the other hand, it is quite clear that there is a tendency during business revivals for velocity to rise in the short run as monetary growth is reduced, thereby softening and delaying the impact of changing monetary growth. Conversely, during a recession, as monetary growth begins to rise, velocity continues downward

---

10 Richard T. Selden, "Monetary Velocity in the United States," Milton Friedman, ed., *Studies in the Quantity Theory of Money* (Chicago: University of Chicago Press, 1956), pp. 192–95.

until the trough of the business cycle is reached, again delaying the impact of changing monetary growth for a brief period.

This observation does not mean that changes in monetary growth are useless as a predictive tool, but, rather than offsetting changes in velocity, they merely insert some slippage into the system. Indeed, from a predictive standpoint this is fortunate. The slippage allows time for a lead to be established and, therefore, makes possible a prediction based partly on a changing monetary growth rate. If business downturns and upturns coincided precisely with changes in monetary growth, it would, of course, be impossible to use that relationship to predict changes in the business trend unless we could in turn predict changes in the rate of monetary growth.

Even though it is quite clear that velocity changes do not fully offset changes in monetary growth, there remains an interesting question as to why such offsets occur in the short run. The data are consistent with the previous argument concerning the effect of changes in liquidity on business and consumers. For example, in the early phase of a declining monetary growth period, liquidity is sufficiently high to allow spenders to economize on cash and thereby turn over the existing money stock more intensively. As liquidity is reduced by further declines in monetary growth, this economizing of cash eventually becomes impossible. When this condition is reached, a reallocation of assets and, ultimately, a change in total spending occur. The converse appears to be true when monetary growth begins to increase as a recession deepens.

Interest rates probably play a part in encouraging cash economizing as the monetary growth rate declines. Such periods are likely to be characterized by high and rising interest rates. Hence, it is more costly to maintain idle funds, and business is encouraged to economize on cash. Conversely, lower rates during a recession mean it is less costly to maintain idle cash, so an increase in the stock of money may not in the very short run lead to additional spending. Fortunately, from our point of view, it is not necessary to understand this relation completely, since we have a long record which demonstrates that velocity does not offset changes in growth of the money stock for a long period.

4. The evidence indicates that the intensity of changes in the rate of monetary growth is positively correlated with the intensity of subsequent changes in the economy. The most severe recessions or depressions which have been recorded since 1909 occurred in 1920–21, 1929–33, and 1937–38. Also, the most severe monetary contractions occurred immediately prior to and during those periods. In early post World War II years, the rate of monetary growth dropped substantially, but the abundance of liquidity prevented a contraction in business. The early post World War II period represents an exception to the conclusions that business declines shortly follow periods of decline in monetary growth and that large business declines follow large declines in monetary growth. This disparity is readily explained in terms of the economy's expansion in response to the enormous monetary increases during World War II, but it makes clear that a mechanical application of the leading monetary indicator technique and explanation is not justified. Variations in the rate of monetary growth since 1951, when a flexible monetary policy was adopted, were quite modest in contrast to earlier periods, although they increased somewhat in the latter 1960's. It is probably not accidental that the economic contractions during that period were also relatively mild. Finally, the most rapid growth in the money stock following contractions occurred after the 1920–21, 1929–33, and 1937–38 downturns. It is significant that the rates of recovery following these contractions were among the most rapid.

Note (in Chart 11) that the decade of the 1960's began and ended with a recession, each recession preceded by extensive monetary restraint. However, in between there were two periods of pause that threatened to become recessions but did not—1963 and 1967. Both slowdowns followed brief periods of noticeable monetary restraint, but the period of restraint was not as long as had preceded prior recessions. Renewed economic expansion occurred on both occasions about two quarters after monetary growth was renewed. The high rate of monetary growth from mid 1965 through 1968 receives the monetarists' blame for the high rate of inflation and high and rising interest rates which characterized that period. The inflation and high interest rate pattern was not changed until well after monetary policy became notably less expansive in late 1968 and especially in 1969.

The economist most responsible for the renaissance and further development of monetarism is undoubtedly Professor Milton Friedman of the University of Chicago. He is uniformly hailed as the intellectual leader of the Chicago School, and is its leading researcher, writer, speaker, and debater. The *Institutional Investor* recently stated: "Their ideas are becoming an increasingly acceptable part of orthodox economic theory, even a guide to the Nixon administration's progress. Indeed, the Chicago School may well be the vanguard of a revolution in economics as sweeping as the one fomented 35 years ago by Lord Keynes."[11] His research in money has been path-breaking and he has also spawned a large number of graduate students, including this author, who have continued work in money.

One of the most persuasive modern pieces of research was conducted by Milton Friedman of the University of Chicago, and David Meiselman, now of Macalester College. Their study

---

[11] Harvey D. Shapiro, "The Chicago School: Apostles of the Money Supply," *Institutional Investor,* February, 1970, p. 36.

was entitled "The Relative Stability of Monetary Velocity and the Investment Multiplier in the United States, 1897–1958."[12] In effect, they attempted to test the relative predictive reliability of the quantity theory, which contends that monetary change is the dominant factor influencing total spending, and hence income trends, and the Keynesian theory of income determination, which contends that autonomous investment expenditures are the dominant causal factor. Fortunately, the evidence from their study was remarkably consistent and unambiguous. The income velocity of the circulation of money was consistently and decidedly more stable than the investment multiplier except during the early days of the Great Depression following 1929. Throughout this long period of evidence, there was a close and consistent relation between the stock of money and consumption or income, and between year-to-year changes in the stock of money and changes in consumption or income. Furthermore, there was a much weaker and less consistent relation between autonomous expenditures and consumption, with the same exception of the Depression, and essentially no consistent relation between year-to-year changes in autonomous expenditures and consumption. The slight relation that existed appears, by several statistical tests, to reflect the influence of money in disguise.

The correlations between money and consumption were not only higher than between autonomous expenditures and consumption, but also they were extremely high in absolute level. For example, from 1897 to 1958 the correlation between the annual values of the stock of money and consumption outlays was 0.985, and 0.695 between the first differences of the series. Correlations between autonomous expenditures and consump-

---

12 Milton Friedman and David Meiselman, "The Relative Stability of Monetary Velocity and the Investment Multiplier in the United States, 1897–1958," *Stabilization Policies,* Prepared for the Commission on Money and Credit (Englewood Cliffs, N.J.: Prentice-Hall, 1963), pp. 165–268.

tion were not only lower than between money and consumption, but also they were generally low in absolute level. For the period studied, the correlation between the annual values of autonomous expenditures and consumption was 0.756, and 0.095 between the first differences.

By the application of statistical techniques, the authors attempted to eliminate the effect of money on autonomous expenditures, and found that the correlation of autonomous expenditures and income became small and sometimes negative. However, when the identical test was applied to the elimination of autonomous expenditures effects on the money stock, the correlation between money and consumption remained about the same as with the simple correlation. The important implication with regard to predictive value is that the quantity theory approach to forecasting income is likely to be more fruitful than the income expenditure approach, i.e., the former corresponds to empirical relations that are far more stable over the course of the business cycle. This means that the business forecaster should rely heavily on monetary change as a predictor of the future business trend, even though other techniques may well be useful in determining the allocation of total spending.

In another study, Friedman and Schwartz demonstrated beyond any reasonable doubt that "the stock of money displays a systematic cyclical behavior."[13] Furthermore, they concluded that for major movements of income "there is an extremely strong case for the proposition that sizable changes in the rate of change of the money stock are a necessary and sufficient condition for sizable changes in the rate of change of money income." For minor movements, they concluded that "while the evidence was far less strong, it is plausible to suppose that

---

[13] Milton Friedman and Anna Schwartz, "Money and Business Cycles," Supplement to the February, 1963 issue of *Review of Economics and Statistics* (Cambridge, Mass.: Harvard University Press, 1963), p. 63.

changes in the stock of money played an important, independent role."

Among the most penetrating and influential research on money has been the work conducted by a group of economists at the Federal Reserve Bank of St. Louis. The St. Louis Federal Reserve research department has been the only unit in the Federal Reserve System that has pursued a monetarist line. Other Federal Reserve banks and the Board's staff generally accepted the income-expenditure theory espoused by new economists. Until recently, the Board has usually played down the role of money, insisting that monetary and credit change was only one of many influences impacting the economy. In general, the Federal Reserve authorities have argued that fiscal mistakes were much more responsible for the economic instability that characterized the period since mid 1965 than monetary policy.

It is not difficult to trace the monetarist predilections of the St. Louis Federal Reserve Bank. The president, Darryl Francis, was once a student of Harry Gunnison Brown of the University of Missouri. Homer Jones, senior vice president of the St. Louis Federal Reserve Bank, was formerly a teacher of Milton Friedman at Rutgers University, later received his Ph.D. from the University of Chicago, and has been a lifelong friend of Professor Friedman. Several other prominent St. Louis researchers were trained at Chicago or UCLA, but some were trained under Walter Heller, a leading fiscalist, whose home base is the University of Minnesota.

Predilections and monetary bias are one thing, and empirical research is another, but the research from St. Louis has been prodigious and convincing. Furthermore, the weekly, monthly, and quarterly output of relevant, well processed monetary and economic data from St. Louis has made their publications "must" reading for everyone who wants to be well informed about recent trends.

In November 1968, Andersen and Jordan published a study

entitled "Monetary and Fiscal Actions: A Test of Their Relative Importance in Economic Stabilization."[14] The results were so startling and contrary to accepted new economics doctrine that a spate of further research efforts was initiated. The Andersen-Jordan tests encompassed the years 1952–1968. After extensive empirical testing of the relative efficacy of monetary-fiscal actions, they concluded: "The response of economic activity to monetary actions compared with that of fiscal actions is larger, more predictable, and faster."[15] Their results "provide no empirical support for the view that fiscal actions measured by the high employment surplus have a significant influence on GNP."[16] They also concluded that their results "provide no support for theories which indicate that changes in tax receipts due to changes in tax rates exert an over-all negative (or any) influence on economic activity."[17] Their correlations did indicate "that an increase in government expenditures is mildly stimulative in the quarter in which spending is increased and in the following quarter. However, in the subsequent two quarters this increase in expenditures caused offsetting negative influences."[18] On the other hand, "the total response of GNP to changes in money or the monetary base distributed over four quarters is consistent with the postulated relationship (i.e., a positive relationship), and the coefficients are all statistically significant."[19]

In a follow-up study, Michael Keran considered the same issue in a longer historical context (1919–1969). He concluded:

---

[14] Leonall C. Andersen and Jerry L. Jordan, "Monetary and Fiscal Actions: A Test of Their Relative Importance in Economic Stabilization," *Federal Reserve Bank of St. Louis Review,* November, 1968, pp. 11–23.

[15] *Ibid.,* p. 22.

[16] *Ibid.,* p. 18.

[17] *Ibid.*

[18] *Ibid.*

[19] *Ibid.,* p. 17.

For the whole period and for each of the subperiods (except the war years 1939–46) the relative impacts of monetary and fiscal influences have been remarkably stable. Changes in the money stock (the indicator of monetary influence) have consistently had a larger, more predictable, and faster impact on changes in economic activity than have changes in federal government spending (the indicator of fiscal influence). This basic relationship is observed in the economically depressed period of 1929–39 and in the prosperous periods 1919–29 and 1953–69.

A historical investigation of the past fifty years reveals that in every case where the monetary variable and the fiscal variable moved in opposite directions, economic activity moved in the direction of the monetary variable and opposite in direction to the fiscal variable. Every cyclical movement in the money stock since 1919 has been followed by a proportional cyclical movement in economic activity.[20]

Nor is the evidence confined to the United States economy. A close correlation between monetary and GNP or spending growth for the seven largest and mostly free market countries of the world was pointed out in a 1963 article.[21] Michael Keran concluded in a February 1970 article as follows:

The purpose of this article has been to review the postwar economic experience of a variety of industrial countries to see whether monetary and fiscal influence bear any systematic relationship to movements in economic activity. The results presented indicate that in spite of admitted differences in economic institutions and differences in the objectives of policy makers between countries, a substantial degree of consistency is observed. For each of the eight foreign countries considered, the monetary influence was important. The estimated coefficient relating the monetary variable to economic

---

[20] Michael W. Keran, "Monetary and Fiscal Influences on Economic Activity— The Historical Evidence," *Federal Reserve Bank of St. Louis Review,* November, 1969, p. 23.

[21] See Beryl W. Sprinkel, "Relative Economic Growth Rates and Fiscal-Monetary Policies," *Journal of Political Economy,* April, 1963 (Chicago: University of Chicago Press), pp. 154–59.

activity was positive and statistically significant. Of the countries in which fiscal measures were available, only in Japan was the positive relationship postulated by economic theory found to hold. . . . The implication in this study is that our confidence in the results of earlier studies which were based on United States data is enhanced.[22]

FORECASTING WITH MONEY

Monetary change is a dominant influence upon the future business trend, but it is not the only factor. Even confirmed monetarists attempt to allow for special factors likely to influence overall economic performance such as expected strikes, existing trends in major aggregates, and, to a lesser extent, the probable changes in government spending.

But if monetary change is a dominant influence, how may it be used in improving one's economic forecast? One simple and largely intuitive, but nonetheless useful, technique is to recognize that spending change as measured by GNP usually lags monetary change by two to three quarters for its major impact. Since monetary change for the recent past is known, one can usually assume that total spending in the next six months will be closely related to monetary change in the past six months. If the money supply has been growing at a stable rate of 4 percent and velocity has been rising at about a 2 percent annual rate, the money data would suggest about a 6 percent annual rate of rise in GNP over the next half year. To make a GNP estimate for the following six months, it is necessary to guess the probable pattern of monetary growth in the immediate six-month period ahead. If inflation is a serious matter and policy makers appear poised to tighten monetary policy and reduce monetary growth, then it would be expected that the rate of

---

22 Michael W. Keran, "Monetary and Fiscal Influences on Economic Activity: The Foreign Experience," *Federal Reserve Bank of St. Louis Review,* February, 1970, pp. 25–26.

rise in economic activity in the second six months ahead would taper. If monetary growth continues to taper for a period of 15 to 18 months, past patterns would suggest that a recession lies immediately ahead. If, alternatively, monetary growth has accelerated during the past six months or so, this force alone would suggest that a quickening of economic activity lies immediately ahead. However, if an economy is in a recession following monetary restraint and the money supply begins to grow more rapidly, past patterns suggest that it would be two to three quarters before the economy would reverse the decline and begin to expand again.

If a recession is expected, due to a contracting pattern of monetary growth, then a perceptive analyst would expect weakness in consumer durable sales, continued weakness in housing until money eased, reduced growth in nondurables, lower inventory accumulation and perhaps even liquidation, and eventually a topping out and probable decline in plant and equipment spending. The above pattern has been typical of mild postwar recessions.

Although the largely intuitive method of utilizing money in predicting the future has been extremely helpful in past years, there has been a growing tendency to attempt to quantify economic relations in either a complex or simple model which simulates the economy. Work on complex econometric models has been under way through most of the postwar years, but these models have not lived up to prior hopes and expectations so far as estimating business cycle turning points is concerned. Most of the large econometric models utilize the framework of the Keynesian income-expenditure theory. Hence, monetarists tend to argue that the impact of monetary change is inadequately incorporated in the existing models. In a study of the monetary theory of nine recent econometric models of the United States, David Fand wrote the following summary:

This paper analyzes the monetary theory of nine recent quarterly econometric models of the United States. We find that the price level and interest rate theory in these models leads to a monetary doctrine and a number of practices which are, in my view, responsible for the poor forecasts in 1968 and 1969. These include: a tendency to minimize the price level consequences of excessive monetary growth; a failure to recognize the impact of inflationary expectations on market interest rates; a reluctance to distinguish between nominal and real quantities; the use of market interest rates as an indicator of monetary policy; and the conviction that the rise in market interest rates since 1966 was due to an increased demand for money, and not the result of excessive growth in the money supply.[23]

A much more promising statistical means of taking monetary change into account is the so-called single equation model developed by economists at the St. Louis Federal Reserve Bank. The approach was first mentioned in the Andersen-Jordan article as an output of their test of the relative efficacy of monetary-fiscal actions.[24] The underlying theory was further developed by Michael Keran.[25] They found approximately two-thirds of the change in GNP from 1953 through 1969 could be explained by changes in the money supply and government spending, with most of the change accounted for by changes in the money supply. They also found that the impact of monetary and fiscal variables was extended over four quarters, and that by estimating monetary and fiscal changes for the period

---

[23] David I. Fand, "The Monetary Theory of Nine Recent Quarterly Econometric Models of the United States" (Paper presented at the 1969 Conference of University Professors, University of Wisconsin, Milwaukee, September 11, 1969), revised January, 1970.

[24] Leonall C. Andersen and Jerry L. Jordan, "Monetary and Fiscal Actions: A Test of Their Relative Importance in Economic Stabilization," *Federal Reserve Bank of St. Louis Review*, November, 1968, p. 23.

[25] Michael W. Keran, "Monetary and Fiscal Influences on Economic Activity— The Historical Evidence," *Federal Reserve Bank of St. Louis Review*, November, 1969, pp. 6–8.

ahead they could generate GNP numbers into the future. According to a recent St. Louis Federal Reserve Bank release, for each $1 billion increase in the money supply, the annual rate of GNP could be expected to rise by $5.5 billion over the next four quarters, whereas a $1 billion rise in government spending would be expected to increase the annual rate of GNP by $0.05 billion over a four-quarter period. By assuming varying rates of monetary growth in the future while taking into account the actual rate of growth in past quarters, it becomes possible to estimate future GNP rates as shown in Table 12.

These projections of total GNP changes are available regularly from the St. Louis Federal Reserve Bank, and they provide a convenient and useful means of taking into account

TABLE 12

Projected Dollar Change in GNP with Different Rates of Change in Money Supply*

Quarter	Assumed Rates of Change in Money Supply†				
	2%	3%	4%	5%	6%
1970/IV	$ 11.1	$ 11.7	$ 12.3	$ 12.9	$ 13.5
1971/I	8.3	9.8	11.3	12.8	14.3
II	6.5	8.9	11.2	13.6	15.9
III	13.3	16.1	19.0	21.8	24.6
IV	8.9	11.8	14.7	17.7	20.6

Projected Dollar Level of GNP with Different Rates of Change in Money Supply*

Quarter	Assumed Rates of Change in Money Supply†				
	2%	3%	4%	5%	6%
1970/IV	$ 996.3	$ 996.9	$ 997.5	$ 998.1	$ 998.7
1971/I	1,004.6	1,006.7	1,008.8	1,010.9	1,013.0
II	1,011.1	1,015.5	1,020.0	1,024.4	1,028.8
III	1,024.4	1,031.7	1,039.0	1,046.2	1,053.5
IV	1,033.3	1,043.5	1,053.7	1,063.9	1,074.1

* Billions of dollars.
† First differences in quarterly data of money supply in billions of dollars. Assumed alternative rates of change in money supply from IV/70 to IV/71.
Note: Estimates based on coefficients from Equation A (I/53 to III/70).
Source: St. Louis Federal Reserve Bank.

alternative assumptions concerning monetary growth in the future. The record has been good, and provides confidence that if one can do a good job of estimating monetary change in the period ahead, one will also be able to estimate the probable trend in the economy.

More recently, economists at the Federal Reserve Bank of St. Louis have developed a small scale econometric model for the United States economy based largely on monetarist principles.[26] Even so, change in government spending is utilized as one of the factors providing a moderate effect on total spending. The St. Louis model consists of only eight equations. Forecasts are obtained by estimating values of the exogenous variables consisting of changes in the money stock, changes in high-employment federal expenditures, potential (full employment) output, and past changes in the price level. The author explains the workings of the model as follows:

The workings of the model are summarized by a flow diagram (Chart 12). Only variables in the current period are shown in the diagram; lagged variables, with the exception of past changes in prices, are omitted. The model is recursive in nature, that is, dependent variables in one equation become independent variables in the next equation. This recursive feature will become evident in the following discussion.

The relationship that determines total spending is the fundamental one among those that determine the endogenous variables of the model. Total spending is determined by monetary actions and fiscal actions (federal spending financed by taxes or borrowing from the public), though no direct information is provided as to *how* such actions affect spending.

The change in total spending is combined with potential (full employment) output to provide a measure of demand pressure. Anticipated price change, which depends on past price changes, is

26 Leonall C. Andersen, "Properties of a Monetarist Model for Economic Stabilization" (Paper presented at Conference on Monetary Theory and Monetary Policy at Konstanz, Germany, June 24, 1970 to June 26, 1970).

CHART 12

Diagram of Monetarist Model

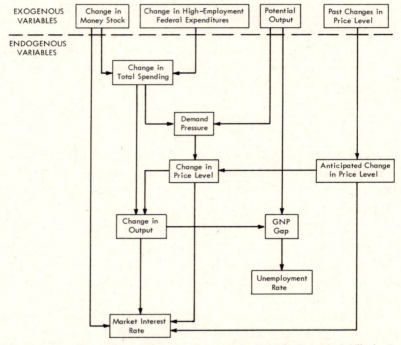

Source: Leonall C. Andersen, "Properties of a Monetarist Model for Economic Stabilization," paper prepared for the Conference on Monetary Theory and Monetary Policy at Konstann, Germany, June 1970.

combined with demand pressure to determine the change in the price level.

The total spending identity enables the change in output to be determined, given the change in total spending and the change in prices. This method of determining the change in total spending and its division between output change and price change differs from most econometric models. A standard practice in econometric model building is to determine output and prices separately, then combine them to determine total spending.

The change in output, the change in prices and in anticipated prices, along with the change in the money stock, determine market interest rates. The flow diagram shows that the market interest rate does not exercise a direct role in the model in the determination of spending, output, and prices.

To determine the unemployment rate, the change in output is first combined with potential output to determine the GNP gap relative to potential output. The GNP gap is then transformed into the unemployment rate.

CONCLUSION

The evidence presented in this chapter argues strongly that monetary change is a major factor determining the future change in economic activity. Since the monetary impact works with a lag, knowledge of past monetary change is a major clue as to the probable trend in economic activity in the months ahead. This knowledge may be either utilized in the form of an intuitive adaptation of the monetary-business relation or formalized, as in the single equation model developed by the St. Louis Federal Reserve Bank or the more sophisticated multiple equation model. Forecasting results have not been perfect, but they have been far better than could be expected from random results, and better than elaborate econometric models which usually utilize a Keynesian specification of the monetary influence. Forecasts need not be perfect to provide useful operational guidance to either public policy formulators or private decision makers. They merely need to be better than chance and alternative forecasting schemes. The monetarist approach has fared well under each criteria. The forecaster ignores monetary change at his peril!

6

Business Fluctuations
and Indicator Aids

Monetarists are frequently accused of ignoring the rest of the world while concentrating on money. In other words, many believe monetarists would argue that only money matters. Such an argument is, of course, a caricature of the facts, but it has been an effective device for attempting to discredit the monetarist approach to economic analysis, for everyone knows that many factors do indeed matter. The relevant question is what other factors the monetarists consider important.

To focus on that issue, we must ask, "Important for what?" A monetarist would respond that money is clearly the dominant, although not exclusive, factor influencing income creation and GNP change. But even so, random events have an influence, and changes in government spending have a modest influence in the two quarters following the change. Tax changes have in the past had no significant influence, and changes in the full employment budget have no demonstrable effect on current or lagged income creation. However, fiscal policy clearly matters greatly when the observer is interested in analyzing such questions as the distribution of resources between the private and public sector of the economy, the allocation of resources within the government sector of the economy, analysis of tax incidence, etc.

This monetarist tends to be a pragmatist and is willing to use any technique that proves useful in answering whatever question is posed. Doctrine may be useful in directing questions to the right issues, but if results are to be the ultimate test, then deciding which factors should be taken into account really depends on what approach works. It is for this reason that monetarists reject fiscal policy as a major factor influencing judgment on future economic and financial markets, while at the same time argue that changes in money make a powerful difference. But a practicing monetarist clearly cannot afford to close his eyes to other developments occurring in the economy, provided they yield information likely to improve judgments concerning the future.

One approach that has had a tolerably good record in anticipating cyclical turns in the past has been the indicator approach developed by the National Bureau of Economic Research. This organization has, since its founding in 1920, devoted a major effort to the analyses of U.S. business cycles or fluctuations. The men most influential in developing the concepts of cyclical analyses emanating from the National Bureau of Economic Research were Wesley Claire Mitchell, Arthur F. Burns, Geoffrey H. Moore, and Julius Shiskin. Although the analytical approach developed by the NBER may not be independent of monetary forces as outlined in the preceding pages, it nonetheless provides another way of looking at the business cycle, and can readily be used to confirm or reject tentative judgments arrived at by the monetary route. In general, monetary trends have a longer lead over business cycle turning points than other leading indicators. In other words, changes in monetary growth lead changes in the NBER leading indicators. Hence, a monetarist can often use trends in the leading, coincident, and lagging indicators to confirm a judgment first formed by analysis of monetary change. There is some reason, however, to believe that changes in the indicators are in response to prior monetary change, so the two approaches may not be completely independent. Nonetheless, confirmation of a monetary analysis by subsequent trends in NBER indicators increases confidence in the monetary hypothesis previously formulated. Since public or private implementation of policy based on a judgment about the economic climate depends primarily on the degree of confidence held, confirmation or rejection of a prior monetary approach is quite useful and well worth the extra effort.

The "business cycle" or "business fluctuation" concept results from the study of the sequence of economic events observed in the movements of economic activity. Unfortunately, each business cycle has many unique aspects, but there is sufficient similarity to justify reference to the business cycle. Since the term "business cycle" may imply a regular periodicity that does not exist, some analysts prefer to use the term "business fluctuations." During periods of business expansion, most aggregate economic series increase, but as the expansion continues, limiting forces gain strength until a reversal occurs and a recession begins. Similarly, as a recession matures, forces making for recovery emerge and finally become dominant, and another expansion ensues. The NBER has dated the months of peaks and troughs of U.S. business cycles from 1854 to the present. Prior to 1961, business expansions prevailed about 60 percent of the time, and economic contractions occurred nearly 40 percent of the time. If war periods are excluded, business contractions extend to about 44 percent of the total. There are a total of 28 business contractions, if each of the brief downturns shortly following World Wars I and II is counted, including the most recent, 1969–70. Omitting the brief contraction following World War II, when transition to a peacetime economy occurred, there have been five postwar recessions.

Although individual business cycles will vary in detail, Arthur F. Burns once described the characteristic movements of economic series during business cycles as follows:

Let us then take our stand at the bottom of a depression and watch events as they unfold. Production characteristically rises in the first segment of expansion; so do employment and money income; and so do commodity prices, imports, domestic trade, security transactions. Indeed, every series moves upward except bond yields and bankruptcies. In the second stage the broad advance continues, though it is checked at one point—the bond market, where trading begins to decline. Bond prices join bond sales in the next stage; in other words, long-term interest rates—which fell during the first half of expansion—begin to rise. In the final stretch of expansion, declines become fairly general in the financial sector. Share trading and stock prices move downward; the liabilities of business failures, which hitherto have been receding, move up again; security issues and construction contracts drop; the turnover of bank deposits slackens; and bank clearings in New York City, though not as yet in the interior, become smaller.

These adverse developments soon engulf the economic system as a whole, and the next stage of the business cycle is the first stage of contraction. Production, employment, commodity prices, personal incomes, business profits—indeed, practically all processes—decline. Of course, the liabilities of business failures continue to rise, which merely attests the sweep of depression. Long-term interest rates also maintain their rise. But in the next stage the downward drift of bond prices ceases; that is, the rise in long-term interest rates is arrested. By the middle of contraction, bond sales join the upward movement of bond prices. More important still, the liabilities of business failures begin declining, which signifies that the liquidation of distressed business firms has passed its worst phase. These favorable developments are reinforced in the following stage. Share trading and prices revive; business incorporations, security issues, and construction contracts move upward; money begins to turn over more rapidly; even total money payments expand. Before long the expansion spreads to production, employment, prices, money incomes, and domestic trade. But this is already the initial stage of general expansion—the point at which our hurried observation of the business cycle started.[1]

Note that the brief description offered by Dr. Burns was strictly descriptive and did not concentrate on fundamental causal factors. Until recent years Dr. Burns, in league with most economists, placed only modest emphasis on monetary influences.[2] He has tended to be eclectic in approach. Only in recent years has he placed heavy emphasis on the importance of monetary change. It may appear somewhat ironic that an eclectic economist is taking the lead in redirecting the Federal Reserve Board toward a monetarist approach. But that does indeed appear to be the case.

LEADING, COINCIDENT, AND LAGGING INDICATORS

Although facts will not speak for themselves, it is important that an analyst be aware of the typical factual pattern of a business cycle. This knowledge will be of aid in properly determining the current state of the business cycle and, hence,

---

[1] Arthur F. Burns, *New Facts on Business Cycles* (New York: 1950), National Bureau of Economic Research 30th Annual Report, pp. 3–31; reprinted in *Business Cycle Indicators*, Vol. I (Princeton, N.J.: Princeton University Press, 1961), pp. 13–44.

[2] See Beryl W. Sprinkel, "The Management of Prosperity: A Review Article," review of Arthur F. Burns' book, *The Management of Prosperity*, in *The Journal of Business*, Vol. 40, No. 2 (April, 1967). Also Beryl W. Sprinkel, "The 1955 Economic Report of the President," *Journal of the American Statistical Association*, Vol. 50 (March, 1955), pp. 240–248.

will sometimes be of use in anticipating future developments. If facts are to be of maximum benefits, they must be interpreted within the framework of an internally consistent and thoroughly tested theory. Unfortunately, there is no shortage of business cycle theories, as any text book on business cycles will demonstrate, but there is a scarcity of tested theories. In order to devise a useful theory consistent with the known facts, it is useful to know those facts. NBER economists have rendered yeoman service in documenting factual trends in the U.S. business cycle over the past century. As might be expected, they found that the turning points of various economic series were not the same, but what is more important, they found that most economic series could be usefully grouped into leading, coincident, and lagging categories. The Department of Commerce issues a monthly publication entitled *Business Conditions Digest* which reports in detail on current trends in the indicators to be discussed, as well as many additional series.

The aggregate economic series most frequently followed by business analysts are included in the coincident grouping. Among the coincident series are such broad measures of economic activity as real and current gross national product, industrial production, nonagricultural employment and unemployment, personal income, retail sales, and manufacturing and trade sales. It is these approximately coincident indicators that are used primarily in defining the peaks and troughs of business cycles. Each coincident indicator does not perfectly coincide with the peaks and troughs of economic activity as determined by NBER, but each comes close, and some kind of composite of these indicators more nearly does so. Although industrial production probably defines the business cycle most faithfully, it is important that many coincident indicators be followed if a realistic picture of the current business trend is to emerge. Chart 13, excerpted from *Business Conditions Digest,* published monthly by the U.S. Department of

CHART 13

Coincident Indicators

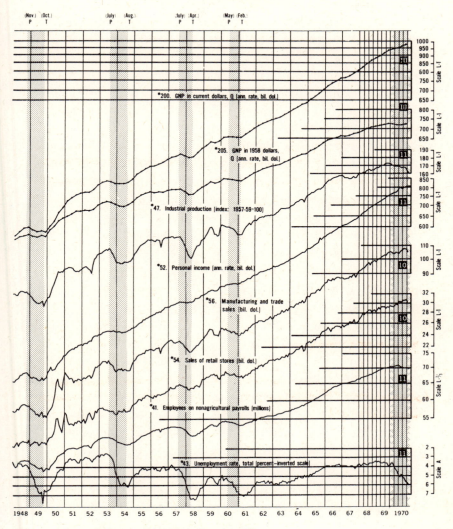

Source: *Business Conditions Digest*, December, 1970.

Commerce, Bureau of the Census, reflects postwar fluctuations in coincident indicators.

Research by the NBER has established that certain economic indicators move in advance or portend changes in the general level of economic activity. These foreshadowing series are called "leading indicators." Many of the series are closely related to future production, employment, and income creation. The leading indicators include such series as new orders for durable goods, plant and equipment contracts, housing permits, new business formation, average hours worked, net corporate profits, and common stock prices. Although no particular series has inevitably led peaks and troughs of economic activity, or even led most turns by a consistent number of months, nonetheless, most leading indicators have led cyclical turns most of the time; some tend to have longer average leads than others. Charts 14 and 15, also excerpts from *Business Conditions Digest,* present the cyclical pattern of many leading indicators in recent periods.

Finally, certain economic series are slow to adjust to the mainstream of economic activity. In other words, they tend to lag behind both the advance signals and the coincident indicators and, consequently, are called "lagging indicators." They include such factors as labor costs per unit of output, bank loan rates, plant and equipment expenditures, manufacturing and trade inventories. Many of the laggers include cost factors which, when they increase, lead to decreased business profitability and, hence, reduce the incentive for increasing such business activities as placing new orders and executing expansion plans. Chart 16, which appears regularly in *Business Conditions Digest,* presents some of the laggers.

Regrettably, few of the indicators fit invariably into the simple categories of leading, coincident, and lagging indicators. Therefore, such a classification tends to be somewhat of an oversimplification. However, there is sufficient consistency

CHART 14

Leading Indicators

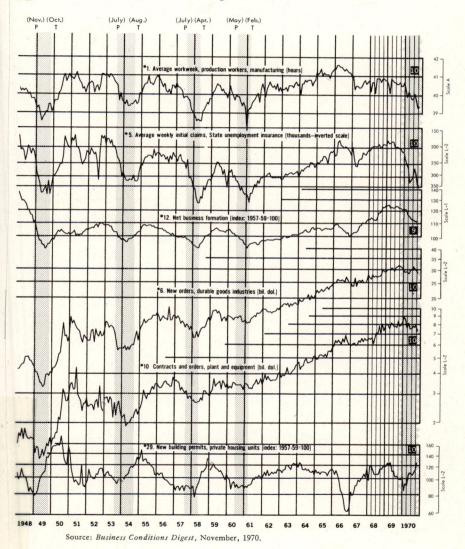

Source: *Business Conditions Digest*, November, 1970.

CHART 15

Leading Indicators

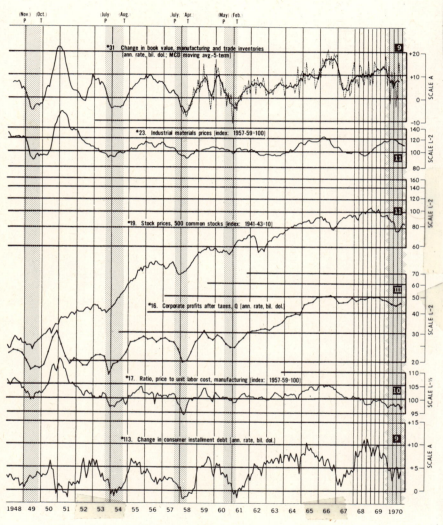

Source: *Business Conditions Digest*, November, 1970.

CHART 16

Lagging Indicators

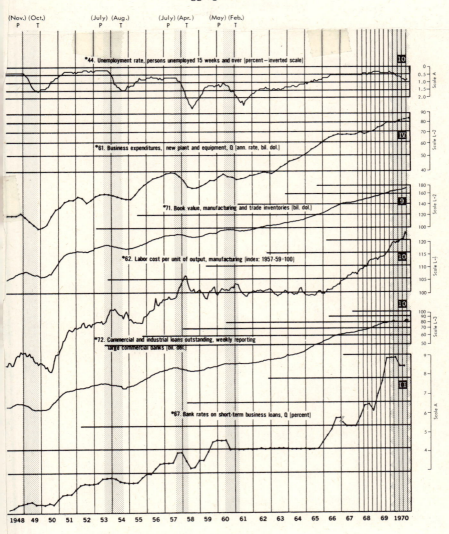

Source: *Business Conditions Digest*, November, 1970.

over many business cycles to make the above classification a useful one. Table 13 gives the average lead or lag of the 26 indicators found to have the most consistent relation in past business cycles.

TABLE 13

Leading Indicators of Business Activity

(record of timing of selected statistical indicators at business cycle turns)

	Peaks		Troughs	
	Number of Cycles	Avg. Lead Months	Number of Cycles	Avg. Lead Months
Leading indicators				
(1) Average hours worked	9	− 6	10	−4
(2) Nonagricultural placements	5	−11	5	−1
(3) Net business formation	5	−20	5	−3
(4) Durable goods new orders	10	− 8	10	−2
(5) Plant & equip. contracts, orders	4	− 8	4	−3
(6) Housing permits	11	−13	11	−5
(7) Mfg. & trade inventory change	5	−14	5	−6
(8) Industrial materials prices	10	− 6	11	0
(9) Common stock prices	22	− 4	22	−4
(10) Corporate profits (net)	10	− 6	10	−2
(11) Price/unit labor cost	10	−11	11	−3
(12) Consumer debt change	7	−12	7	−4
Coincident indicators				
(13) Nonagricultural employment	5	− 4	5	−1
(14) Unemployment rate	7	− 4	7	+2
(15) GNP (current dollars)	9	0	10	−1
(16) GNP (1958 dollars)	8	0	9	−3
(17) Industrial production	10	0	11	0
(18) Personal income	9	+ 1	10	−2
(19) Manufacturing and trade sales	4	− 4	4	0
(20) Retail sales	10	+ 1	11	0
Lagging indicators				
(21) Unemployment rate, 15+ weeks	4	+ 1	4	+2
(22) Plant and equipment expenditures	10	0	10	+2
(23) Manufacturing & trade inventories	5	+ 2	5	+2
(24) Unit labor cost	10	+ 8	11	+9
(25) Commercial and industrial loans	6	+ 2	6	+2
(26) Bank loans rate	10	+ 5	11	+5

(− Lead + Lag)
Source: National Bureau of Economic Research.

RATIONALE UNDERLYING THE LEADING INDICATORS

Rationale for the leading indicators can be developed on at least three levels of discussion: (1) development of a theoretical framework which explains why various series lead the economy; (2) discussion of criteria applied by the NBER in choosing these particular leaders from among the many available; and (3) explanation of the observed pattern of the leaders in a manner that will increase confidence that future patterns with regard to business fluctuations will be similar to past behavior.

THEORETICAL FRAMEWORK

Until recently, no one had attempted to provide a basic theoretical rationale for the leading indicators. In a recent article[3] Julius Shiskin argued that the observed three-stage pattern of movement in the leaders, followed by a similar change in the coincident, and eventual confirmation by the laggers could be integrated into the monetarist's explanation of business fluctuations. He compared changes in the NBER leading indicators with changes in monetary and fiscal variables from 1919 to 1968. The monetary policy variables chosen were the rate of change in the money supply narrowly defined and broadly defined. The fiscal policy variables were the administrative budget surplus for the period prior to 1940 and for the period since World War II. He examined two alternative series, the national income accounts surplus and the "high employment" surplus. Table 14 records the results. He concluded as follows:

As can be seen from the summary figures in Table [14], the change in the money supply reached its turns earlier than the index of

---

[3] Julius Shiskin, "Economic Policy Indicators and Cyclical Turning Points," *Business Economics* (Brooklyn, N.Y.: Long Island University, September, 1970).

TABLE 14. Timing of Economic Policy Variables Compared to Index of Leading Indicators and Leading Indicators Compared to Aggregate Economic Activity

Series (1)	Reference Turns Covered (2)	Matched Timing Comparisons (3)	Number of... Leads (4)	Rough Coincidences (5)	Lags (6)	Reference Turns Skipped (7)	Extra Specific Cycle Turns (8)	Mean Lead (−) or Lag (+) (Mos.) Actual (9)	Adjusted for Smoothness* (10)	Standard Deviation (11)	Matched Timing Comparisons as a Percent of Reference Turns Total (12)	Leads (13)	Lags (14)
Economic policy variables compared to leading indicators													
Percent change in money supply:													
1919–40, 1946–68	18	18	16	4(2)	0	0	2	−10.4	− 5.4	6.7	100	89	0
1946–68	9	9	9	1(0)	0	0	2	− 9.1	− 4.1	4.4	100	100	0
Percent change in money supply plus time deposits:													
1919–40, 1946–68	18	18	16	4(2)	0	0	0	−10.0	− 6.0	6.7	100	89	0
1946–68	9	9	9	1(0)	0	0	0	− 8.6	− 4.6	4.3	100	100	0
Federal surplus or deficit (inverted): Admin. budget (1919–40) or NIA (1946–68) basis	18	12	9	1(0)	3	6	4	− 9.2	− 8.2	12.7	67	50	17
NIA basis, 1946–68	9	4	3	0(0)	1	5	2	− 9.2	− 8.2	12.2	44	33	11
High employment basis, 1947–68	9	4	3	1(0)	1	5	2	− 2.5	− 1.5	4.1	44	33	11
Change in fed. surplus or deficit (inverted):													
NIA basis, 1946–68	9	5	0	1(0)	5	4	4	+11.2	+13.2	9.3	56	0	56
High employment basis, 1946–68	9	5	2	1(0)	3	4	4	+ 1.0	+ 3.0	6.8	56	22	33
Leading indicators compared to aggregate economic activity													
Manufacturers' new orders, 1921–68	19	17	16	7(1)	0	2	2	− 7.5	− 6.5	8.4	89	84	0
Average workweek, 1921–68	19	17	13	4(2)	2	2	2	− 5.0	− 4.0	5.6	89	68	11
Housing authorized by building permits, 1919–1968	21	19	17	5(1)	1	2	8	− 8.0	− 7.0	7.9	90	81	5

See footnote on facing page.

leading indicators on all but two occasions during the period 1920–67. The exceptions, both of which occurred in the 1920's, hardly damage the generalization because the money supply series is very erratic and, when the leads are short, some coincidences or lags are likely merely as a result of chance. The leads in the change in the money supply series over the index of leading indicators are, of course, shorter than over the business cycle turns. There are no cases where the leads in the change in the money supply cross opposite turning points in the index of leading indicators. Furthermore, there are no extra cycles in the money supply series when it is compared with the leading indicator index. In general, then, the record for the change in the money supply is better when the comparison is made with the leading index reference dates than with the business cycle dates. The results for the budget series are quite different. They match only about one-half and lead only about one-third the turning dates in the leading indicator index. Moreover, they do not meet the conditions required to qualify as leading, coincident, or lagging indicators when compared either to the conventional business cycle turning dates, or to the leading index reference dates.

Furthermore, if monetary change does have an almost immediate as well as a lagged effect upon income creation, as previously argued, it is reasonable to believe that sensitive NBER leading indicators such as stock prices, new orders, and average hours worked would be affected before turning points

NOTE TO TABLE 14.

Peaks and troughs in the composite index of the leading indicators are used as reference turns for the comparisons with the economic policy variables, whereas the NBER reference dates (i.e., business cycle peaks and troughs) are used for the comparisons with the leading indicators. Rough coincidences include exact coincidences (shown in parentheses) and leads and lags of three months or less (which are included also in the lead and lag columns). The total number of timing comparisons is the sum of the leads, exact coincidences, and lags; it can be less than the number of the reference turns covered by the series because the number of specific turns in a series is not necessarily the same as the number of reference turns in that period and because some specific turns in a series do not correspond to reference turns.

* Mean lead or lag plus one-half the MCD span, less 0.5 if the MCD span is odd or less 1.0 if the MCD span is even. This is an estimate of what the mean lead or lag would be for a moving average of MCD span, with moving average placed in terminal month of span. The MCD spans for the above series are: percent change in money supply, 11 mos.; percent change in money supply plus time deposits, 9; administrative budget surplus, 5; NIA surplus, 3; manufacturers' new orders, 3; average workweek, 3; housing authorized by building permits, 3; high employment surplus or deficit, 3; change in fed. surplus or deficit, NIA accounts, 6; change in high employment surplus or deficit, 6.

would be reached in coincident indicators of economic activity. Regardless of whether "ultimate truth" is contained in the monetary and leading indicator hypothesis, it clearly is a fact that some forecasters, including the writer, have in the past successfully relied on the relationship posited. Early change occurs in monetary growth, followed by changes in the leading, coincident, and lagging indicators, respectively. Consequently, it has been possible to monitor the changing business scene by utilizing this device. Since leading indicators are sensitive, they also tend to be volatile. Therefore, it is sometimes difficult to determine if a change is really under way. Judgments can frequently be improved if leading indicators are viewed in light of the prior monetary change. If short-run movements in the NBER indicators appear to be inconsistent with monetary trends, the careful analyst would be inclined to deemphasize the latest indicator change as a random event rather than a basic change. For example, if monetary growth had been weak for many months, short-run strength in the leading indicators would tend to be discounted. Weakness in the leaders would be more tenable. Frequently, subsequent revisions and/or new data confirm the prior expectation. Conversely, a strengthening in the monetary trend would be expected to presage strengthening in the leaders, followed by a rise in the coincident, and finally the lagging, indicators. Continued weakness in the leaders in such an environment would be suspect.

CRITERIA APPLIED

When the list of indicators was last revised in 1967, Moore and Shiskin developed an explicit scoring system for evaluating and selecting the "best" indicators.[4] They explained their approach as follows:

---

[4] Geoffrey H. Moore and Julius Shiskin, *Indicators of Business Expansions and Contractions* (New York: National Bureau of Economic Research, Inc., 1967), pp. 8–28.

The current study has extended the use of explicit criteria and objective standards employed by Mitchell, Burns, and Moore in establishing previous lists. This has been accomplished by a plan for assigning scores to each series within a range of 0 to 100. The scoring of each series, admittedly arbitrary in many respects, reflects our desire not only to make as explicit as possible the criteria for selecting indicators, but also to increase the amount of information available to the user to aid in evaluating their current behavior.

The scoring plan includes six major elements: (1) economic significance, (2) statistical adequacy, (3) historical conformity to business cycles, (4) cyclical timing record, (5) smoothness, and (6) promptness of publication. When the subheads under most of these elements are counted, some twenty different properties of series are rated in all. This list of properties provides a view of the many different considerations relevant to an appraisal of the value of a statistical series for current business cycle analysis.[5]

Although any type of scoring system used for evaluating indicators of economic activity must be somewhat arbitrary, their system insures consistency of treatment. By several different tests it is clear that there is considerable similarity in behavior of indicators within each group and considerable difference from group to group.

EXPLANATION OF SERIES

Average Work Week, Production Workers, Manufacturing

Since manufacturing industries are more prone to be cylically sensitive than other industries, the lead nature of various employment and order series is most evident in this industry. Since it is typically less costly to adjust the workweek than to reduce the number of employed, the length of the workweek

---

[5] *Ibid.*, p. 3.

typically leads employment. Business operates in an uncertain environment. Reductions in the workweek are more readily reversed if orders improve than would be layoffs. Reductions in the workweek enable the employer to keep his labor force intact for future use, whereas layoffs may be unavailable when again needed. Also, when reductions in overtime are possible, this will achieve a lower cost per hour than will a commensurate reduction in the work force.

Net Business Formation

The number of net new businesses formed leads the business cycle, while the number of businesses discontinued is roughly coincident with cyclical change. As with other factors related to the investment process, the timing of net new businesses is closely associated with changes in profits. Substantial increases in profits and profit margins tend to induce, with a slight lag, the creation of a large number of new businesses. As costs rise and profit increases become less widespread in the advanced stages of the business cycle expansion, the number of new businesses declines. A business contraction reduces new business formation, but before the cycle trough is reached, the number of firms and industries experiencing rising profits increases and induces an increase in new business formations.

New Orders, Durable Goods Industries

New orders for durable goods is one of several series that represent investment commitments by businesses. Several studies by the National Bureau of Economic Research have demonstrated that the volume of activity in these early stages of the investment process tends to fluctuate in advance of changes in such broad measures of activity as production, income, and employment. This order series has shown a persistent tendency to lead the production output of the industries receiving the orders, as one might expect. Again, the many factors that contribute to the early declines in orders during business expansions are rising cost-price ratios, tighter money conditions, and the rapid accumulation of inventories. Improvement in the above factors is typically associated with an improvement in the orders trend. The size of order backlogs should be observed in relation to changes in orders, since high backlogs may delay the impact of declining orders, whereas low backlogs may hasten the effect.

Contracts and Orders, Plant and Equipment

This series is the most comprehensive measure of new investment commitments by business enterprises. Just as new orders for durable goods reflect changing profit prospects, so do orders and contracts for plant and equipment. It is important to recognize that although this contract and order series leads business peaks, actual plant and equipment spending is a lagger, reflecting the time needed for adjusting actual outlays after the early signs of weakness develop.

New Building Permits, Private Housing Units

The new building permits series is smoother than the erratic housing starts series, but reflects the same basic pressures and cyclical pattern. Permits are particularly sensitive to such short-range factors as the state of the money market and changes in housing legislation. In addition, such longer-range factors as changes in construction costs, marriage rates, and vacancy rates are influential. Since permits represent an early stage in the construction process, they lead such factors as residential construction employment and expenditures, tend to lead production of construction materials and household appliances, and also have an impact on the demand for furniture and other household furnishings. New orders for materials used largely in housing are closely related to starts, as are residential mortgage commitments.

Changes in Manufacturing and Trade Inventories

Changes in manufacturing and trade inventories are extremely volatile and account for the bulk of cyclical change during mild business recessions. These changes have shown a persistent tendency to reach cylical turns before GNP. Inventory changes do not become negative before business cycle peaks, but they tend to become smaller. Likewise, decreases in inventories usually become smaller before troughs in the business cycle. NBER studies indicate that it is the purchased material component of total inventory change that is primarily responsible for the early timing of changes in the total.

Industrial Material Prices

This index includes the daily prices of 13 raw materials which sensitively reflect forces affecting open markets and organized exchanges. Attempts to build or pare down materials inventories tend to be reflected promptly in the index. Therefore, changing profitability of business which affects inventory change is reflected in prices paid. These prices also tend to lead business cycle turning points.

Stock Prices

Profits and interest rates are closely associated with the pattern of stock prices in the business cycle. As explained in this book, changes in monetary growth and in interest rates tend to alter the desirability of holding stocks, and their prices typically move in advance of the business cycle turning points.

Corporate Profits after Taxes

Since actual and potential profits play a central energizing role in a free market economy, they play an important role in the generation of the business cycle. Profits provide the incentive and funds for investment, they generate business optimism and pessimism, and they encourage business expansion and contraction. Rising costs in the last stages of a business expansion and a slower rate of increase in physical production contribute to an adverse profit trend before the business cycle peak is reached. The opposite forces work during a business decline.

Ratio, Price to Unit Labor Costs

This index is the best available monthly index of profit margins, which are a major factor impacting total corporate profits. Changes in profits change the incentive to produce.

Change in Consumer Installment Debt

Change in consumer installment debt represents the difference between extensions and retirements. Debt retirement is largely a function of prior contracts, while extensions relate to current commitments. This series has in the past displayed wide cyclical movements and consistent leads.

ANALYTICAL TECHNIQUES

In observing changes in the above series, several adjustments must be made in order to detect a meaningful change. As is true in most data analysis, the first elementary step involves the elimination of seasonal movements. Also, in some cases it is necessary to use moving averages to smooth erratic elements in the series. Several summary measures are designed to show how widespread and how fast the movements of cyclical developments are occurring.

When evaluating trends in the indicators, it is desirable to rely on the impression given by the total group rather than to fix attention on only one or a few indicators, since each indicator does not work every time. One device for combining data and giving an impression of the pervasiveness of the cyclical movement is called the "diffusion index." The diffusion index is a simple scheme for summing figures and producing a type of index number. To construct a diffusion index for each group, add the number of items that are rising at a particular point in time, and take this number as a percentage of the total indicators in that group. In other words, a diffusion index represents the percent of indicators expanding at a given point in time. Such a series will show how widely diffused expansionary or contractionary forces are in the sector under consideration. Even after making seasonal adjustments, using moving averages when necessary and computing diffusion indexes, the series is still erratic at times.

It is useful to compute diffusion indexes for each of the leading, coincident, and lagging indicators so that the development in one set may be compared with developments in the other sets. Chart 17 shows that a *diffusion index* of the leading indicators tends to move ahead of the index of coincident indicators. The laggers, of course, are the last to reflect a changing business trend.

Diffusion indexes may also be used to show the percentage of companies, industries, or geographic areas experiencing rises over the time interval measured. The scope of expansion or contraction usually narrows before peaks and troughs in business cycles, and diffusion indexes measure these phenomena.

CHART 17

Diffusion Indexes

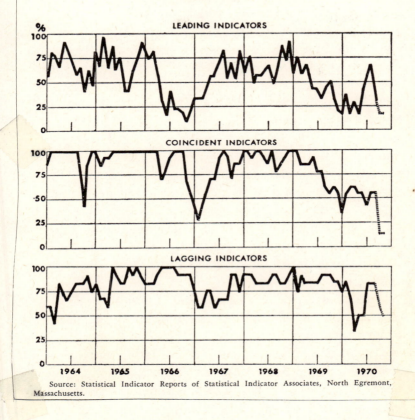

Source: Statistical Indicator Reports of Statistical Indicator Associates, North Egremont, Massachusetts.

Therefore, diffusion indexes are useful predictive devices, because they usually reach their highs and lows before business cycle peaks and troughs. They also serve to point out the important fact that there is rarely a period when all business activities are moving in the same direction. At all times, cross currents are encountered which complicate the task of the analyst.

After studying a large number of diffusion indexes, Geoffrey H. Moore made the following conclusions regarding their properties and what they reveal about the economy.[6] (1) Cyclical movements in the economy are general, but far from universal. Diffusion indexes seldom show all economic series going in the same direction. (2) There is little evidence that cyclical movements have become either more or less general in recent years. (3) The leads or lags that certain series exhibit to one another are usually reflected in diffusion indexes constructed from the components of the series. (4) The scope of a business cycle expansion diminishes before the peak in total economic activity is reached, and the scope of a contraction diminishes before the trough in total economic activity is reached. (5) Once expansion in the economy has become general, when measured in such a way that cylical factors are exposed, it stays general for a considerable time. These periods are usually longer than those in which contraction is general. (6) The scope of a contraction shortly after it begins is correlated, though often only loosely, with the severity of the contraction.

Another statistical technique useful in business cycle analysis compares the behavior of the current business cycle phase with behavior during the corresponding phase of previous business cycles. Such a technique is useful in placing current cyclical movements in proper historical perspective. It is especially useful in recession periods to compute change in a wide range of indicators in the first six months and first year of prior recoveries. Almost inevitably, the rise in past business expansions has been much more rapid than our memory suggests.

Another useful summary measure, represented regularly in *Business Conditions Digest,* is referred to as "amplitude adjusted" general indexes. These indexes combine various series measuring different types of economic activity such as production, employment, and prices in a single index. The technique standardizes the month-to-month percentage changes of each

---

[6] *Ibid.,* pp. 79–86.

series so that all series are expressed in comparable units. *Business Conditions Digest* adjusts each series so that its average month-to-month change, without regard to direction, is one. This approach facilitates an interpretation of the current month's change with respect to earlier periods as well as with other series. The individual amplitudes in adjusted series have been weighted and combined into a single index. This index also has been adjusted so that its average month-to-month change is one. This index provides a composite measure of the amplitude and pattern of the business cycle. For example, if the index shows an increase in the current month of 1.5, this means it is rising 50 percent faster than its average rate of increase in the past; if the increase is only 0.5, it is rising only half as fast as the historical average. This index should be interpreted with the knowledge that economic activity tends to rise most rapidly in the early stage of a business cycle expansion, and slows as the cycle matures.

It is also possible to compute a composite index for the leading, coincident, and lagging indicators. This index is useful in determining whether the cycle trends in the series are widespread and likely to be cyclical in nature, or due to isolated phenomena, such as a strike. An example of such indexes appears in Chart 18.

Another useful technique for identifying peaks and troughs of business cycles involves "timing distributions" of current highs or lows showing the number of individual series reaching highs during each of the recent months of an expansion, or lows during recent months of business contractions. As new highs or lows are reached, the current highs or lows will be moved ahead. Comparison of the current timing distributions with those for periods near earlier business cycle peaks and troughs is useful in deciding whether recent evidence suggests a turning point is at hand. *Business Conditions Digest* presents detailed timing distributions each month.

CHART 18

Composite Indexes

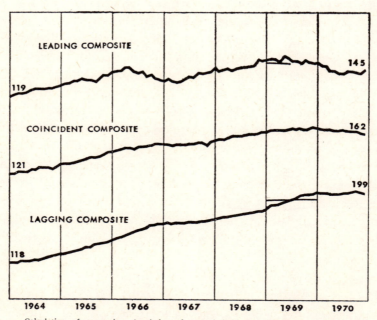

Calculation of composite: An index of each individual indicator is computed with 1957–1959 = 100. To obtain the group indexes, individual indicator indexes within each group are added and divided by the number of series in the group.

Source: Statistical Indicator Reports of Statistical Indicator Associates, North Egremont, Massachusetts.

Repetitive Aspects of Business Cycles

There exists no foolproof method of determining in advance the length or depth of a recession once it is under way, or the length and extent of a recovery currently in progress. Nonetheless, the prudent and enterprising observer is not helpless. The National Bureau of Economic Research has carefully documented and codified most of the relevant facts concerning the 28 U.S. business cycles since 1854. Knowledge of what usually happens during a business cycle is of great aid in estimating what will happen in the current one. Many observers, caught up in the milieu of the present, are far too prone to assume that existing conditions are unique. Sometimes they are, but usually the present is merely repeating the past in many significant respects. Since one cannot study the future, it is important to study and know the past as a guide to interpreting the present and projecting the future. An organized search for similarities between current economic trends and past trends is likely to be far more fruitful than a search for existing but frequently insignificant differences. Even to isolate significant unique differences, the analyst must know the past. Knowledge of the past can hopefully limit future mistakes in analysis to at least those pertaining to unique conditions rather than to errors in analyzing recurring trends. Furthermore, one's self respect and confidence are more readily restored following an error based on a new set of circumstances than an error due to ignorance of history, even though each may be equally costly.

Despite many differences in detail, Geoffrey H. Moore of the NBER has isolated the following significant similarities of past business cycles.[7]

1. Recovery from the lows in output, employment, and profits has usually taken place at a faster pace after severe depressions than after mild contractions.

2. However, the magnitude of a cyclical advance in stock prices typically varies inversely with the severity of the previous business decline. In other words, the market has tended to react with confidence after a mild recession, but with caution after a severe one.

3. Despite a faster economic pace after severe contractions, reattainment of previous peak levels has taken longer because the preceding recession was deeper.

---

[7] See various essays written by Geoffrey H. Moore in *Business Cycle Indicators* (Princeton, N.J.: National Bureau of Economic Research), Vol. I.

4. Nearly every business expansion has carried total output, employment, and profits beyond the levels reached at the previous peak.

5. The rates of advance in total economic activity during expansions have been more uniform throughout the expansion than the rates of decline throughout the contraction. Therefore, a more accurate projection of the ultimate rate of advance of a business expansion can be made early in the expansion than can be made of the ultimate rate of decline at the beginning of a contraction. Comparative data of present and previous business expansions are frequently useful in forming a view regarding the strength of the current rise.

6. The rate of growth in output, employment, and profits has been consistently larger in the initial stages of a business expansion—the first six to nine months—than in later stages. After the initial phase, slower growth has been the rule, especially after the preceding peak level has been attained.

7. The average length of nonwar business expansions since 1854 has been about 26 months prior to the decade of the 1960's, with only two—other than those occurring during war periods—lasting longer than 37 months. The expansion following the Great Depression of 1929–33 lasted 50 months. Only five expansions out of 26 lasted less than 20 months. There has been a general tendency within the past 40 years for recoveries to last longer and declines to be shorter than previously, with the exception of the long-lived 1929–33 decline, and also the abortive 25-month 1958–60 recovery.

8. The weakness in the NBER leading indicators in the early months of a recession is closely correlated with the ultimate severity of the contraction. An experiment performed by Moore in the fall of 1960 suggested that the existing contraction would be milder than all contractions since 1920 except that of 1926–27, which was among the least severe of the previous 25 business cycle contractions in the National Bureau's

records dating back to 1854.[8] It is now possible to state that the 1960–61 recession was milder than any downturn from 1920 to 1961 except for the small dip in 1926–27.

It is clear from the above brief review of past business cycles that the experience of the expansion of the 1960's was unusually long in duration. This raises the question, "Why?" Until the slowdown of 1969 and 1970 it had become fashionable in some quarters to argue that the business cycle was dead or dying and that growth forces were so strong that we need not fear recessions in the future. But recent events belie such an interpretation. A more popular interpretation pointed to the new economics doctrine and policies which reigned supreme during most of the 1960's, and attributed the long period of economic growth to the judicial application of flexible fiscal policies. In particular it has frequently been argued that the 1964 tax cut, adopted at a time when the actual budget was in deficit but the full employment budget was in surplus, thereby exerting a "fiscal drag," accounts for the unusually long economic expansion. This argument is appealing, but unfortunately doesn't fit the facts too well.

The major changes in the business expansion in the 1960's that need explanation were (1) the slowdown in the economy in the first half of 1963; (2) the acceleration in activity in the last half of 1963; (3) the slowdown in the first half of 1967; (4) the speed-up in the last half of 1967; and (5) the recession beginning in late 1969 and extending through most of 1970. As indicated in Chart 19, changes in monetary growth led each of these changes in economic tempo by two to three quarters and were consistent with the longer term monetary evidence. Fiscal change as reflected in Chart 20 appeared inconsistent with each. The high employment budget surplus was declining prior to the 1962 slowdown, therefore exerting less restraint, according

---

8 Geoffrey H. Moore, statement on the current economic situation before the Joint Economic Committee of the Congress, December 7, 1960.

CHART 19

Money, Velocity, and Business

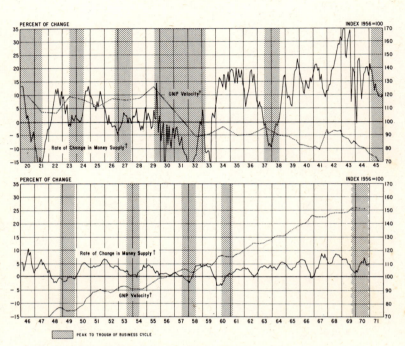

* All commercial banks demand deposits adj. + currency (seas. adj.).
† Annual rate of monthly change, 6-month moving average.
‡ Annual data before 1939; quarterly since 1939.
Jagged area represents a significant slowdown in business activity.
Source: U.S. Department of Commerce, Federal Reserve Board, National Bureau of Economic Research, Inc.

to conventional fiscal theory. Restraint increased prior to the 1963 expansion. The deficit was becoming greater, presumably exerting stimulus prior to the 1967 slowdown, and did not change markedly before recovery in the last half of 1967. The surplus became less restrictive prior to the 1969 slowdown after the massive change in 1968 as a result of the surtax, which did not slow the economy unless one is to believe that the tax increase worked with a 15-month lag.

CHART 20

Fiscal Measures

(quarterly totals at annual rates, seasonally adjusted)

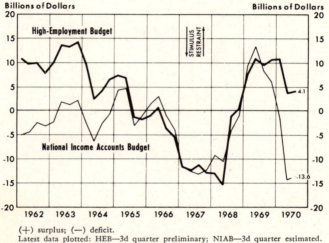

(+) surplus; (—) deficit.
Latest data plotted: HEB—3d quarter preliminary; NIAB—3d quarter estimated.
Prepared by Federal Reserve Bank of St. Louis.
    Sources: U.S. Department of Commerce, Council of Economic Advisers, and
Federal Reserve Bank of St. Louis.

The 1964 tax cut became effective March 1, and there is no evidence that the economy accelerated shortly before, at the time of the tax cut, or shortly thereafter. A stable growth pattern of economic activity in 1963–64 and 1965 is consistent with the relatively stable monetary growth during that period. Therefore it would appear that flexible fiscal policies have been much overrated as an explanation of the unusual economic trends of the 1960's, and that monetary change offers a much more believable rationale.

Careful analysis of developing economic trends as measured by the leading, coincident, and lagging indicators, in the light of the above long-standing patterns, will greatly improve current economic judgments. Analysis of the NBER indicators can be most effective when conducted within the framework of a continuing analysis of monetary trends.

Evaluation of Indicator Approach

In a broad sense, there can be no reasonable doubt that the indicators, when properly presented and adequately analyzed, record the tendency of some series to lead business cycle turning points, others to coincide, and the remaining to lag. The indicators also truly reflect the tendency for the scope of business expansions to become more narrow as the business cycle ages, and for the scope of contraction to become less as the business trough approaches. Therefore, in hindsight an analyst can usually point with justifiable pride to the fact that indicators again faithfully recorded classic tendencies inherent in the U.S. business cycle. But the most critical question is: Does the indicator approach enable the analyst to recognize these changes as they are occurring, and can he use this information to predict the next turning point with a high degree of accuracy? The candid answer must be a qualified no, but it should be followed by an equally candid admission that the future can never be known with certainty, and that no other forecasting approach has a virtual monopoly on accurate predictions. Perhaps a fairer question might be: Does the indicator approach provide clues which will improve the ability of the careful analyst to anticipate the next turning point? Here the answer must certainly be yes. Since progress toward the solution of important and difficult tasks can seldom come with great leaps forward, a prudent analyst must gratefully accept whatever guidance is available. The results achieved by business analysts in anticipating postwar business cycle swings were usually improved substantially because of the availability of the NBER indicator methodology, especially when interpreted in the context of the existing monetary environment.

But why is the approach not capable of nearing perfection? A brief review of the inherent limitations would be a prudent exercise.[9] First it should be recognized that the indicators sometimes give what in hindsight prove to be false signals. But, unfortunately, we search for a foresight mechanism. The indicators are sensitive not only to impending major cyclical declines but also to minor declines, as well as periods of level economic activity. Some wags contend that the leading indicators forecasted seven of the past four recessions! There is some truth to this accusation. For example, the leaders weakened in 1951, but the economy expanded modestly on net balances as the rise in defense activity more than offset weakness in the private sector. In 1956, the indicators again suggested weakness in the economy, but the recession was delayed until 1957, perhaps due to a large backlog of capital appropriations and a high level of unfilled orders. Again in 1962 the indicators declined, but the economy merely leveled off and later strengthened. They weakened prior to the slowdown in the first half of 1967, and also prior to the 1969–70 recession. Weaknesses were correctly reflected before each of the postwar recessions, but sometimes the leaders strengthened briefly before the downturn, as in 1948 and 1960. At all times it is extremely important to interpret the indicators within the entire business complex, including private trends as well as monetary policies, and not merely to apply mechanically the indicator approach.

A second and related difficulty is the tendency for the leaders to record a variable lead time between cycles. It is to be expected that some leading indicators have a longer lead in any particular cycle than other leaders, but that can be al-

[9] Also see Frank E. Morris, *Business Cycle Indicators* (Princeton, N.J.: National Bureau of Economic Research), Vol. I, pp. 110–19.

lowed for if the typical leads are kept in mind. For example, housing starts and new business incorporations usually have longer leads than such leaders as new orders and the average workweek. But, regrettably, there is also considerable variability in the lead of any particular indicator from cycle to cycle. Sometimes allowance for this variability can be made by reference to such economic factors as the size of backlogs of unfilled orders, unspent appropriations, and the level of building contracts, but much of the difficulty of interpretation inevitably remains.

Furthermore, economic activity may be affected by political and international developments that are basically noneconomic in character and usually are not encompassed in the indicator statistical system; nevertheless they have important economic consequences. Modern examples of such developments include the Korean conflict during the 1949–53 expansion, which turned out to be unusually long, the Viet Nam War, and the recurring steel and automobile strikes. Even the threat of strikes may accelerate inventory accumulation and thus distort the true economic picture that would otherwise be reflected by the leaders.

Despite heroic attempts to devise mathematical methods of processing the data, thereby eliminating irregular and seasonal movements, some erratic movements remain. It is also unfortunately true that the leading series tend to be the most erratic. Therefore, it is most difficult to distinguish between random interruptions of the underlying trend and true cyclical changes in the series. To complicate matters more, revisions of the data occur rather frequently. Therefore, the analyst does not always know what has actually happened in the past, practically never knows what is happening at present, and is even less certain about what will happen in the future!

Finally, the leading indicator technique for predicting business cycle fluctuations was not initially grounded in a cohesive, unifying theory. But, as previously mentioned, Julius Shiskin argues that it can be incorporated in the monetarist approach which is developed in this book. It is also possible to explain why individual indicators react as they do with respect to the business cycle. Past experience suggests that careful analysis of indicator trends will be of considerable aid to the analyst, particularly if used in conjunction with the monetarist approach.

To quote an earlier work of this economist and statistician who has done much to improve the indicator approach:

> The difficulties of using the indicators are formidable. In interpreting current changes we are sometimes confronted with false signals, pauses in the underlying trend, variability in the performance of our most trusted series, shifts in attitudes arising from external events, and errors of measurement. Progress has slowly, but steadily, been made to reduce these difficulties. . . . However, while the inherent difficulties of forecasting changes in our vast and complicated economy may be reduced, they will never be completely eliminated, so that we shall always have to contend with a margin of error in our forecasts.[10]

The fainthearted and defeatists should never attempt to analyze current business trends for the avowed purpose of estimating the future course of economic activity. This task is not and cannot be completely a science, as a large element of judgment will inevitably remain. A wise professor of business forecasting, the late Garfield V. Cox of the University of Chicago, once responded to this student's question concerning how he was able to reach a precise quantification of his views about the future state of business: "I am always uncomfortable with any statistical projection of the future. I therefore choose the statistical projection with which I am least uncomfortable and thereby minimize my discomfort." For those interested in

---

[10] Julius Shiskin, "Business Cycle Indicators: the Known and the Unknown," *Business Conditions Digest*, September, 1963, pp. 69–79.

minimizing their discomfort concerning the probable future course of the economy, an understanding and application of the indicator approach is helpful. It provides a useful, even though imperfect, supplement to the monetarist approach stressed in this book.

CHAPTER 7

Money and Inflation

THE POST 1965 INFLATION

Beginning about mid 1965, the U.S. economy entered the most serious inflationary surge since the early postwar years. Not only did prices rise, but for several years they rose at an accelerating pace. The post 1965 inflation was especially disturbing because it followed many years of relative price tranquility extending from 1951. During the fourteen-year period ending in mid 1965, wholesale prices rose only 0.4 percent per year, consumer prices increased at a 1.3 percent annual rate, while the GNP price deflator rose 2.2 percent per year. That mild inflation contrasted sharply with the 1969 price performance, when wholesale prices increased 4.8 percent, consumer prices jumped 6.1 percent, and the GNP price deflator rose 5.1 percent.

As in many other areas of analysis, the monetarists and fiscalists offer differing answers as to the cause of the inflation, as well as policies needed for bringing the inflation under control. In general, the fiscalists argue that the failure to enact promptly a tax increase sufficient to cover the rising costs of the Viet Nam escalation, which began in mid 1965, accounted for the accelerating inflation in subsequent years. That answer, of course, follows from their heavy emphasis on the importance of the full employment deficit as a factor stimulating total spending. The monetarists, on the other hand, argue that the fly in the ointment was not the growing deficit but rather the rapid increase in the money supply, which resulted from a much easier monetary policy.[1] Both groups recognize that the economy had at long last achieved approximate full employment of resources by late 1965, when unemployment declined to only 4 percent of the labor force compared to an average of 5.5 percent from 1960 through 1965. Also, the operating rate in manufacturing industries had risen from a 1961 low of 74.5 percent to about 90 percent by year-end 1965. These facts meant that real economic growth could not draw on an unemployed pool of productive resources, but would come only from growth in the labor force and capital resources, and future improvement in productivity. Thus, a rapid surge in final demands would inevitably place upward pressure on prices. The essence of the disagreement turns on what factor or factors brought forth the rapid increase in total spending beginning in the last half of 1965.

As previously noted, both monetary and fiscal measures moved rapidly toward stimulus in the last half of 1965 and early 1966. But monetary restraint was brought to bear from spring 1966 to late in the year while the deficit continued to increase. The slowdown in the economy in the first half of 1967 was accompanied by a significant easing in inflationary pressures. The wholesale price index of industrial commodities, a sensitive price index, reached a peak annual rate of rise of about 4 percent in mid 1966 and by year end was rising at a

---

[1] For an excellent discussion of these two competing viewpoints see David I. Fand, "A Monetary Interpretation of the Post-1965 Inflation in the United States," *Banca Nagionale Del Lavaro Quarterly Review* (Rome, Italy: Banca Nagionale Del Lavoro, June, 1969).

nominal rate of about 1 percent. The slower moving consumer price index declined from a peak rate of about 4 percent to a low of about 1.6 percent in the spring of 1967. The GNP price deflator rate of rise slipped from nearly 4 percent in mid 1966 to a little under 3 percent by mid 1967.[2]

But the tendency toward less inflation was short-lived. In late 1966, monetary policy shifted toward massive ease as measured by monetary growth and related variables, and with the usual lag, total spending rose sharply about mid 1967. Inflation became even more intense because resources were fully utilized; hence increased spending was promptly reflected in higher prices.

As previously noted, the tax surcharge of mid 1968 did not significantly slow economic activity as expected by the new economists, and total spending continued to rise rapidly with accompanying accelerating inflation, as would be expected from the rapid growth in the money supply in 1968. Following a return to a tighter monetary policy, especially during much of 1969, economic activity did begin to taper late in the year, and with the usual lag, price increases became less marked by the early part of 1970. Industrial material prices and wholesale prices, which are most sensitive, responded first, suggesting less rise in the consumer price index and the GNP deflator in subsequent quarters, provided monetary policy did not again shift to excessive ease.

The monetarist explanation of inflation is essentially that the money supply per unit of output rose, resulting in a rapid increase in spending which placed strong demand pressure on prices. The reason for the rapid increase in the money supply traces back to the rapid increase in monetary aggregates largely under the control of the Federal Reserve (see Table 15).

---

[2] Geoffrey H. Moore, "The Anatomy of Inflation" (Report before the Subcommittee on Fiscal Policy of the Joint Economic Committee, U.S. Congress, October 8, 1969).

TABLE 15

Change in Monetary Aggregates
(annual rates of change)

	Money Supply	Monetary Base	Bank Reserves
Mid 1960 to mid 1965	3.2%	+3.2	+3.5
Mid 1965 to April 1966	6.4%	+4.9	+8.4
April 1966 to Nov. 1966	0.6%	+1.4	−4.7
Nov. 1966 to Dec. 1968	7.0%	+6.5	+8.2
Dec. 1968 to Dec. 1969	3.9%	+3.1	+3.0

Statistics: Federal Reserve Bulletin, Federal Reserve Bank of St. Louis.

Sometimes the existence of a large deficit encourages the Federal Reserve to provide financing assistance and hence brings about a rapid increase in monetary aggregates. Therefore, a balanced budget may well provide greater assurance that monetary growth will be moderate. But, clearly, shifts in the budget deficit are not always closely related to changes in monetary aggregates. For example, in 1966 the deficit was increasing, but growth in monetary aggregates declined. Again in 1968 following the tax surcharge the budget shifted toward surplus, but monetary growth accelerated because of the prevailing fear of "overkill," which resulted in an easier monetary policy.

Monetarists argue that the method of financing a deficit or the disposition of a surplus is far more important as a determinant of a change in spending than the size or change in the deficit or surplus. If a deficit is financed with new money as a result of an easing monetary policy, total spending and inflation are stimulated. On the other hand, if a deficit is financed by nonbank buyers of government debt, investors provide money to the government but have fewer funds available to offer to other potential borrowers and spenders. Hence, private spending is restrained while government spending is financed from the existing money supply.

A surplus does not exert a significant restraint on total

spending if government debt is retired and funds are returned to the private sector of the economy. If, however, the surplus funds are impounded by the Treasury, or total bank reserves are reduced so that retirement of debt privately held leads to no increase in deposits, private spending is restrained. Changes in the money supply give a better clue to future spending and inflation than changes in the budget deficit or surplus.

Clearly, the tendency for new economist policy makers to measure monetary restraint by changes in interest rates rather than changes in monetary aggregates was at least partially responsible for rapid growth in the money supply in the latter 1960's. From 1965 through 1969 interest rates rose most of the time, suggesting, from the fiscalist viewpoint, that monetary policy was tight. Yet, as noted above, monetary aggregates expanded at an unusually rapid rate. As will be argued in the next chapter, an easy money policy as measured by monetary aggregates inevitably leads to tight money as measured by interest rates. The unwillingness to make this very important distinction undoubtedly added many percentage points to the various measures of inflation during the past several years. Since current policy makers do make this distinction and are dedicated to maintaining steady but moderate growth in the money supply, this is another reason for believing that inflationary pressures will gradually ease.

LONGER-TERM U.S. EVIDENCE

Monetarists argue then that if the money supply rises relative to real production, inflation will ensue. The greater the rise of the ratio money supply/real GNP, the greater the expected rise in prices. Furthermore, they argue that although variation in velocity or turnover of money could conceivably initiate excessive spending and consequent inflation, as a practical matter the demand for money function, i.e., velocity function, is relatively stable. Therefore, serious inflations in the past have been initiated by rapid growth in the money supply, not by increased velocity. If this relatively simple hypothesis fits the recent past, as appears to be the case, is there confirming evidence from prior periods in the U.S. as well as from other countries? The answer is definitely yes. The existence of additional evidence would serve to greatly strengthen convictions about the relationship between the money supply and inflation if it covered a long period of time, and was maintained regardless of the state of economic development, cultural, and banking system differences.

There is perhaps no relation between economic variables that has been more intensively researched and more firmly established than the money supply-inflation relation. Yet doubt and disagreement abound. The difficulty is partly due to the imperfections of the data on money supply, real output, and prices for earlier U.S. history, as well as modern and earlier histories of many other countries. And part of the difficulty lies in the nature of the scientific method. Hypotheses can be rejected or confirmed; they cannot be proved. Despite the manifold deficiencies, there is sufficient evidence supporting the money supply-inflation relation to provide considerable confidence in its veracity.

Massive U.S. price increases in the 19th and 20th centuries have usually been associated with wars.[3] The following periods stand out, as reflected in Chart 21: the War of 1812, the Civil War, World War I, World War II, a small price surge during the Korean War, and another rise during the Viet Nam War. Although data are sketchy for the earlier period, there is evidence to indicate that much of the increased government outlays were financed with new money, and the money supply

---

3 *Wholesale Prices Historical Chart Book* (Washington, D.C.: Board of Governors of the Federal Reserve System).

CHART 21

Wholesale Prices

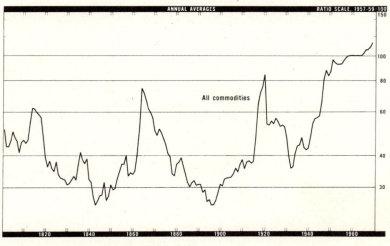

Source: *Wholesale Prices Historical Chart Book.*

surged as did government deficits. Since production could not increase commensurately, prices rose.

As indicated in Chart 22, the ratio of money supply/real GNP began to rise in 1898 and continued upward at a moderate pace until 1916.[4] The price level, which had been declining for many years, likewise began to move moderately upward until more rapid monetary growth occurred from 1915 to 1920. Data for the World War I period indicate that from early 1915, when the money stock was about $12 billion, to early 1920 there was a doubling in the money supply, and the money

---

[4] The general statistical procedure for obtaining *constant-dollar* (*real*) *GNP* is to divide current dollar estimates by appropriate price indexes. The resulting figures are then combined into designated subtotals and total GNP.

When these deflated subtotals and total are compared with comparable figures expressed in current dollars, an average price relationship is implied. Thus, the current dollar total in a given year divided by some one figure would yield the constant dollar figure. These divisors are called "implicit price deflators."

CHART 22

Money and Inflation
(United States)

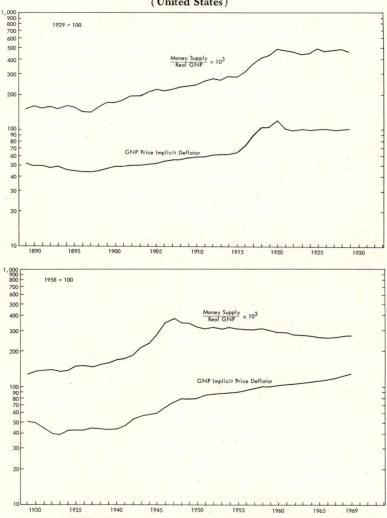

Note: From 1889–1929 the money supply is defined as currency plus demand deposits and time deposits. The base year used for the Implicit Price Deflator is 1929. From 1929–70 the money supply is defined as currency and demand deposits and the base year used is 1958. The narrow definition of the money supply is not available for the early years.

Source: Federal Reserve Board; U.S. Department of Commerce; Milton Friedman and Anna Schwartz, *Monetary Statistics of the United States*, National Bureau of Economic Research (New York: Columbia University Press, 1970), pp. 15–19. Simon Kuznets, *Capital in the American Economy*, Table R–22, Variant III. Data prepared by Harris Trust and Savings Bank.

supply per unit of output rose 77 percent.[5] All commodity wholesale prices slightly more than doubled in the same period. Following the monetary deflation of 1920–21 and subsequent price decline, the money stock grew moderately for the remainder of the decade from about $21 billion in late 1921 to nearly $27 billion by the end of 1929. The 1920's were generally characterized by economic growth and stable prices and the money supply growth was in line with increases in real output.

But from the end of 1929 to early 1933 the money stock declined 27 percent while the broader series, including time deposits, decreased one-third.[6] As usual, the impact of monetary restraint was more severe on production than prices, but as indicated in Chart 22, GNP prices did decline about 20 percent from 1929 until 1933.

During the Great Depression years from 1933 to the early 1940's, the money supply per unit of output rose moderately, as did prices. But as full employment of resources was achieved after World War II began, the money supply rose rapidly relative to output, and prices also zoomed. In fact, actual prices undoubtedly rose more rapidly than the prices reflected in official indexes, since price control and rationing created black markets. However, after the elimination of controls, prices rose and equilibrium was established by 1948.

Since 1947 the money supply per unit of output moved slowly downward until 1966, and rose in subsequent years. Even so, prices drifted upward at a modest pace until the past four years, when inflation became more serious. In other words, the moderate and nearly continuous rise in velocity in the postwar years was sufficient to generate some inflation. Such factors as rising interest rates, or perhaps increased confi-

---

[5] Milton Friedman and Anna Schwartz, *Monetary Statistics of the United States,* National Bureau of Economic Research (New York: Columbia University Press, 1970), pp. 15–19.

[6] *Ibid.,* pp. 25–29.

dence in the stability of the economy, resulted in some reduction in the demand for money to hold.

One of the most interesting differences in price performance following the Civil War, World War I, and World War II was the fact that following the first two wars prices dropped sharply, whereas the pace of the rise moderated following World War II. The explanation clearly lies in the influence of the 1946 Employment Act, which placed responsibility on the federal government to maintain high rates of income and employment. Consequently, the money supply was not reduced following World War II as was the case following the other two wars. Hence, total spending and income creation remained firm and supported the inflated price level. Whereas sizable unemployment was permitted in earlier periods, there appears to be no reason to believe that it will be permitted in the present environment. Although five recessions have occurred since World War II, in only the first case was there any tendency for prices to decline, and then only modestly. The rate of rise slackened significantly in the other four recessions, however. As indicated previously, each recession was preceded, and indeed precipitated by, reduced monetary growth which led to reduced income creation. Unfortunately, monetary growth occasionally became excessive in boom periods, thereby unleashing the inflationary pressures brought under control during the prior recessions.

Clearly, the long-term price record of the U.S. economy is consistent with the proximate explanation offered by the monetarist: changes in the money supply must be related to growth in output. Inflations are tamed in pauses, recessions or depressions preceded by reduced monetary growth or monetary contraction. As the nation was recently reminded in the 1969–70 recession, economic adjustments are painful affairs. Inflations and inflationary expectations are broken only by creating widespread disappointments among workers, consumers, businessmen, and investors. Hence, monetarists argue that once inflation is brought under control it is extremely important to avoid future excessive expansion in the money supply, lest the gain be for naught. Serious inflation is not inevitable, nor has it been characteristic of most of our modern history. It all depends on how the money supply is managed relative to the economy's capacity to expand output.

LOOKING AT OTHER COUNTRIES

Economists can seldom perform a "test tube" experiment where all variables are carefully controlled and cause and effect can be firmly established. Resort must be made to observing relevant phenomena over long periods of time in the same country or searching foreign countries for evidence which confirms or rejects a prior hypothesis. The recent histories of several Latin American countries have provided some very interesting evidence bearing on the monetarist view with regard to the cause of inflation.[7] Many of our southern neighbors have experienced very serious inflation; others have suffered moderate inflation, while a few have enjoyed unusual price stability. If the monetarist explanation is approximately correct, we should find that growth in the money supply per unit of output was much greater in the countries with serious inflation than in those with more stable prices. Indeed that is the case! Charts 23A through 23P present the story.[8]

---

[7] Also see Karl Brunner, "The Drift into Persistent Inflation," *Wharton Quarterly* (Philadelphia: University of Pennsylvania, Wharton Graduate School, Fall, 1969).

[8] These graphs depict the consumer price index increase relative to the growth in the ratio of money supply to real GNP x 10^3. The general statistical procedure for obtaining the consumer price index is to establish a base period (1957–58), assign that period the number 100, and assign every other year some other number relative to the rise or fall in prices as compared to the base period. Since a GNP price deflator is not available for these nations, estimates of real GNP were obtained by dividing current dollar estimates by the consumer price index. The money supply for each country is available.

CHART 23A

Money and Inflation
(Chile)

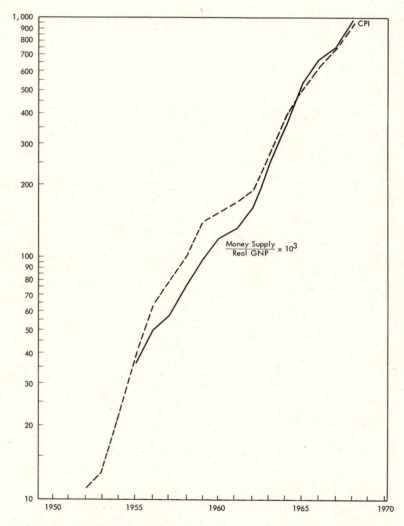

Source: International Monetary Fund, *International Financial Statistics*, August 1968; 1968/70
Supplement, April 1970. Data prepared by Harris Trust and Savings Bank.

CHART 23B

Money and Inflation
(Colombia)

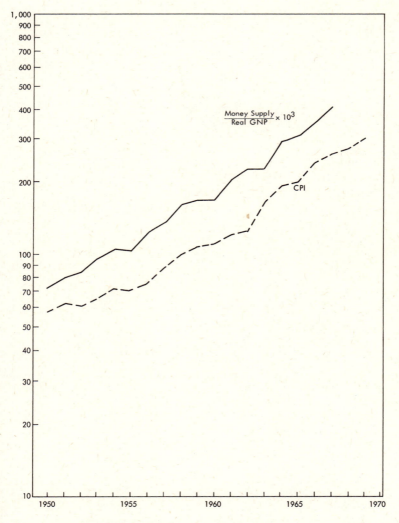

Source: International Monetary Fund, *International Financial Statistics*, August 1968; 1968/70 Supplement, April 1970. Data prepared by Harris Trust and Savings Bank.

CHART 23C

Money and Inflation
(Brazil)

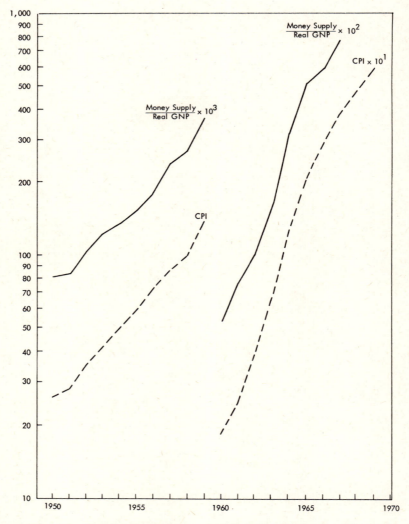

Source: International Monetary Fund, *International Financial Statistics,* August 1968; 1968/70 Supplement, April 1970. Data prepared by Harris Trust and Savings Bank.

CHART 23D

Money and Inflation
(Ecuador)

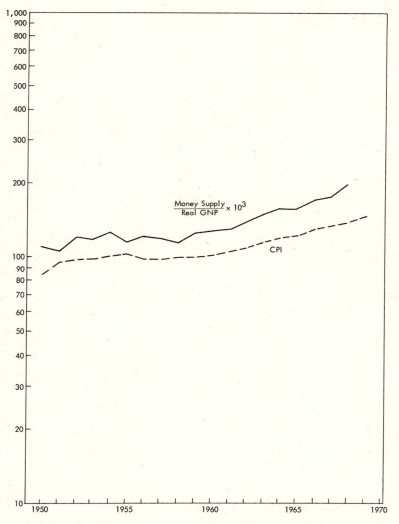

Source: International Monetary Fund, *International Financial Statistics*, August 1968; 1968/70 Supplement, April 1970. Data prepared by Harris Trust and Savings Bank.

CHART 23E

Money and Inflation
(South Korea)

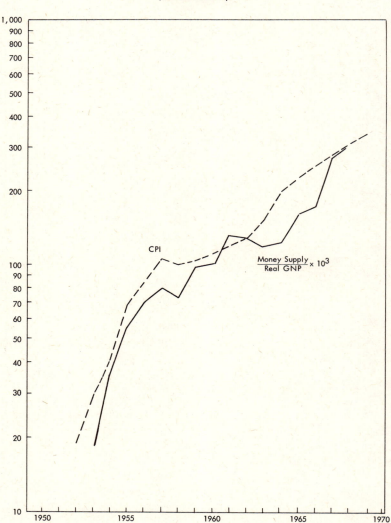

Source: International Monetary Fund, *International Financial Statistics*, August 1968; 1968/70
Supplement, April 1970. Data prepared by Harris Trust and Savings Bank.

CHART 23F

Money and Inflation
(Peru)

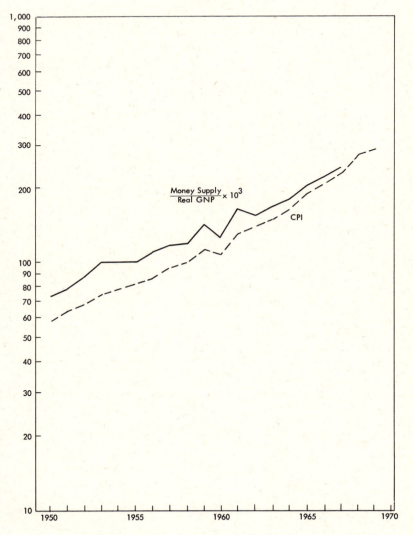

Source: International Monetary Fund, *International Financial Statistics*, August 1968; 1968/70 Supplement, April 1970. Data prepared by Harris Trust and Savings Bank.

CHART 23G
Money and Inflation
(Mexico)

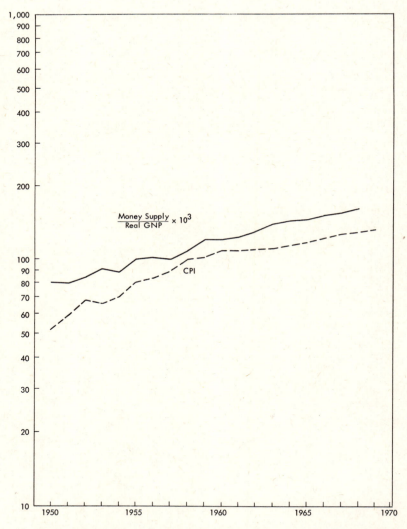

Source: International Monetary Fund, *International Financial Statistics*, August 1968; 1968/70 Supplement, April 1970. Data prepared by Harris Trust and Savings Bank.

CHART 23H

Money and Inflation
(Argentina)

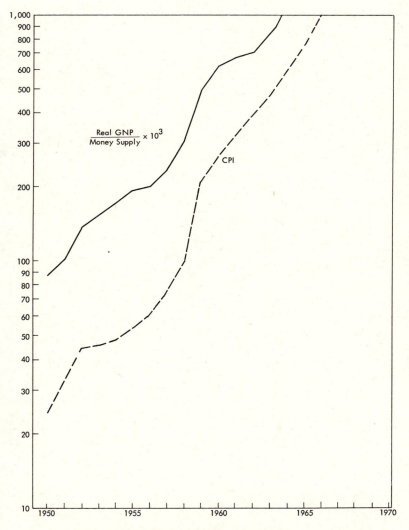

Source: International Monetary Fund, *International Financial Statistics*, August 1968; 1968/70 Supplement, April 1970. Data prepared by Harris Trust and Savings Bank.

CHART 231

Money and Inflation
(Switzerland)

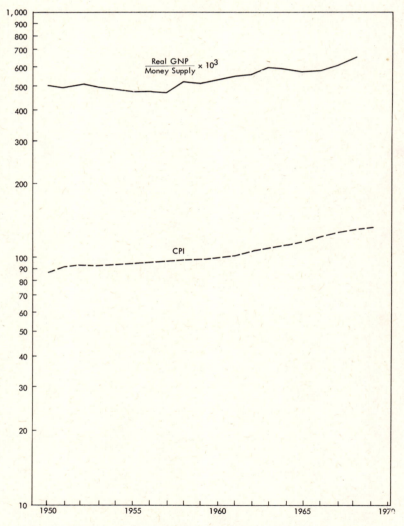

Source: International Monetary Fund, *International Financial Statistics*, August 1968; 1968/70 Supplement, April 1970. Data prepared by Harris Trust and Savings Bank.

CHART 23J

Money and Inflation
(France)

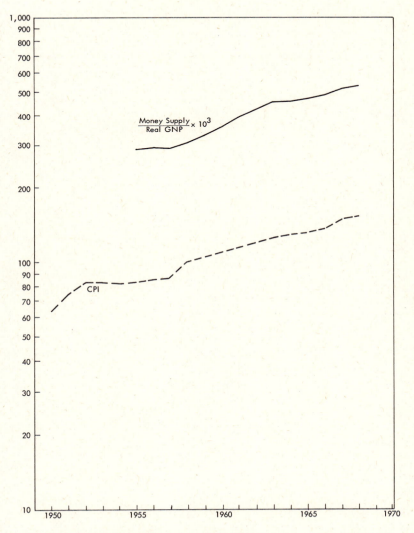

Source: International Monetary Fund, *International Financial Statistics*, August 1968; 1968/70 Supplement, April 1970. Data prepared by Harris Trust and Savings Bank.

CHART 23K

Money and Inflation
(United Kingdom)

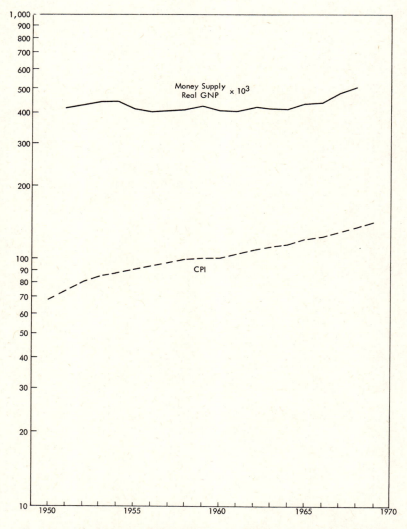

Source: International Monetary Fund, *International Financial Statistics*, August 1968; 1968/70 Supplement, April 1970. Data prepared by Harris Trust and Savings Bank.

CHART 23L

Money and Inflation
(West Germany)

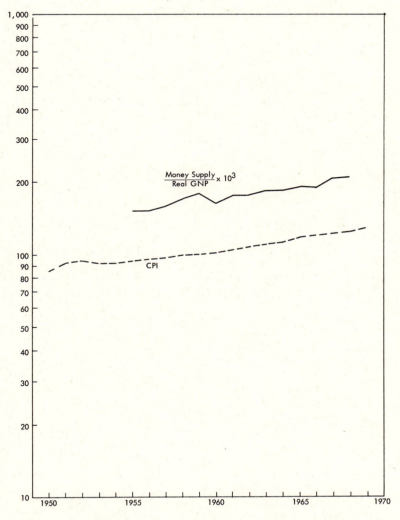

$$\frac{\text{Money Supply}}{\text{Real GNP}} \times 10^3$$

CPI

Source: International Monetary Fund, *International Financial Statistics,* August 1968; 1968/70 Supplement, April 1970. Data prepared by Harris Trust and Savings Bank.

CHART 23M

Money and Inflation
(Canada)

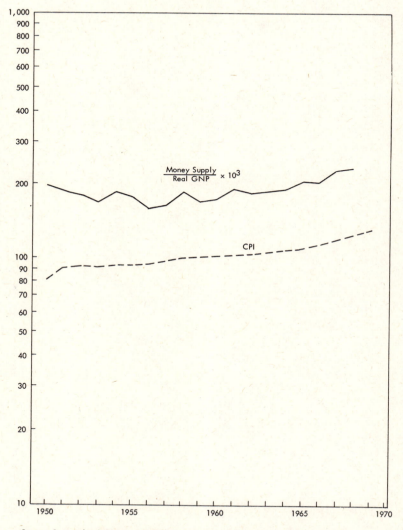

CHART 23N

Money and Inflation
(Japan)

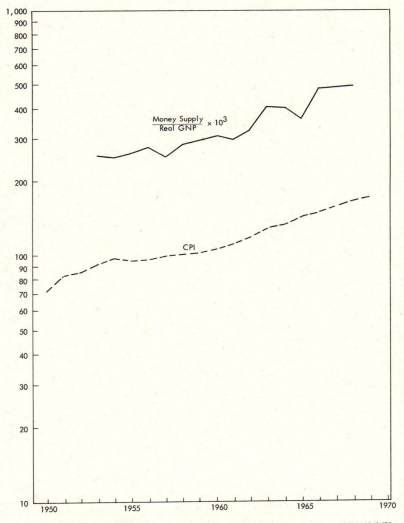

$$\frac{\text{Money Supply}}{\text{Real GNP}} \times 10^3$$

CPI

Source: International Monetary Fund, *International Financial Statistics*, August 1968; 1968/70 Supplement, April 1970. Data prepared by Harris Trust and Savings Bank.

CHART 230

Money and Inflation
(Italy)

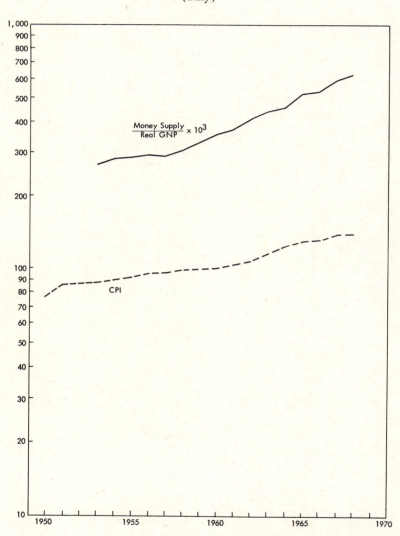

Source: International Monetary Fund, *International Financial Statistics*, August 1968; 1968/70 Supplement, April 1970. Data prepared by Harris Trust and Savings Bank.

Rapid inflation has become endemic in Argentina, Brazil, and Chile during recent years. The proximate cause is not difficult to isolate. In these countries the money supply per unit of output has risen very rapidly. At the other extreme of the spectrum, Ecuador and Mexico have experienced only modest inflation, while the growth in their respective money supplies per unit of output has been fairly modest. Colombia and Peru have chosen a middle course, with moderate money supply growth per unit of output, and have suffered moderate inflation.

TABLE 16

Money and Inflation—1955–68
(compound annual rates of change)

	Money Supply/ Real Gross National Production (%)	Consumer Price Index (%)
Brazil	35.3	37.9
Chile	29.0	27.6
Argentina	22.6	26.6
Colombia	11.2	10.4
Peru	7.7	9.0
Ecuador	4.4	2.3
Mexico	3.8	3.6

Source: International Financial Statistics, International Monetary Fund.

During the same period of time, South Korea suffered an annual rate of inflation of 12.5 percent, with their money supply per unit of output rising at a 14.1 percent rate. The most interesting aspect of their experience was the reduced rate of money supply per unit of output growth extending from 1957 to 1964. During the same period their rate of inflation tapered as indicated in the chart. As Chart 23A discloses, Chile had a somewhat similar experience in the early 1960's, but in each case subsequent rapid expansion in the money supply restored serious inflation.

Neither is confirming evidence for the monetarist limited to developing countries as discussed above. Most free world developed countries have experienced only moderate inflation in recent years, and money growth per unit of output has also grown moderately (Charts G through O). In general, those developed countries that have permitted only modest growth in the money supply per unit of output have experienced the least inflation, while those with more rapid monetary growth have suffered the most. However, since the variations are less extreme, the rank order of the two series is not as close as appears to be the case for Latin America.

TABLE 17

Money and Inflation—1955–68
(compound annual rates of change)

	Money Supply/Real Gross National Production (%)	Consumer Price Index (%)
Italy	6.2	3.1
Japan	4.9	4.3
France	4.8	4.9
West Germany	2.5	2.2
Canada	2.2	2.2
Switzerland	1.6	2.3
United Kingdom	1.4	3.1

Source: International Financial Statistics, International Monetary Fund.

To further strengthen the argument that rapid growth in the money supply was the force that propelled total spending upward, the following comparison between monetary and GNP growth rates was computed for the same countries. The money supply series was compiled independently of the GNP series. Again the rank order of the two series is strikingly similar. Countries with high monetary growth developed high GNP growth, mostly inflation, whereas those countries having less growth in the money supply also had a smaller rise in total spending. Restrained monetary growth was clearly the key to preventing inflation brought on by excessive spending. Velocity or demand for money remained relatively stable.

TABLE 18

Money and GNP Growth—1955–68
(compound annual rates of change)

	Money Supply (%)	Gross National Product (%)
Brazil	38.9	42.6
Chile	34.7	33.2
South Korea	30.0	26.2
Argentina	24.9	28.9
Colombia	16.5	14.8
Japan	14.7	14.0
Peru	12.5	13.8
Mexico	12.4	11.2
France	10.4	10.4
Italy	9.2	12.0
West Germany	8.9	8.7
Ecuador	8.0	6.5
Switzerland	6.7	7.6
Canada	5.9	8.0
United Kingdom	3.9	6.4

Source: International Financial Statistics, International Monetary Fund.

ANCIENT HISTORY

Nor is the evidence on the relation of money to prices confined to modern history. In early periods, the money supply consisted almost exclusively of gold and silver. In a review entitled *The History of Prices before 1750*,[9] Professor Earl J. Hamilton attributes observed price changes in Europe to "changes in the ratio of the money supply—resulting from changes in the stock of bullion—to the physical volume of trade in terms of money."[10] A few direct quotes will serve to give the flavor of the incomplete evidence that is available:

[9] Earl J. Hamilton, *The History of Prices before 1750* (XI Congrés International des Sciences Historiques, Stockholm, Sweden, 1960).

[10] *Ibid.*, p. 154.

"Though we cannot measure the advance anywhere, scholars generally agree that prices in silver or gold rose in England, France, Spain and elsewhere in the thirteenth century and turned downward from around 1315 to 1350. Fairly reliable statistical data indicate that prices rose sharply following the Black Death and fell, with notable interruptions, from around 1380–1390 to the last quarter of the fifteenth century. Though no one knows even approximately how much, scholars agree that the output of silver and perhaps of gold rose a great deal in Europe during the thirteenth century, fell in the first half of the fourteenth, and remained low until about 1475.[11]. . .

"Since we have no infallible measure of either prices or any major force that might have governed prices, a doctrinaire explanation is not warranted. It seems, however, that changes in the ratio of the money supply—resulting from changes in the stock of bullion—to the physical volume of trade in terms of money were chiefly responsible for variations in the price level. In his excellent study of "Mining and Metallurgy in Medieval Civilization," [in *The Cambridge Economic History of Europe,* Vol. II (1952), pp. 437 ff.] Professor John U. Nef, despite the complete lack of quantitative data, gives convincing evidence that the European output of precious metals rose sharply in the thirteenth century. There may have been a considerable increase in gold imports from Africa. Apparently the money supply outstripped the increase in physical trade and the fall in velocity of circulation presumably resulting from rising incomes. A decrease in the ratio of the money supply (resulting from a catastrophic drop in production of the precious metals through exhaustion of many deposits, the ravages of war and civil disorder, plagues, the increased cost of production as prices rose in conjunction with a fixed or slowly rising mint price of bullion and a decline in prospecting) (cf. John U. Nef, *op. cit.,* Vol. II, pp. 456–458) to the physical volume of trade seems to have been the chief factor in falling prices.[12]

". . . The chief factor in the Price Revolution of the sixteenth and

---

[11] *Ibid.,* pp. 152–53.
[12] *Ibid.,* p. 154.

seventeenth centuries was the great addition to the money supply. The increased output of silver in Europe, particularly in Germany, beginning in the last quarter of the fifteenth century [John U. Nef, "Silver Production in Central Europe, 1540–1618," *Journal of Political Economy*, XLIX (1941), pp. 577 ff.] arrested the downward trend of prices which had lasted about a century and, along with gold imports from the Antilles, caused prices to turn upward early in the sixteenth century. But it was the explosive increase in world silver production after the conquests of Mexico and Peru, the discoveries of the almost incredibly rich mines of Zacatecas, Guanajuato and Potosí and the introduction of the mercury amalgamation process of mining in the middle of the sixteenth century that gave rise to the Price Revolution. This is shown by the fact that a sharp rise in silver prices began earlier and was more violent in Andalusia, the region that received all the bullion that legally came into Europe from the New World, than in any other area in Europe for which we have satisfactory price data. New Castile, the Spanish region in closest contact with Andalusia, was next to experience the Price Revolution. An unfavourable balance of payments induced by relatively high Spanish prices, and, to a much lesser extent, royal expenditures for war and diplomacy pushed the precious metals into other European countries. Of course, some bullion leaked into other countries directly from the New World, perhaps in small volume up to the death of Philip II and in increasing amounts thereafter. Both the lag of French and English prices behind those of Spain and the similar rise in each country indicate that specie from the New World was the leading factor forcing silver prices upward in all three.[13] . . .

"An increase in the physical volume of trade relative to the money supply times velocity appears to have been primarily responsible for the declining trend of specie prices from the culmination of the Price Revolution through the first third of the eighteenth century. That the dynamic factor in the rising trend of specie prices after about 1735 was an increase in the production of gold and silver,

---

[13] *Ibid.*, pp. 155–56.

particularly in Brazil and Mexico, [cf. Adolf Soetbeer, *Edelmetall-Produktion und Wertverhaltniss zwischen Gold und Silber seit der Entdeckung Amerika's bis zur Gegenwart* (*Gotha, 1879*), *pp. 109–110*], is shown by the coincidence of this increase and the price upturn at such widely distant and economically diverse points as Madrid, Valencia, London and Philadelphia.

"The strategic role of changes in the supply of gold and silver money in Spanish price movements is demonstrated by the fall of prices during the war with France and England in 1719–1720 and during the War of the Austrian Succession, and the stability of prices while Spain participated in the last thirteen months of the Seven Years' War; for some specie continued to flow out, and Spain's weakness at sea enabled her enemies to reduce or shut off imports from the New World. Prices rose after suspension of hostilities permitted the inflow of bullion impounded during the conflicts. Paper money filled the void in 1779–1783, but prices rose more in the first two years of peace, when the specie pent up in the New World arrived, than in four years of war and paper-money inflation."[14]

Although detailed evidence is lacking, the facts that are known from ancient history appear to support the argument that a rise in the money supply per unit of output is both a necessary and sufficient condition for inducing inflation. Never has a serious inflation occurred without a sharp increase in the money supply per unit of output, and such a rise in the money supply inevitably fosters inflation. It has apparently ever been thus and when faced with the evidence, a monetarist is inclined to conclude that probabilities point toward the same relation in the future. In one sense, this conclusion is indeed fortunate, for the money supply in modern economies is subject to control by monetary authorities. If governments are to respond to the world-wide desires of their citizens to avoid serious inflation, they must control monetary growth in line with output in-

---

[14] *Ibid.*, pp. 156–57.

creases. The medicine will work if applied! But unfortunately the early stages of inflation are usually so pleasant that governments are frequently encouraged to finance deficits with new money while permitting rapid growth in the money supply. Although the acquisition of money by the individual is a costly exercise involving work, production, or sale of assets, the added short-run cost to a government of creating money is very low; hence, there exists world-wide tendency to inflate. A clearer understanding of the cause of inflation combined with pressure from concerned citizens will be necessary to slow price increases in the next decade. Fortunately, increased emphasis upon controlling monetary growth by U.S. officials as well as by many other central bankers around the world suggests that all is not yet lost. We can have relatively stable prices if the political will is sufficient.

MONITORING PRICE CHANGES

In making short-run analyses of changing inflationary pressure, there are several techniques that provide excellent early warning signals. In this age of inflation, prices seldom decline, as previously noted. Therefore, in one sense, inflation is almost always with us. Rather than concentrating attention on the level of prices, which is usually going up, it is desirable to focus on the rate of rise which has changed significantly in the years since World War II. Only recently have U.S. price indexes been reported in seasonally adjusted form, which is useful for making revealing short-run analysis. However, even after the seasonal adjustment, there remain sporadic month-to-month movements which, if left in the data, serve to obscure the developing trend. Once again we are faced with the desire to have both a sensitive measure that reflects short-run changes and a smooth measure which is not beclouded by erratic movements. Unfortunately we can't have both. But a useful compromise is available. By computing a seasonally adjusted annual rate of rise averaged over a six-month period, it is possible to get a series that is reasonably sensitive yet devoid of most erratic movements. Therefore, by directly watching changes in the rate of rise rather than changes in the level of prices, a careful analyst will be much better informed about what is actually happening to prices.

A careful observer should not be satisfied with knowing only what has recently happened to prices. He should like to have some early indications of what to expect. It is the thesis of this book that changes in total demand are primarily a result of prior changes in the money supply. Clearly, changes in total demand relative to the capacity of the economy to increase production are the major factors accounting for changes in prices. Therefore, it follows that changes in the rate of growth of the money supply should precede changes in total demand which, in turn, should be closely related to changes in prices, especially as full employment of resources is approached.

Indeed that appears to be the case, as indicated in Chart 24. This chart plots the annual rate of change in the money supply since 1948 against the annual rate of change in consumer prices, both seasonally adjusted and smoothed over a six-month period. The relation is far from perfect, but it is clear that changes in money usually precede changes in the consumer price index.

Cooling of the early post World War II inflation began in 1948, well after monetary growth declined. Renewed monetary expansion began in late 1949 and prices zoomed, especially after the beginning of the Korean War, and the rate of increase dropped promptly in 1951, even though monetary expansion did not contract until 1952. The bulge in monetary growth during the recession of 1954 did not reincite inflation until well after the recovery was under way in 1956 and unemployment

CHART 24

Changes in Money and Inflation
(annual rates of change in money supply and consumer price index—
6-month moving average)

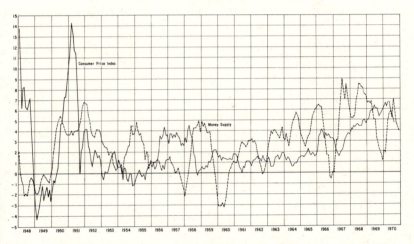

Source: Federal Reserve Board; CPI: Geoffrey H. Moore, "The Anatomy of Inflation" (Statement before the Subcommittee on Fiscal Policy, Joint Economic Committee, U.S. Congress, October 8, 1969), Chart I. Data prepared by Harris Trust and Savings Bank.

of resources was much reduced. Monetary restraint in 1955, 1956, and 1957 induced the recession of 1957–58, and with the usual lag, inflation receded. The economic expansion of 1958–60 was short-lived, due to the prompt adoption of monetary restraint in 1959. Because of widespread underutilization of resources, serious inflation was not renewed. The recession of 1960–61 resulted in some further reduction of inflation.

In the first half of the 1960's underutilization of resources was widespread and monetary growth was unusually stable, except for a brief period in 1962. By the last half of 1965 approximate full employment of resources was achieved, monetary growth spurted for about three quarters, and by early 1966 prices began to escalate sharply. For seven months in 1966 severe monetary restraint was applied and with a brief lag, price increases began to abate. But alas, monetary growth zoomed in 1967 and most of 1968 and price rises soared to new heights. Monetary restraint was imposed in 1969 and early 1970 and again these measures brought the price rise under control during 1970.

It seems fair to conclude that price inflation is stimulated by rising and high monetary growth once the economy achieves practical full employment of resources. Monetary restraint brings a slowing in the economy and later a slowing in inflationary pressures. These facts, plus the voluminous evidence cited earlier, strongly suggest that if monetary growth is stabilized and kept in line with the growth of productive capacity, inflation will be modest, at worst.

Sensitive measures of price change combined with measures of demand and supply pressures as described above provide a good early warning system for detecting changing prices. An added tool for observing changing price trends involves an awareness of which price indexes are early movers and which respond only slowly. In an excellent paper,[15] Dr. Geoffrey H. Moore provides insight concerning the usual timing sequence between several price, cost, and expectation variables. He concludes the following:

1. Common stock prices, as measured by Standard and Poor's 500 stock index, have led at every turn in the CPI. The leads have averaged about a year at peaks and a half-year at troughs. However, the leads have varied greatly in length and there have been some swings in stock prices—for example, in 1961–62—that are not matched by corresponding swings in the CPI. Stock prices are, of course, especially sensitive to investors' appraisals of domestic and international events, many of which have little to do with the factors

---

[15] Geoffrey H. Moore, "The Anatomy of Inflation" (Statement before the Subcommittee on Fiscal Policy, Joint Economic Committee, U.S. Congress, October 8, 1969).

that determine the prices that consumers pay. But some factors influence both stock prices and consumer prices, causing them to move in a rough correspondence, but with the effects showing up much earlier in stock prices, and of course greatly magnified in degree.

2. The prices of industrial materials traded on commodity markets also tend to lead the turns in the CPI. To a lesser extent, so do the prices of industrial commodities in the wholesale markets generally. Price changes in these markets are generally passed on, with a lag, to the retail markets. The processing that the industrial materials and components undergo as they enter into finished goods for sale to consumers adds a cost element which itself generally lags behind these prices.

3. The Consumer Price Index includes services as well as commodities, and the prices of these services lag behind the total index as well as its commodity price component. Some of these service prices, such as rents or utility charges, lag as a consequence of being fixed by contract or by regulation, or simply by custom.

4. Rates of increase in labor compensation per manhour appear to move in roughly coincident fashion with rates of increase in consumer prices, while rates of increase in labor costs per unit of output usually lag behind both the compensation rates and the prices.

5. Records of selling price expectations held by manufacturers, wholesalers and retailers, compiled by Dun and Bradstreet, Inc., suggest that such expectations lag behind actual price changes. Similar data on consumers' expectations, compiled by the University of Michigan Survey Research Center, reveal a similar pattern.

The data supporting these conclusions are found in Tables 19 and 20.

SUMMARY

Rapid growth in the money supply per unit of output is usually a necessary and sufficient condition to bring serious inflation. The more rapid the growth in the money supply in

TABLE 19. Cyclical Peaks in Rate of Change in Selected Prices, Wages, Costs, and Price Expectations[1]
(seasonally adjusted annual rates except where indicated)

Series	Peaks					Median at Peaks
CPI, total	Feb. 1951	Oct. 1956	Nov. 1959	April 1966	—	
500 common stock prices[2,4]	Jan. 1951	Sept. 1955	Jan. 1959	April 1963	Sept. 1968	
Industrial material prices[2]	Nov. 1950	Dec. 1955	Nov. 1958	Nov. 1964	—	
WPI, industrials[5]	Jan. 1951	Nov. 1955	May 1959	July 1966	—	
GNP deflator	Feb. 1951	Aug. 1956	N.C.	Aug. 1966	—	
CPI, services	N.A.	June 1957	Sept. 1959	Sept. 1966	—	
Selling prices, mfg., & trade[3]						
Actual	Feb. 1951	Nov. 1956	Aug. 1959	Aug. 1966	—	
Anticipated	May 1951	Feb. 1957	Nov. 1959	Feb. 1967	—	
Compensation per man hour[6]	Nov. 1950	Aug. 1956	Feb. 1960	May 1966	—	
Unit labor cost[6]	Feb. 1951	Feb. 1956	Aug. 1960	Aug. 1966	—	

Series	Lead (+) or Lag (−) at Peaks in CPI, Total, in Months					Median at Peaks
500 common stock prices[2,4]	−1	−13	−10	−36	—	−12
Industrial material prices[2]	−3	−10	−12	−17	—	−11
WPI, industrials[5]	−1	−11	− 6	+ 3	—	− 4
GNP deflator	0	− 2	N.C.	+ 4	—	0
CPI, services	N.A.	+ 8	− 2	+ 5	—	+ 5
Selling prices, mfg., & trade[3]						
Actual	0	+ 1	− 3	+ 4	—	+ 1
Anticipated	+3	+ 4	0	+10	—	+ 4
Compensation per man hour[6]	−3	− 2	+ 3	+ 1	—	− 1
Unit labor cost[6]	0	− 8	+ 9	+ 4	—	+ 2

N.A.—Not available. N.C.—No timing comparison.
[1] Six-month or two-quarter span except series on selling prices, manufacturing, and trade.
[2] Not seasonally adjusted.
[3] Diffusion index. Copyrighted by Dun and Bradstreet; may not be reproduced without permission from source.
[4] Additional peaks were observed in April 1961 and April 1967.
[5] Additional peak observed in July 1953.
[6] Private nonfarm, all persons.

TABLE 20. Cyclical Troughs in Rates of Change in Selected Prices, Wages, Costs, and Price Expectations[1]
(seasonally adjusted annual rates except where indicated)

Series	Troughs					Median at Troughs
CPI, total	Feb. 1949	Dec. 1954	Oct. 1958	June 1961	April 1967	
500 common stock prices[2,4]	Dec. 1948	Sept. 1953	Jan. 1958	Feb. 1960	Oct. 1966	
Industrial material prices[2]	June 1949	Aug. 1951	Jan. 1958	July 1962	Oct. 1966	
WPI, industrials[5]	May 1949	Jan. 1954	Feb. 1958	Dec. 1960	July 1967	
GNP deflator	May 1949	Nov. 1953	N.C.	Aug. 1961	May 1967	
CPI, services	N.A.	N.A.	Dec. 1958	Aug. 1961	Aug. 1967	
Selling prices, mfg., & trade[3]						
Actual	N.A.	May 1954	May 1958	May 1961	May 1967	
Anticipated	N.A.	Aug. 1954	Aug. 1958	Feb. 1963	Aug. 1967	
Compensation per man hour[6]	Nov. 1949	Feb. 1955	May 1958	Feb. 1961	May 1967	
Unit labor cost[6]	Aug. 1949	Feb. 1955	Aug. 1958	Aug. 1961	Aug. 1967	

Lead (+) or Lag (−) at Trough in CPI, Total, in Months

Series						Median at Troughs
500 common stock prices[2,4]	−2	−3	−9	−18	−6	−6
Industrial material prices[2]	+4	−40	−9	+13	−6	−6
WPI, industrials[5]	+3	−11	−8	−6	+3	−6
GNP deflator	+3	+13	N.C.	+2	+1	+3
CPI, services	N.A.	N.A.	+2	+2	+4	+2
Selling prices, mfg., & trade[3]						
Actual	N.A.	−7	−5	−1	+1	−3
Anticipated	N.A.	−4	−2	+20	+4	+1
Compensation per man hour[6]	+9	+2	−5	−4	+1	+1
Unit labor cost[6]	+6	+2	−2	+2	+4	+2

N.A.—Not available.   N.C.—No timing comparison.

[1] Six-month or two-quarter span except on selling prices, manufacturing, and trade.

[2] Not seasonally adjusted.

[3] Diffusion index. Copyrighted by Dun and Bradstreet; may not be reproduced without permission from source.

[4] Additional troughs were observed in June 1962 and March 1968.

[5] Additional trough was observed in Nov. 1951.

[6] Private nonfarm, all persons.

relation to the capacity of the economy to produce goods and services, the more rapid the inflation. Data from Latin America and the developed nations of the free world strongly support the above assertions. Since the money supply is readily controllable, why do governments so frequently permit inflation, despite widespread support for a stable price level? Certainly the answer is partly that too many nations believe that manipulation of fiscal policies can provide a satisfactory preventive for inflation. In country after country such an approach has not worked unless accompanied by moderate monetary growth, but there are two supporting reasons. First, inflation in the initial stages is very satisfying. Nearly everyone enjoys higher incomes, and it may take awhile to realize that real incomes are not advancing commensurately. Expectations as well as realizations change only slowly. But an additional contributing factor must be the recognition by government officials that the process of going from a serious inflation toward price stability is usually a very painful one and many governments do not have that much fortitude. The existing government might look good in the annals of history, but that is of course small comfort to a politician if, in fact, he is voted or thrown out of office. A defeated politician can do little to improve the welfare of his constituents. To make matters worse, there is a good chance that his successors will receive the kudos for finally bringing the inflation under control.

Controlling inflation is indeed a painful process. First monetary restraint raises interest rates in the short run. Such a move is hardly a popular policy. Somewhat later, income growth begins to abate, owing to fewer jobs being created, reduced overtime, and eventual increased unemployment. Workers grow restive not only because their real incomes are probably not increasing due to the continued price rise, but also because overtime is dropping and some of the previously employed are losing their jobs. The young with lower seniority and the disadvantaged tend to be first to receive the axe.

In the meantime, investors seldom fare well. Bondholders watch their investment values decline as interest rates rise. As a group, equity holders also lose as stock prices recede. Potential home buyers are unhappy because they have increasing difficulty acquiring money, and sellers are disappointed because price concessions become necessary to sell homes.

As weakness in the economy spreads, businessmen become disenchanted because their costs continue to mount while their volume slips. In fact, no one is happy and retribution may well occur at the voting booth unless the adjustment is prompt and inflation recedes quickly. But that isn't the way it usually works. As noted previously, less inflation usually occurs only after widespread disappointments occur among consumers, businessmen, investors—in fact, nearly everyone. Therefore it is not difficult to understand why few governments have both the sagacity and tenacity to pursue a set of policies designed to bring inflation under control. In the last half of the 1950 decade, President Eisenhower tenaciously followed anti-inflationary policies with the result that prices did indeed stabilize but two recessions were induced in 1957–58 and 1960–61. The elimination of inflationary expectations made continued price stability possible in the first half of the 1960's but the 1960–61 recession, with attendant economic costs, undoubtedly contributed to the political defeat of Richard M. Nixon in the 1960 campaign. It is doubly important that once success has been achieved, inflationary policies be avoided like the plague; otherwise, all the pain will have been for nothing except to accumulate one more bit of experience demonstrating both the veracity of the monetarist claims and the political costs of restoring price stability.

What about the oft repeated claim that rapid wage increases, not the money supply, actually cause inflation? The wage push theory is especially popular among businessmen, for they recognize that wage costs are a substantial portion of total costs, and if they are to maintain a satisfactory profit, prices must be raised. There of course can be no denying the fact that rapid wage increases are likely to lead to attempts to raise prices to retain or even improve profit margins. But will the posted price increases stick? This all depends on the state of final demand. If demand is rising, the new prices will be confirmed in the marketplace. But if monetary restraint is battling inflation, final demands in many markets will weaken, making it impossible to sustain higher prices. In that event, rapid wage increases will squeeze profits, increase unemployment, and eventually contribute to the stabilization of prices.

When serious inflation is underway and widely expected, all contracts dealing with the future value of money reflect inflationary expectations. As will be argued later in detail, interest rates rise in order to compensate for the decline in the value of money. Lenders may insist on equity kickers of one sort or another, in addition to high interest rates, in order to maintain purchasing power. Workers bargain for and receive large increases for future years since it is believed that purchasing power will be subsequently reduced. Rents extending into the future escalate. The only way of preventing market participants from arranging contracts to allow for reduced purchasing power in the future is to convince them that inflation will not occur. Performance must precede conviction and on this score many modern governments have been found sadly lacking.

The individual observer can do little to bring inflation under control, but he can be aware of what is happening to prices and what is likely to happen. By observing sensitive measures of the rate of change in prices, he will be aware of change long before most market participants, and may be able to benefit in the marketplace if his ability to act matches his knowledge. If he also concentrates on changing demand pressures, as measured by monetary growth, in relation to the economy's capacity to produce, he will be one more jump ahead of others. Finally, knowledge of the typical sequence of price and cost changes will enable him to concentrate his attention where the action is, rather than being led down popular, but frequently misleading byways.

Serious inflation is indeed one of the scourges of mankind for well known reasons. But all is not lost! Modern governments, including the United States, have recently become increasingly aware of what can be done to prevent serious inflation in the future. The price records extending back many centuries and covering many countries confirm the argument that serious inflation cannot occur if only moderate growth in the money supply is permitted.

8

Money and
the Bond Market

INTRODUCTION

The basic real rate of interest is determined by nonmonetary factors such as real savings and real productivity. The real rate of interest refers to the market rate of interest adjusted for expected changes in the purchasing power of money. Many variables affect the real rate of savings and capital productivity. Fortunately, from our point of view, most of the determinants of the basic real rate of interest are slow moving and do not change drastically over time. It is the intent of this chapter to concentrate on monetary factors which in many economies account for most of the cyclical and secular change in market rates of interest. Since asset values fluctuate with market rates of interest, not real rates, investors must concentrate their attention on changing monetary variables which account for most changes in market interest rates.

CONFUSION BETWEEN CREDIT
AND MONEY

As Professor Friedman has frequently pointed out, much of the misunderstanding concerning the relationship between money and interest rates stems from a failure to distinguish between three ways in which the word "money" is used.[1] When we refer to someone's making money, we really mean earning income. When we refer to someone's borrowing money, we mean that he is entering into a credit transaction on the borrowing side. We are also referring to credit markets when we speak of the money markets. Finally, when we talk about money in the sense developed in this book, we are talking about coins and currency carried in our pockets plus checking accounts to our credit at commercial banks. It is especially important that we keep the "credit" sense of money distinct from the quantity of money.

When we are talking about credit, it is proper to say the interest rate is the price of credit. Therefore, we can conclude that an increase in the quantity of credit will tend to reduce interest rates. Conversely, a decrease in the supply of credit will tend to raise interest rates. Unfortunately, the tendency to confuse the terms "credit" and "money" frequently leads to the conclusion that an increase in the quantity of money will tend to reduce interest rates and that a decrease in the quantity of money will tend to raise rates. But this is true only in the short run, and then the cause and effect relation runs in the opposite direction, as explained shortly. Clearly, the relation between the quantity of money and interest rates is much more complicated than suggested by the simplistic view that more money means lower interest rates.

---

[1] Milton Friedman, "Factors Affecting the Level of Interest Rates," *Savings and Residential Financing* (1968 Conference Proceedings), pp. 12–13.

Although the interest rate is the price of credit, it is not the price of money. The inverse or reciprocal of the price level is the price of money. As previously argued, an increase in the quantity of money tends to raise prices and reduce the value of money; conversely, a smaller supply of money reduces prices and raises the value of money. To see what happens to interest rates when an increase in the quantity of money occurs, a more complicated analysis is needed.

THE LIQUIDITY EFFECT

The conventional Keynesian analysis of the effect of an increase in the money supply on interest rates argues that to induce money holders to voluntarily hold an increased supply of money, interest rates must decline. This effect may be referred to as the "liquidity effect." Until recently, most economists would have used only the above version in explaining the impact of a changing money supply on interest rates. Some would have argued that the very forces by which the money supply increases in our economy, i.e., largely open market purchases of Treasury bills, leads to higher prices for Treasury bills and ultimately to lower rates on other assets as portfolios are adjusted to the lower Treasury bill rate. This analysis is indeed correct so far as it goes, but it stops much too soon and, in fact, misses the major effect of a changing money supply on interest rates.

The liquidity analysis does not fit even a casual reference to empirical relations between money supply and interest rates. For example, it is well known that in many of the South American countries we previously surveyed, such as Chile and Brazil, interest rates are very high. But we know that monetary expansion in those countries has been very high, not low as the liquidity theory would imply. If we seek a country where interest rates are low, like Switzerland, we find that monetary expansion is also low, not high, as the liquidity argument implies. Or if we search the modern history of the United States we find that interest rates dropped drastically during the period from 1929 to the mid 1930's. Yet, as previously noted, the money supply declined 29 percent from 1929 to 1932. During the first half of the 1960's, when monetary growth was moderate at about 3 percent, interest rates were much lower than they have been since mid 1965, when monetary growth averaged much more. It appears that high interest rates are typical of countries with high rates of monetary growth and serious inflation and not vice versa. Many years ago, Gibson, an English financial writer, published several articles drawing attention to the close correlation between the level of interest rates and commodity prices. Keynes was impressed by these data and named the relation "The Gibson Paradox," after the author who first indicated a price-interest rate relation. Since it was known that countries with high serious inflation also had rapid monetary growth, it appeared paradoxical that more money caused higher, not lower, interest rates. The facts just do not fit the theory that more money causes lower rates. Since the facts cannot be changed, we must go back to the drawing board to uncover some missing elements in a viable theory of interest rates.

THE INCOME AND PRICE EFFECTS

Monetarists argue that an increase in the money supply does indeed tend, in the first instance, to raise asset prices and lower interest rates. But that isn't the end of the story. They also contend that more money leads, with an appropriate lag, to more spending. More spending occurs on both consumers goods and services as well as investment goods. If sufficient idle resources are available to accommodate increased spending with increased real production, then real incomes rise with no significant short-run effect upon prices. Since incomes are higher, resulting from higher sales, production, and employment, there is an increase in the demand for loanable funds. The higher income effect resulting from more money in the economy tends to raise the demand for funds and place upward pressure on interest rates.[2] Therefore, the income effect of higher monetary growth raises interest rates in a direction of change contrary to the initial liquidity effect.

But the story cannot stop there. Suppose more rapid monetary growth continues and practical full employment of labor and capital resources is achieved. Additional increases in total spending are reflected in higher prices. The income effect tended to reverse the liquidity effect which lowered interest rates, and now the price effect serves to drive interest rates even higher. Why should this be?

Participants in the credit markets become aware of the fact that prices are rising and probably begin to expect that further increases will be forthcoming, since reversal of an inflationary trend can be achieved only gradually. The borrower recognizes that if he borrows now and pays back later, the value of the money, i.e., purchasing power, will be less at the time the loan is repaid. Presumably it will be less difficult to pay back a loan with inflated dollars than with stable dollars. Therefore, he is interested in increasing his demand for loanable funds. Lenders are aware of the inflationary phenomena as well and insist on receiving the basic real rate of interest plus more to compensate for reduced purchasing power of the money to be repaid at a subsequent date. These demand and supply pressures result in higher rates of interest as well as a proliferation of other devices, such as equity participations, designed to maintain the purchasing power of the money loaned.

We now may conclude, on the basis of the above argument,

---

[2] *Ibid.*, pp. 17–20.

that an increase in the quantity of money leads in the first instance to somewhat lower interest rates, but that once income and prices are stimulated, interest rates go up, not down. The greater the amount of money pumped into the economy, the larger the rise in incomes, prices, and, consequently, interest rates. Hence, more money leads to higher, not lower, interest rates. We should expect to find that countries experiencing the highest rate of monetary growth relative to output, and hence the highest rate of inflation, also have the highest interest rates. And indeed that is the case. The above explanation of the apparent Gibson Paradox was first developed by Irving Fisher in 1896 in his essay entitled "Appreciation and Interest."[3] Once again, we find that what is old is not always wrong and what is new is not necessarily correct. The following excerpt from Fisher appears as fresh as if it were just written.

Four general facts have now been established:
(1) High and low prices are directly correlated with high and low rates of interest; (2) Rising and falling prices and wages are directly correlated with high and low rates of interest; (3) The adjustment of interest to price (or wage) movements is inadequate; (4) This adjustment is more nearly adequate for long than for short periods.

These facts are capable of a common explanation expressing the manner in which the adjustment referred to takes place. Suppose an upward movement of prices begins. Business profits (measured in *money*) will rise, for profits are the difference between gross income and expense, and if both these rise, their difference will also rise. Borrowers can now afford to pay higher "money interest." If, however, only a few persons see this, the interest will not be fully adjusted[4] and borrowers will realize an extra margin of profit after

---

[3] Irving Fisher, *Appreciation and Interest,* American Economic Association (Evanston, Ill.: Northwestern University, 1896), pp. 75–76.

[4] "It seems scarcely necessary to add as an independent cause of mal-adjustment the accumulation (or in the opposite case, depletion) of bank reserves, for this is but another symptom of mal-adjustment due to imperfect foresight. An increase of

deducting interest charges. This raises an expectation of a similar profit in the future, and this expectation, acting on the demand for loans, will raise the rate of interest. If the rise is still inadequate, the process is repeated, and thus by continual trial and error the rate approaches the true adjustment.

When a fall of prices begins, the reverse effects appear. Money profits fall. Borrowers cannot afford to pay the old rates of interest. If, through miscalculation, they still attempt to do this, it will cut into their real profits. Discouraged thus for the future, they will then bid lower rates.

Since at the beginning of an upward price movement the rate of interest is too low, and at the beginning of a downward movement it is too high, we can understand, not only that the averages for the whole periods are imperfectly adjusted, but that the delay in the adjustment leaves a relatively low interest at the beginning of an ascent of prices and a relatively high interest at the beginning of a descent. This would explain, in part at least, the association of high and low prices with high and low interest. The fact that the adjustment is more perfect for long periods than for short, seems to be because in short periods the years of non-adjustment at the beginning occupy a larger relative part of the whole period.

ANALYTICAL IMPLICATIONS

As recently pointed out by Professor David I. Fand, the Fisher analysis yields several useful implications for analysis of current and prospective interest rates.[5]

1. Market interest rates reflecting inflationary expectations need to be distinguished from the real rate of interest (or rate of return) which takes account of price level changes.

---

gold supply, as in 1852–53 (see Tooke and Newmarch, "History of Prices", vol. V, p. 345) may first find its way into the loan market instead of into circulation. But if foresight were perfect, this would not happen, or if it did happen, borrowers would immediately take it out (or increase the liabilities against it) to avail themselves of the double advantage of low interest and high prospective profits from the rise of prices about to follow."

[5] David I. Fand, "Money Matters," *Barron's,* December 1, 1969, p. 5.

2. Market rates may rise or fall, even if real rates are stable.

3. A market rate may be viewed as the sum of the real rate plus the expected changes in prices—the premium for inflationary expectations. Thus, if a real long rate is 5 percent and prices are expected to rise at a rate of 4 percent, the corresponding market long rate will rise to include a 4 percent inflation premium, and settle at 9 precent.

4. High (but stable) market rates reflect an inflationary process that has been fully anticipated, higher rising rates indicate that the inflationary expectations are not yet fully anticipated, and reflected in the level of market rates.

5. Market rates may change in response to changes in real rates, even in a regime of stable commodity prices. Nevertheless, most of the observed changes in market rates can apparently be explained by the distributed lag function of past price changes, without introducing changes in real rates.

Therefore, analysis of the impact of changing monetary growth on interest rates is more complicated than is frequently presumed. Modern day populists are invariably in favor of "easy money," by which they really mean low rates of interest. But this desire is usually translated into always being in favor of rapid growth in the money supply brought about by an expansive monetary policy. If the above argument is correct, an easy money policy will inevitably bring tight money in the sense of high and rising interest rates. Conversely, the monetarists are usually in favor of moderate monetary growth, which inevitably leads to lower interest rates once an existing inflation has cooled. The experience of the past several years has once again recalled the economic truths espoused by Irving Fisher three quarters of a century ago. Monetary growth per se probably has very little impact on the real rate of interest, but it inevitably has a major effect upon the observed market rate of interest.

SOME FACTS CONCERNING
THE ARGUMENTS

Recently Phillip Cagan and Arthur Gandolfi of Columbia University attempted to measure the liquidity effect upon interest rates of changing monetary growth.[6] For the full period from 1910–65 they found that an increase in monetary growth of one percentage point led to a decline in interest rates for seven months that reached 2.6 basis points. In subsequent months interest rates rose, presumably in response to the income and price effects. For a decline in monetary growth the pattern was simply the reverse. These results appear to conform to other evidence that indicates monetary change has a major impact on income change with a two to three quarter lag.

As previously noted, Irving Fisher gave the first adequate explanation of the relation between interest rates and inflation. He asserted, among other views, that interest rate movements lag behind price changes and that there is a marked correlation between interest rates and a weighted average of past price level changes, reflecting effects that are distributed over time. Fisher and most subsequent researchers found the lagged effect to be very long indeed, ranging from a mean lag of 10 years on short-term rates to much longer for long-term rates.

A recent detailed study by Wm. P. Yohe and Denis S. Karnosky of the St. Louis Federal Reserve Bank found much shorter leads.[7] They concluded: "The present study has found mean lags of less than one year for the effect of price level changes on both long-term and short-term interest rates. In

---

[6] Phillip Cagan and Arthur Gandolfi, "The Lag in Monetary Policy as Implied by the Time Pattern of Monetary Effect on Interest Rates," *The American Economic Review*, May, 1969, p. 277.

[7] Wm. P. Yohe and Denis S. Karnosky, "Interest Rates and Price Level Changes, 1952–69," *Federal Reserve Bank of St. Louis Review*, December, 1969, p. 18.

CHART 25

Yields on Highest Grade Corporate Bonds

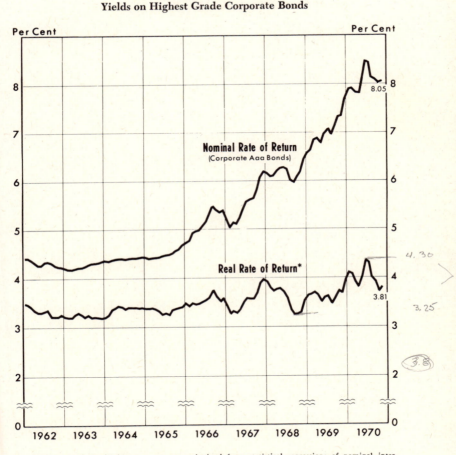

Per Cent

Per Cent

Nominal Rate of Return
(Corporate Aaa Bonds)

8.05

Real Rate of Return*

3.81

4.30

△1%

3.25

3.8

1962 1963 1964 1965 1966 1967 1968 1969 1970

* Estimates of "real" interest rates were obtained from statistical regressions of nominal interest rates on current and lagged price changes and on variables thought to influence "real" interest
rates (i.e., the level of and changes in output and changes in the deflated money stock). See William P. Yohe and Denis S. Karnosky, "Interest Rates and Price Level Changes, 1952–69," *Review*,
Federal Reserve Bank of St. Louis, December 1969.
     Latest data plotted: November estimated.
     Prepared by Federal Reserve Bank of St. Louis.

contrast, earlier studies yielded mean lags of anywhere from seven to thirty years."[8] They explained their different results primarily on the grounds of better statistical procedures for estimating the lag and institutional changes which have resulted in prompter and larger effects of price changes on interest rates in more recent years. They concluded that "most significant is the finding that price level changes, rather than 'real' rates, account for nearly all the variation in nominal interest rates since 1961. Furthermore, the addition of variables to the regression to account explicitly for the 'real' rate components of nominal rates does not appreciably alter these findings."[9]

Chart 25 published regularly by the St. Louis Federal Reserve Bank presents the yields on highest grade corporate bonds on both a nominal or market rate of return as well as on a real rate basis. As can be noted at a glance, the great bulk of the enormous rise in interest rates since 1962 can be explained by the increased rate of inflation expectations. High interest rates are usually associated with serious inflation. And, of course, the relation works in reverse. If inflation is indeed being brought under control as most monetarists contend, interest rates should recede significantly from recent high peaks. In a stable, moderate monetary growth environment, the populist objective of lower interest rates is indeed plausible!

---

[8] *Ibid.*, p. 26.
[9] *Ibid.*, p. 36.

9

Money and
the Stock Market

STOCK PRICES AND MONETARY GROWTH—
LEADING INDICATORS

Both monetary change and stock prices lead business cycle turning points, and both series can, therefore, be classified as leading indicators of economic activity. But since monetary changes have a longer lead over business cycle turning points than stock prices, it follows that monetary change leads stock prices. It was an awareness of these simple leading relationships that was responsible for sparking the investigations reported in *Money and Stock Prices.*[1] Additional evidence bearing on the pervasive influence of monetary change is presented here.

On the average, the monthly Standard & Poor's index of 425 industrial stock prices has turned downward four months prior to past business cycle peaks. However, not even the stock

---

[1] Beryl W. Sprinkel, *Money and Stock Prices* (Homewood, Ill.: Richard D. Irwin, Inc., 1964).

217

market has invariably turned ahead of past business cycle peaks. For example, the monthly average peak of the 1927–29 bull market in stocks was reached in September 1929, whereas the business peak was attained in June 1929. In that exceptional period, stock prices lagged behind the business cycle turning point. In the 1954–57 bull market, stocks hit a double peak as measured by some price indexes—one in July 1956, and another in July 1957. The first occurred 12 months prior to the 1957 business cycle peak, somewhat longer than average, whereas the second peak was coincident with the 1957 business peak. Again in 1959, stock prices registered a double peak. The first occurred in July 1959, ten months prior to the subsequent business cycle peak, and the second was reached in December 1959, five months before the business cycle high. Prior to the 1969–70 recession, stock prices reached their peak many months ahead, in December 1968. But, in general, in the past 40 years stock prices turned down prior to the peak in business activity. During the same period, stock prices hit their trough prior to the trough in business activity, with the exception of 1921 when stock prices lagged the business cycle trough by one month. In the 1960–61 recession, stock prices reached a low in October 1960, four months prior to the business cycle trough. Again, in 1970, stocks began to rise well ahead of a resumed economic expansion.

It should be remembered that infrequently the stock market experiences a cycle all its own, apparently unrelated to the business cycle. In 1939 and 1940, when war broke out in Europe and for awhile went badly for the Allies, the U.S. stock market broke sharply despite strong underlying monetary and economic trends. Again in 1962, the market suffered a sharp break; however, a pause in economic activity followed, not a recession. The break in stock prices was approximately coincident with weakening monetary trends, but favorable liquidity trends restored most of the losses within several months; stock prices eventually rose to new highs before liquidity trends became unfavorable. A sizable stock market break occurred in 1966, approximately coincident with declining monetary growth. The economy again paused in 1967, and stock prices rose subsequent to an easing in monetary policy in late 1966.

Knowledge of the facts concerning the usual lead relation between stock price changes and business cycle changes points up the extreme difficulty of attempting to forecast the first from a forecast of the second. Although stock price data are available currently, business data usually become available one to four months after the facts are generated by the economy. One never knows for certain the current state of the economy, and seldom knows its recent state except in a few major industries such as steel and autos, where weekly data are generally available. Data revisions further complicate the matter. Unless one can confidently project the business trend more than six months beyond the last observed data, assuming that data will not be revised later, it will be impossible to say what will happen to the stock market price trend.

Yet many analysts base their views of future stock prices on short-run business forecasts. It is no wonder that these forecasts seldom detect stock price turning points and usually are correct only when present price trends are continued into the future. Since the most probable price trend, in the absence of overwhelming evidence to the contrary, is one that continues in the same direction, it is possible with such forecasts to be right most of the time. However, the misses will occur at the very time when accuracy is worth a great deal of money, namely, at the turning points of the stock market. It is painfully clear from the above data that short-run economic forecasts are frequently useless in estimating future stock price trends at turning points, even if the economic projections are correct. In fact, short-run economic forecasts are likely to be completely misleading at those points where the direction of stock price movements is the opposite of the business trend.

It is clear that the usual relation between stock and economic trends is for stock prices to turn down when aggregate business activity has hit new highs and is still rising. Stock prices typically continue down until well after the upper turning point of the business cycle has been passed, but turn up before the business cycle trough. Later, when the business cycle turns upward, the stock market is usually well above its lows. In fact, stock prices and economic activity typically move in the same direction a little over two-thirds of the time, but go in opposite directions nearly one-third of the time, and this is the third that is most interesting, most difficult to predict, and yet potentially most profitable.

An alternative to using the prospective business trend to formulate views on the future stock market trend is expressed by the old market maxim, "Sell on good news and buy on bad news." It is clear that cyclical stocks should be sold when basic business news is good and bought when business news is bad. Yet this rule does not tell us at what point during the good news sales should be made nor at what point during bad news stocks should be bought. We must not forget that market and business trends go in the same direction over two-thirds of the time.

Many attempts have been made to develop systems for forecasting the future of stock prices. Few have proved adequate over a long span of time. Many sage investors contend that it cannot be done on a basis consistent enough to make it a worthwhile part of an investment plan. Yet the quest continues.

Unless one is to adopt a defeatist attitude or rely on long "short-run" business forecasts or on hunches, a stock market forecast must be based on something that occurs *prior* to a change in the trend of stock prices. Some have suggested that the composite of leading indicators developed by the NBER should be used. Yet stock prices themselves are among the most reliable leading indicators. Clearly, it makes little sense to attempt to use stock price changes to forecast stock price changes; some critics contend that the Dow theory, which is based on past market action, attempts to achieve just that remarkable feat.

As indicated earlier, changes in the rate of monetary growth have consistently preceded business cycle turning points. Stock prices usually do so. In fact, the average lead of changes in monetary growth prior to the business cycle peak is about 15 or 16 months, compared with a 5- or 6-month average lead of stock prices. Changes in monetary growth lead cyclical upturns by an average period of 8 months, whereas stock price upturns occur about 4 or 5 months prior to business upturns on the average. Therefore, changes in monetary growth lead changes in stock prices by an average of about 9 months prior to a bear market and by about 2 or 3 months prior to bull markets.

However, the data indicate only the *average* lead of changes in monetary growth prior to a change in stock prices. Although averages may be useful statistical summaries for some purposes, they may be very misleading in other cases. Well known is the story of the gentleman who drowned in attempting to wade across a river that averaged only one foot deep. Analysts must also be interested in the variability of the data. Although there are statistical measures of variability readily available, perhaps the most convincing test of the usefulness of the monetary growth-stock price relationship is to apply it.

It should also be carefully noted that there is no apparent inherent theoretical reason why the average lead of monetary change over stock price changes should be about 9 months prior to bear markets and about 2 or 3 months prior to bull markets. In fact there has been a tendency for the monetary lead over bear markets to shorten in recent years. Our present understanding of why monetary change affects equity prices does not provide the answer. Perhaps a greater awareness of the influence of money is partly responsible. Substantial variation in the future lead time would seriously limit the usefulness of the liquidity aid to timing investment changes. Since we do not fully understand why the leads have been of the duration recorded in the past, we cannot be certain they will be repeated in the future. Even though we cannot be sure of future lead times, both theoretical arguments and empirical evidence strongly suggest that monetary changes will provide some useful guidance to future investment timing decisions.

TURNING POINTS IN MONEY AND STOCK PRICES

Chart 26 displays the same monetary growth series as previously cited, along with Standard and Poor's index of 425 industrial stock prices. Peaks and troughs of monetary growth are chosen in hindsight, and the encompassed period of time is shaded. In other words, all periods of declining monetary growth are shaded, and periods of expanding growth in the money supply are unshaded. In all periods of designated declining monetary growth except two in the 1960's, the beginning contraction periods precede a later recession. In the brief but sharp 1962 and 1966 periods of monetary contraction, the economy did not undergo an adjustment large enough to receive a NBER designation as serious as recession, but on each occasion the economy leveled out and paused for two quarters.

Note that all bear markets, except in the late 1930's and early 1940's when war broke out, began in a period of declining monetary growth, and all bull markets began in a period when liquidity was being restored to the economy. In most periods monetary growth declined for a year or a little longer before a bear market developed. But the lead of monetary expansion

CHART 26

Monetary Growth and S&P's Index of 425 Industrials

(annual rate of change)

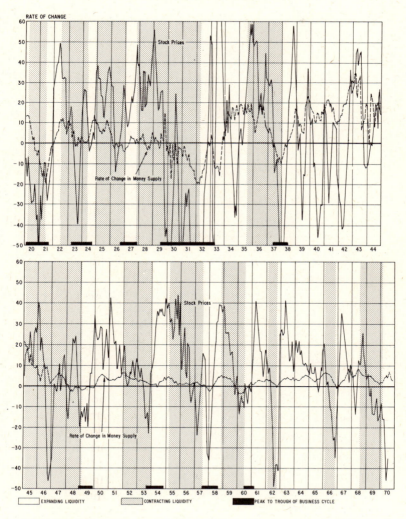

Source: Federal Reserve Board and Standard and Poor's. Data prepared by Harris Trust and Savings Bank.

over a rising stock market was much shorter, generally one to three months. There have been no exceptions to the above statements.

Unfortunately the leads have not been of equal length on either the bear or bull side of the market. Excluding the two sharp breaks in 1962 and 1966, the average lead of declining monetary growth over stock market peaks has been about 11 months, with the average lead of designated expanding money over stock market troughs approximately 2 months (Table 21). In several cases the later decline in stock prices was quite moderate, making it unlikely that investors could have gained by knowledge of contracting liquidity. This was especially true in 1923, 1926, 1946–49, and 1953. However, all serious declines in stock prices were encompassed by periods of contracted liquidity including 1919–21, 1929–32, 1937–38, 1956–57, 1959–60, 1962, 1966, and 1969–70.

Periods to be designated as monetary contraction were chosen from peak rates of monetary growth to trough rates when the swing in monetary growth was sufficient to induce either a pause, recession, or depression. It would, of course, be possible to designate other periods of fluctuating monetary growth which were not closely related to subsequent adjustments in the economy. But in all other cases, the periods of monetary change were brief, like 1939 or 1940, or mild, like numerous other short wiggles in the monetary growth series.

Although we can be reasonably confident that major bull markets cannot develop without expanding monetary growth, and that major bear markets cannot occur without contracting monetary growth, we cannot be nearly so certain about the length of monetary change prior to major market movements. The lead of expanding monetary growth before bull markets has inevitably been short, usually 1 to 3 months; the lead before bear markets has been much more erratic, ranging from zero in 1962 and 1966 to a typical lead of 12 to 15 months. Clearly,

TABLE 21

Turning Points in Money and Stock Prices—1918–70
(lead before downturns)

Monetary Growth Rate Peaks*		Stock Price Peaks		Months Series Lead	
December	1918	October	1919	10	
September	1922	March	1923	5	
November	1924	February	1926	15	
December	1928 (April 1928)	September	1929	9	(17)
July	1936 (June 1935)	March	1937	8	(21)
January	1945	May	1946	16	
December	1951	January	1953	13	
February	1955	July	1956	17	
November	1958	July	1959	8	
January	1962	December	1961	−1	
January	1966 (October 1964)	January	1966	0	(15)
July	1968 (July 1967)	December	1968	5	(17)
			Range	17 to −1	(21 to −1)
			Average	8.8	(12.8)

(lead before upturns)

Monetary Growth Rate Troughs		Stock Price Troughs		Months Series Lead	
June	1921	August	1921	2	
August	1923	October	1923	2	
December	1926	December	1926	0	
March	1932	June	1932	3	
December	1937	May	1938	5	
February	1949 (July 1948)	June	1949	4	(11)
November	1953 (March 1954)	September	1953	−2	(−6)
January	1958	December	1957	−1	
May	1960	October	1960	5	
September	1962	October	1962	1	
November	1966	October	1966	−1	
December	1969 (February 1970)	June	1970	6	(4)
			Range	6 to −2	(11 to −6)
			Average	2.0	(2.1)

* Computed on a 6-month moving average.
Money = Demand deposits and currency.
Source: Federal Reserve; Dow Jones; Harris Trust and Savings Bank.

changing monetary growth is not the only factor influencing stock price changes. Equally obivous is the fact that fluctuating liquidity changes appear to have a major impact on equity prices and should not be ignored in making equity investment decisions that require an explicit or implicit forecast of the future.

A more sensitive measure of the possible impact of changing monetary growth on equity prices can be achieved by plotting the annual rate of change in money against the annual rate of change in stock prices (Chart 27). A six-month moving average was used for each series. The relation is quite clear, even though far from perfect. In general, the leads appear to be much shorter when viewed in this manner, and money continues to lead changes in equity prices most of the time. The changes in stock prices remain quite volatile despite the imposition of a six-month moving average.

In the 1920's, fluctuations in the two series appeared to be closely related most of the time, with monetary growth usually maintaining a short lead. Declining monetary growth presaged the stock market collapse in 1929 and led the upturn in 1932. But the decline in 1934 and early 1935 was not indicated by a decline in monetary growth. The 1937 market break was preceded by reduced monetary growth when the Federal Reserve raised reserve requirements in an attempt to absorb excess reserves. The abortive 1938 recovery was preceded by increased monetary growth, and even during the war years there was a fairly close relation, with money usually in the lead. However, at the end of the war in 1945 and 1946 the equity market was stronger than suggested by the monetary series. The bear market from 1946 to 1949 danced to the tune of money, and stronger markets followed an expanding money supply in 1949. In the decades of the 1950's and the 1960's there was a noticeable positive relation between the two series, even though the relation was not one-to-one.

CHART 27

Liquidity Changes and Stock Prices

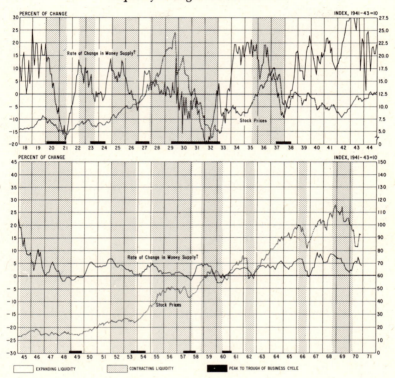

* All commercial banks demand deposits adjusted + currency (seasonally adjusted).
† Annual rate of monthly change, 6-month moving average.
Price index scale different on upper and lower charts.
Source: Standard & Poor's Industrial; National Bureau of Economic Research, Inc.; Federal Reserve Board.

In general, it appears useful to maintain a current series on changing monetary growth and changing stock prices. When rates of change are compared, it is clear that changing monetary growth has a relatively short lead over responding equity prices.

In recent years researchers have published evidence relating changes in monetary growth to fluctuations in stock prices. In addition to *Money and Stock Prices*,[2] A. James Meigs, Vice President of The First National City Bank, one of the leading monetarists, has published two interesting papers on money and stock prices.[3] In a recent article,[4] Michael Palmer presented evidence of the close relation between changes in the money supply and common stock prices in the last decade. Even Federal Reserve officials now argue that their actions have an impact on equity prices. In describing the results of research with a large econometric model at the Board, Governor J. Dewey Daane stated: "The way monetary policy affects consumption is, in considerable part, through its impact on the value of equities. I suppose it will come as a surprise to no one that monetary policy is revealed to have a potent effect on the stock market. And it turns out, according to this research, that fluctuations in equity prices seem to have a measurable *direct* effect on consumption."[5]

Now that the attention of economists and investment analysts is focusing on this relation, research efforts will undoubtedly improve. But we need not wait to use the relation and begin developing an understanding of why it exists.

WHY MONEY AFFECTS STOCK PRICES

The facts are that all cyclically related stock price movements since at least 1918 have been closely associated with monetary change. Even the stock market breaks and subsequent recoveries in 1962–63 and 1966–67 which were associated

---

[2] *Ibid*.

[3] A. James Meigs, "Business Economics," *Sketches From a Fed-Watcher's Notebook*, September, 1969, pp. 33–35; "Monetary Policy and Stock Prices in the 70's—Another Point of View" (Speech at Argus Seminar, Phoenix, Arizona, November 23, 1969).

[4] Michael Palmer, "Money Supply, Portfolio Adjustments and Stock Prices," *Financial Analysts Journal,* July–August 1970, pp. 19–22.

[5] J. Dewey Daane, "New Frontier for the Monetarists" (Remarks before Northern New England School of Banking, Dartmouth College, Hanover, New Hampshire, September 8, 1969).

with mere pauses in economic activity were contemporaneous with sharp changes in monetary growth, even though the usual lead relation on the downside did not exist. Clearly, the 1969–70 bear market was suggested by the tighter monetary policy being pursued. Some, of course, contend that the connection is spurious and that the oft observed relation in the past will not hold for the future. One can never know the future with certainty, but the reasonable consistency of the relation in the past suggests that fundamental rather than ephemeral forces were at work. Furthermore, since 1957 when the author began working with these ideas, the association has persisted. The mere fact that the relation has been so consistent for so long does not demonstrate that it will continue to hold in the future, but it does cast doubt on any assertion that the observed relation is a fabric of hindsight application which bears no implications for future investment decisions. Foresight predictions are, of course, a much more severe test of the predictive power of a theory than hindsight forecasts. By either test, the monetary approach remains reasonably well intact, albeit not completely unscathed.

Some may contend that other factors cause changes in both monetary growth and stock prices, and that changes in the first in no sense "cause" the second to change. This may be true, but it would be more convincing if one could determine what the "other factors" might be. In any event, so long as changes in monetary growth continue to lead stock price changes, one need not be convinced that the relationship is causal. If one contends that business conditions bring about both the decline in monetary growth and in stock prices, it is difficult to explain why both series begin declining when business activity is still rising, and why both series begin rising prior to a subsequent upturn in economic activity. Furthermore, it was demonstrated previously that monetary growth is determined primarily by monetary policy actions taken by the Federal

Reserve Board, rather than by the impact on the banking system of changing business conditions.

If we are to argue that changing monetary growth in some sense causes changes in stock prices, a plausible explanation must be developed. The following hypothesis is suggested.

The initial causal force is conceivably related to the changing liquidity of the economy relative to the liquidity desires of economic units, including businesses and consumers. The demand of the community for money grows as incomes rise and interest rates decline, i.e., asset values grow. As incomes rise, the community desires to hold a larger volume of money to accommodate the larger transaction volume. Also, demand for money increases as interest rates decline, for the cost of maintaining idle cash is less. Transaction demand for money increases over the long-term trend of the economy, and also during the expansion phase of the business cycle. If monetary growth is reduced at that time by Federal Reserve action, it becomes necessary for the community to adjust growing liquidity needs relative to existing liquidity.

Neither individuals nor businesses, separately or in aggregate, can increase the stock of money in the economy, since in our economic system the basic source of liquidity must be the Federal Reserve System. But separate economic units can attempt to improve their own liquidity position. The extent to which one spending unit succeeds in doing so is, however, at the expense of another. How is an adjustment to changing liquidity attempted? First, spending units attempt to conserve on cash balances when liquidity decreases during the expansion phase of the business cycle. There is an additional incentive to do so during periods of rising economic activity, for interest rates typically rise also. Therefore, it becomes more costly in terms of sacrificed income to hold large cash balances. Such adjustments tend to increase the velocity or turnover of money. It has been previously observed that velocity tends to rise during the expansion phase of the business cycle. But as the liquidity squeeze continues relative to liquidity desires, it becomes necessary to make additional adjustments. There is an attempt to shift from less liquid to more liquid assets. This force may be evidenced by fewer purchases of readily marketable assets such as stocks, and by a tendency to shift from stock purchases to bond purchases—a more liquid type of asset. Finally, some convert less liquid assets into cash and near substitutes. There is an increased volume of stocks offered for sale. In order to entice purchasers, the price declines. Eventually, further attempts at liquidity adjustment through the financial markets become more difficult and costly, and total spending is affected adversely. Perhaps the last resort is an attempt to acquire liquidity by spending less relative to income. When a sizable number of spending units resort to this device, total spending declines, corporate profits drop, and the economy enters a recession. But prior to the recession, stock prices and corporate profits decline.

But why the upturn in stock prices at the very time when prospects for employment and earnings are deteriorating? It seems unlikely that investors in the aggregate can properly forecast the subsequent upturn in economic activity when individual professional forecasters have so much difficulty. Again, there may be a basic force operating on investors and the economy bringing this development about, even though not predicted by the investing public.

As incomes and asset values decline, the desire for liquidity on the part of economic units recedes, assuming there is no cumulative crisis of fear or a further liquidity squeeze resulting in a crisis. If at the same time the Federal Reserve encourages growth in the money stock and, consequently, the basic liquidity of the economy, some investors become willing to give up some of their excess liquidity. For an individual unit, this may be done by ceasing to sell readily marketable, less liquid assets, and eventually by buying such assets. There may be a tendency for investors to shift out of liquid assets into less liquid assets. Again, the changing interest rate pattern encourages this shift. Interest rates typically decline in a recession so that the return on fixed-value assets is lower than previously relative to the dividend yield on stocks. During the declining phase of the economy, some investors are willing to hold more cash, since interest rates are lower; therefore, velocity recedes. However, as liquidity increases, stock prices are likely to respond by ceasing to decline and eventually by rising, even though the short-run trend in business activity continues to deteriorate.

Let us trace the sequence of events over the business cycle in somewhat more detail. First, assume the economy is in balance in the sense that the amount of money desired by the community is equal to the existing stock, and that investors are content with their present diversification of assets. Now, let us suppose that an increased rate of monetary growth occurs in response to open market purchases by the Federal Reserve Open Market Committee.[6] If the purchase were from a commercial bank, the bank would have excess reserves in place of government securities, and there would be an incentive to rearrange its portfolio since excessive liquidity would exist. If the purchase were from a nonbank seller, the seller would be likely to hold the cash only temporarily and deposit it in a commercial bank, thereby adding to banking system excess reserves. Therefore, in either case the liquidity of the banking system would be increased, and in the last case the nonbank seller would have a higher ratio of money to total assets than prior to the sale. In neither case would the seller of government securities be in a position of balance, even though he were willing to sell the

---

[6] For an elaborate discussion of this adjustment mechanism see Milton Friedman and Anna J. Schwartz, "Money and Business Cycles," *The Review of Economics and Statistics,* Supplement (Cambridge, Mass.: Harvard University Press, February, 1963).

securities to the Federal Reserve Open Market Committee at the favorable price offered. There would exist an incentive to rearrange investment portfolios by exchanging cash for a less liquid asset. The commercial banking system would, in the process of using its excess reserves, increase total assets and also the stock of money.

It seems reasonable to expect that both the nonbank and bank holders of redundant balances would attempt first to purchase securities comparable to those just sold, i.e., fixed interest securities which entail low risk. But in the process of buying these securities, prices would be bid up, and buyers who had excess cash would search further along the investment spectrum. Banks would then attempt to expand loans, and other investors might add to other higher risk, fixed-coupon obligations, and eventually equities, real property, etc.

As the process of monetary expansion and asset adjustment develops, the primary impacts are diffused throughout the economy in several ways: (1) the scope of assets affected widens; (2) creators or builders of assets find that the price of assets has been increased, and it becomes profitable to step up the rate of production. This rise in asset value encourages business enterprises to increase capital expansion, while demand for homes, an important nonfinancial effect, encourages home building, and demand for consumer durable goods tends to raise production of these items, and so on. Therefore, it is apparent that the initially redundant cash balances concentrated in the hands of those first affected by the open market purchases trigger a series of responses throughout the economy.

It can readily be seen that the monetary stimulus is spread from the financial markets to the markets for currently produced goods and services. As the prices of financial assets are bid up, they become expensive relative to nonfinancial assets, so that there is an incentive for investors to adjust their total portfolios of assets by acquiring nonfinancial assets. At the same time, the prices of existing nonfinancial assets rise, and they become expensive relative to newly constructed nonfinancial assets. The rise in the prices of nonfinancial assets tends to encourage the direct purchase of current assets services rather than the purchase of the assets. This tends to raise the demand for current productive services both for producing new capital goods and for purchasing current services.

The foregoing explanation is quite consistent with many of the observed regularities of the business cycle, including the pattern of security price changes. The rate of growth of the money supply is usually increased by the Federal Reserve System early in a business contraction. Recalling the explanation above, we would expect the initial impact of increased monetary growth to be reflected first in financial markets. The attempt to restore holdings of fixed-coupon securities would result first in a rise in bond prices. Later, as investors adjusted their movements along the investment spectrum, equity prices would rise, and finally, as nonfinancial asset prices were bid up, the flow of payments for goods and services would increase. That is the pattern found in the typical business contraction. The above sequence of events transmitted from a Federal Reserve open market purchase explains why bond prices typically move ahead of stock prices which, in turn, rise before the trough in the business cycle which coincides with the increase in production of goods and services. It is important to recognize that the Federal Reserve and the commercial banking system play a central role in the transmission mechanism that results in the cyclical fluctuations of the stock and bond markets. Monetary contraction would have the opposite effects on the financial markets and production recited above.

The central element in the transmission mechanism is the banking system which initiates balance sheet adjustments throughout the economy as investors attempt to adjust their actual stocks to their desired stocks. In this stock-flow explanation, money is a stock in a portfolio of assets, similar to the stock of financial assets or nonfinancial assets such as houses, buildings, and inventories. It yields a flow of services like other assets. It is subject to change by action of the Federal Reserve System, and in the view expressed above, this change is the central motivating force resulting in business cycle disturbances and the related fluctuations in stock prices.

As previously noted, changes in the rate of growth in the money supply are fairly closely related to changes in the rate of change in stock prices. Similarly, changes in the growth rate of the money supply are associated with changes in the rate of change in corporate profits before taxes, with the money supply usually shortly in the lead (Chart 28). Corporate profits are a function of sales volume and profit margins. Reduced monetary growth affects total spending and sales volume over a period of many months, with the initial impact mild but nearly immediate, and with the effect distributed over a considerable period of time approximating a year. Reduced sales growth emanating from reduced monetary growth results in reduced profit growth almost immediately. As the monetary squeeze continues, income growth continues to decline, until eventually incomes actually decline during the recession period. During the later part of a business expansion, corporate profits actually recede, as do other leading indicators. Since costs continue to rise even after industrial prices weaken, reduced margins add to the declining volume and profits decline sharply. These phenomena are usually compounded by the fact that improvement in productivity weakens, or productivity actually declines during the late phase of a business expansion and in the early period of economic contraction. Increased attention to cost control during the recession period eventually relieves the pressure on profit margins. Usually monetary expansion begins early in the contraction phase of the business cycle. Increased monetary growth begins to reduce the downward pressure on

CHART 28

Money Supply and Corporate Profits
(annual rate of change)

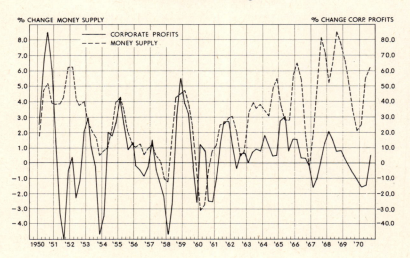

total spending and sales, and eventually leads to an actual increase in sales and output. Improving profit margins reverse the profit trend even before volume improves, and as volume increases, profits expand for both volume and margin reasons.

Not only is monetary change closely related to subsequent changes in corporate profits and stock price changes, but also a monetarist explanation is consistent with the standard theory of stock price determination. It has long been argued that the price of a stock is equal to the discounted value of expected earnings. The major factors thus determining the value of a stock are expected earnings and the interest rate. In a recent article, Michael W. Keran demonstrated that during the past 15 years the major factors determining stock prices were expected corporate earnings and current interest rates, which in turn were influenced by the money supply.[7] He concluded that, "According to this analysis, changes in the nominal money stock have little direct impact on the stock price, but a major indirect influence on stock prices through their effect on inflation and corporate earnings expectations."[8]

In this broader context, changes in the money supply can be viewed as a proxy for the factors that both directly and indirectly influence stock prices. Changes in money directly influence the willingness of asset holders to buy or sell common stocks as they react to changing liquidity pressures. But perhaps, as Keran argued, the indirect effects are even more important. As previously argued, changes in money influence the rate of income creation or business activity. Since corporate profits are a residual, change in the rate of growth in national income exerts a magnified influence on the trend in corporate profits. A mere slowing in the rate of rise in the economy, for example, often causes an absolute decline in corporate profits. Theory tells us that expected corporate profits are a major variable influencing stock prices. Profit expectations are formed by past trends in corporate profits. If profits have been flat for some time, a current downtrend in profits could result in a significant downward revision in corporate profit expectations, since most recent trends heavily influence current views.

If prior monetary growth were highly expansive, inflation could result in high and rising interest rates as market participants came to expect serious inflation in the future. Furthermore, the short-run impact of a tighter monetary policy would raise interest rates. An inflationary environment, responding to a prior expansive monetary policy, followed in turn by a

---

[7] Michael W. Keran, "Expectations, Money, and the Stock Market," *Federal Reserve Bank of St. Louis Review*, January, 1971, p. 16.

[8] *Ibid.*, p. 31.

tighter policy which tended to slow the economy, would exert serious downward pressure on common stock prices due to liquidity, profits, and interest rate influences. Conversely, a period of expanding economic growth in response to stable and moderate monetary growth occurring at a time characterized by waning inflationary pressures would be highly beneficial to equity prices. Expanding money would create liquidity pressures toward common stock acquisition and rising corporate profits would raise profit expectations, whereas reduced inflationary expectations would result in lower interest rates.

One might expect rising inflation expectations to raise both the current interest rate and expected corporate earnings by the same proportion and hence not affect stock prices. But, as Keran pointed out, it is not necessary that inflation expectations just balance each other through the interest rate and corporate earnings effect except in long-run equilibrium when actual and expected inflation are equal.[9] He noted two ways in which the inflation effect upon expected earnings and interest rates may logically differ. First, due to different time horizons, investors in bonds may evaluate inflation expectations differently than the holders of stocks. But perhaps more importantly, even if stock and bond investors have the same inflation expectations, it is possible that inflation expectations may raise interest rates more than expected earnings. If inflation leads to expectations of cost increases in excess of price increases, real earnings expectations are lowered relative to real interest rates. The latter possibility appears especially plausible when it is recognized that sensitive wholesale prices respond much more readily to demand changes than labor rates which make up a sizable proportion of most production costs. Hence, in the early phase of a developing inflation, stock prices may respond favorably as expected earnings rise more than interest rates. But later,

---

[9] *Ibid.*, p. 24.

perhaps after monetary restraint is applied, interest rates continue to rise, it becomes more difficult to raise prices, and costs continue their upward movement. Thus, rising inflation expectations depress stock prices because of rising interest rates along with flat or declining real earnings. Conversely, declining inflation expectations have a favorable impact on stock prices through both lower interest rates and a more favorable cost pattern as costs eventually rise less rapidly, in line with the more stable price trend.

Viewed in this theoretical framework, the massive weakness in common stock prices in 1969 and the first half of 1970, despite only a modest business recession, becomes somewhat more understandable. First, corporate profits after taxes had been on a virtual plateau for four years prior to the weakness which developed in late 1969 and early 1970. Volatile monetary policies from mid 1965 until recently promoted volatile economic performance characterized by stop-go economic growth, making it impossible to maintain stable growth in corporate earnings. Furthermore, growth in the money supply was so expansive as to engender a developing and accelerating inflation which was not reflected in rising corporate profits. Undoubtedly the rapid growth in federal spending during the early years of the Viet Nam conflict also added to the developing inflation. The "new money" financing of the deficit was even more potent.

As inflation became more serious, inflationary expectations were elevated. This phenomenon was reflected in high and rising interest rates. In late 1968, monetary policy began to shift toward less monetary expansion. The short-run impact was to place additional upward pressure on interest rates but by then costs were rising rapidly. Tightening liquidity directly placed selling pressure on common stock prices. But by late 1969 the economy began to slow, and corporate profits after taxes declined. Interest rates were still rising as inflation continued to accelerate. Undoubtedly the Cambodian invasion in April 1970 was an additional adverse development, as it represented a threat that inflation would become even more serious and interest rates would rise further. Stock prices continued to be weak for three or four months after monetary growth began to expand when direct liquidity pressures provided support for equities.

In short, 1969 and the first half of 1970 represented the worst of worlds so far as equity prices were concerned, despite the fact that the business downturn was modest. Earnings turned sharply downward following a flat trend for several years, and interest rates rose sharply, first in response to an accelerating inflation and later in response to a tightening monetary policy. It should be noted in passing that if policies of 1969 and early 1970 succeed in slowing the inflation, while later policies of 1970 and 1971 stimulate real economic growth, interest rates and earnings expectations will be highly favorable for equity prices.

Monetary change is not the only factor affecting corporate profits, interest rates, and stock prices, but it appears to be a major one. Either monetary change causes changes in corporate profits, interest rates, and stock prices, or they are subject to a common cause. Since monetary growth is determined largely by actions of the Federal Reserve System, it is difficult to accept the view that some other force causes changes in these variables.

As asserted previously, there is no way of proving that the above explanation is the correct one. But it is consistent with the observed relation of typical economic and stock price trends over the business cycle. Until a contradiction is discovered and a superior explanation is offered, the above rationale should be provisionally accepted. Although it is comforting to our intellect to be able to explain seemingly contradictory developments, this cannot be a valid test of the theory that changes in monetary growth affect stock prices, both directly and indirectly, in a predictable way. The only acceptable test is one of predictive power: "Show me." Based on forecasting power, the monetary theory of stock price fluctuation appears to fare well, even though not perfectly.

CHAPTER 10

The Role of Money
in Investment Policy

TIMING—ONLY ONE OF SEVERAL
INVESTMENT HAZARDS

Some may say that the monetary approach to timing investment in stocks and bonds cannot be considered as an aid to formulating investment policy but that it is, rather, a speculative tool. If, by speculative, the critic means that from time to time a view is formed as to whether the most likely trend in the market is up or down, then the observation is correct. However, many consider the formulation of a point of view concerning the direction of the market to be applauded more than criticized, for refusal to face this issue is to ignore one of the important potential hazards to successful investing, as we just relearned in 1969–70. Unfortunately, complete disregard of a hazard does not make it disappear. An imperfect solution may be better than no solution at all. The monetary aid to timing stock and bond commitments is based on careful analysis of past data and attempts to analyze current developments in the light of long-lasting relations that have been subjected to

242

extensive tests. It is difficult to believe that a relation that has covered longer than a half-century and persisted through periods of prosperity and depression, war and peace, rapid economic growth and stagnation, highly developed commercial and central banking systems and rudimentary financial systems, will not hold most of the time in coming years. Furthermore, as previously stressed, the results of this study are consistent with the long-lived and thoroughly tested quantity theory of money.

It must be candidly noted that severe stock price fluctuations have been less prevalent in most of the post World War II period; hence, any investment timing technique has been less useful than previously. If we finally reach the millennium when all business cycles are eliminated, perhaps no attention need be devoted to the problem of timing equity investments. Furthermore, if we could be absolutely certain that all future recessions would be mild, the potential gains from successful investment timing actions would probably be minor except on those occasions when financial markets magnified developments in the real economy, as in 1969 and 1970. Since stock prices have moved upward throughout much of the past twenty years, a buy-and-hold policy would have been almost as good as timing purchases and sales of equity securities by changing liquidity trends. But nothing was lost by basing action on liquidity trends, and much could have been gained in the 1969–70 market break by watching monetary growth. In a sense, a proper application of the liquidity timing device may be looked on as partial insurance against cyclical risk. If the economy and stock markets become even less volatile in the future, application of monetarist principles are unlikely to prove costly. On the other hand, if a serious business and stock market decline were to develop in the future for reasons not evident at present, the liquidity approach would probably prove valuable. So long as monetary trends remain favorable, the investor's confidence in the future trend in equity prices should be strengthened. Conversely, a deteriorating liquidity trend should help alert the investor that equity prices may decline. In summary, even in a world of apparent increasing stability, a careful analysis of monetary trends should at least strengthen confidence in investment decisions as well as provide some insurance against being lulled into what might prove to be a false sense of security.

Although many investors say that they make no attempt to forecast stock price trends, their actions frequently belie their words. Any calculated decision, including the decision to do nothing, must be based on some estimate as to what the future holds. Therefore, candid admission of a point of view, which can be subjected to explicit analysis and testing, is more prudent than avowals of "no opinion" when in fact the investor is acting as if a carefully formed opinion existed. In other words, when a viewpoint is explicitly developed, the resulting decision is likely to be more carefully considered than if an implicit seat-of-the-pants view is permitted to affect the investment decision making process. An explicit forecast can be tested; hence, new results can be added to present knowledge.

The manner in which the monetary approach is adapted to a personal or institutional investment policy should vary with the objectives of the investor. Those placing most emphasis on maximum long-run capital appreciation might want to be more bold in applying the principle than those who are interested primarily in steady income and moderate capital gains. It should be recognized that aggressive application of this approach in the past would have avoided most bear markets, and therefore would have contributed to the preservation of principal. However, income would have fluctuated significantly, even though excellent long-term growth in income would have occurred. It is believed that the liquidity theory can be adapted in some degree to all types of investment programs, be they institutional or personal, defensive or aggressive.

The monetary approach has some implications for security selection, but the usual problem of choosing the proper security based on investment objectives remains formidable. One objective of investors using monetary theory for timing stock purchases and sales should be to hold stocks most likely to do best during bull markets. Stocks which do best in bull markets may not be the same stocks which do best over the entire business cycle or best over the longer pull. For example, a cyclically volatile stock with only average long-term growth performance may be converted into a rapidly growing investment medium if the investor holds the stock only during the upward market phase. Therefore, successful application of the liquidity timing theory may tend to increase the relative attraction of "cyclical" stocks, assuming, of course, that business activity and stock prices continue to fluctuate in both directions. This observation appears even more possible when the dividend yield differential is taken into consideration. Perhaps the type of equity most ideally suited for shift over the cycle is growth stocks that are also cyclically sensitive. Diversification requirements will perhaps dictate a balance in the portfolio between aggressive and defensive equities in many investment programs, so that prudence must be exercised in emphasizing cyclically sensitive stocks. Regardless of the makeup of the portfolio, the monetarist theory directs investor attention toward reducing holdings of stocks whose prices are particularly sensitive during periods generally unfavorable to equity prices, and it encourages stock commitments when monetary growth is expanding.

Application of monetarist principles to the bond portion of investment accounts is equally fraught with difficulties. We know that the short-run effect of an easier monetary policy is to reduce interest rates for a few months. Cagan's[1] results indicate

---

[1] Phillip Cagan and Arthur Gandolfi, "The Lag in Monetary Policy as Implied by the Time Pattern of Monetary Effect on Interest Rates," *The American Economic Review* (Evanston, Ill.: American Economic Association, May, 1969).

that liquidity effects have extended over about seven months in the past before the income effect began to work in the opposite direction. Rising incomes in response to an easier monetary policy raise demand for money and tend to raise interest rates. But of even greater importance in recent years has been the Fisher[2] effect of rising prices and price expectations on interest rates. Despite the relatively easy money policy (in fact, because of it) from 1965 to 1969, investors suffered the largest bear bond market in modern times. This suggests that when the money supply grows rapidly at a time of full utilization of resources, investors should be very wary of holding long maturity bonds because they inevitably depreciate in a developing inflationary environment. Conversely, as inflation subsides, usually during a recession or pause in economic activity, long-term bonds represent good investment commitments. Clearly, portfolio managers usually should not shift all bond commitments from short to long maturities based on inflationary or cyclical expectations, but some rearranging of maturities seems prudent.

Even with careful monetary analysis it is not always possible to avoid being caught in an adverse bond market trend. For example, most monetarists argued that the economy was moving into a recession in late 1969, and that inflationary pressures would gradually ebb. If such a pattern were to develop, this expectation suggested an easing trend in interest rates during most of 1970, and tended to justify longer bond maturities. Indeed a recession did develop, and interest rates declined significantly in the first three months of the year. But businessmen clung tenaciously to high profit expectations and sold a large amount of bonds in the first half of 1970. This pressure most likely could have been absorbed in a trend of declining rates, but the announcement of the Cambodian excursion cre-

---

[2] Irving Fisher, *Appreciation and Interest*, American Economic Association (Evanston, Ill.: Northwestern University, 1896), pp. 75–76.

ated widespread fears of further inflation, added uncertainty, and caused a loss of confidence. The frantic scurrying for liquidity resulted in a sharp interest rate rise extending well into June 1970, when most long-term bonds reached another new low. Only after the withdrawal from Cambodia, combined with the growing realization of profits squeeze and reduced inflationary pressures, did bond prices rise sharply, in line with the expectation of analysts who utilized the monetarist approach to interest rate analysis. Clearly, there is no way of avoiding serious losses in investment markets from time to time regardless of the analytical approach taken. It is the contention of this book that maintenance of a continuous and careful analysis of the business scene, based on the monetarist view of how markets function, will increase the prospects of gain while reducing, but not eliminating, the potential for loss.

PITFALLS IN APPLICATION

In addition to unpredictable outside forces like the beginning of a war, which inevitably upset markets, there are other difficulties inherent in applying the monetarist approach. These difficulties can be largely overcome if they are promptly recognized. Since no one expects to anticipate future market behavior perfectly, it should be no surprise that monetarists do not have a monopoly on foresighted ability. However, by understanding monetary factors and applying them carefully, it is contended that results will be much better than chance and frequently better than alternative approaches; at a minimum, supplementing other proved investment strategies with monetarist insights will improve understanding and, if implemented, investment performance.

The foregoing evidence established that there is an observable and, to a large extent, predictable relation between changes in the rate of monetery growth (liquidity) and changes in the prices of stocks and bonds. A rationale based on the modern version of the quantity theory of money appears to "explain" the relationship. Although it is possible to apply this relation to investment policy, there are many difficulties in addition to possible future changes in lead times that should be recognized in order to avoid dangerous pitfalls. It should be noted that peaks and troughs in monetary growth were selected in hindsight and that favorable and unfavorable liquidity periods for stock prices were determined by those selections. Hindsight selection is always easier than foresight decision making. It requires little knowledge and judgment to be an excellent Monday morning quarterback. Nonetheless, it is reasonable to believe that a careful analysis of monetary theory and policy can, within a narrow range of error, select critical liquidity turning points at the times they occur. Since the monetary-stock price relation was developed in 1957, there have been several opportunities to test abilities to select turning points in monetary growth. In each case, it was relatively easy to make the proper identification, even though the decisions were not without accompanying doubts and concerns. Once again, it should be pointed out that a monetarist approach will not detect fluctuations in stock prices which are unrelated to underlying business cycle phenomena.

It is relatively easy to determine bear market signals with high accuracy because of the usual long lead between the change in trend of monetary growth and the subsequent action point—usually 9 to 12 months. This means that the observer usually has at least a year in which to make up his mind as to whether there has or has not been a change in the monetary growth trend, assuming past patterns are repeated. The longer the basic liquidity trend continues downward, the more investment policy should be based on the assumption that the stock market is nearing its peak. Conversely, if a downward trend in monetary growth is interrupted by a protracted upward trend reaching new highs before 9 to 12 months have elapsed, the bear market signal should probably be considered cancelled. This situation has seldom occurred.

The major difficulty in application lies in the determination of the trough in the rate of monetary growth shortly before a bull market action point is designated. This problem is a serious one due to the short lead time between the liquidity trough and the bull market signal—only a few months, if past patterns continue to prevail. Fortunately, data on the stock of money are available with only a ten-day lag. Sometimes it may be necessary to allow more than a two-month rise in monetary growth before reaching an action point. However, somewhat superior results would have occurred in the past if only a one- or two-month lag had been permitted.

As discussed previously, the determination of a reversal in monetary growth toward expansion in March 1970 was relatively easy if careful attention was devoted to analysis of the economy, policy objectives of the Nixon Administration, and policy proclivities of the newly-appointed chairman of the Federal Reserve Board. However, in hindsight the May 1970 stock market trough occurred three months after the reversal in monetary policy—a little longer than usual. Purchases made during those three months would have been at very favorable prices, but each purchase prior to May 26, 1970 would have looked very bad in the meantime. The pervasive fears that shook the marketplace after the beginning of the Cambodia experience undoubtedly placed a great premium on acquisition of liquidity. Hence, to continue buying in that period required faith and conviction in the monetarist position that many investors did not have. It is at a time like that when knowledge of the economy and economic policy can strengthen the nerve and enable an astute investor to move against the crowd. But it isn't easy. There are always special reasons why the money relation will not work "this time," but it usually does!

There were many occasions in the past, as indicated in Chart 6, when monetary growth turned up for a period of two or three months and later declined to new lows. Obviously, the careful analyst must utilize additional information in order to form a confident judgment as to whether a recent reversal in a long-time monetary growth decline will be a lasting one. It is here that knowledge of our monetary system, economic theory, current monetary policy, and current economic conditions is crucial. Good intuition, luck, and conviction also help.

Since the adoption of a flexible monetary policy in 1951, the Federal Reserve has rather consistently pursued a restrictive monetary policy during periods of rising economic activity and an easy policy during periods of declining production and employment. But the above statement is somewhat oversimplified. The Federal Reserve has been understandably reluctant to base monetary policy on projections of economic soothsayers.

During much of the 1960's explicit forecasts tended to play a growing role in the formation of economic policies. By the mid 1960's, following the 1964 tax cut, confidence was very high that fine tuning of economic policies based on explicit economic projections was the wave of the future. But as the remaining portion of the 1960's unfolded it became increasingly clear that either the forecasts were very bad or the theories being used for formulating policies did not yield credible results. Inflation became increasingly serious, and nothing effective was done to control it until 1969.

The new administration also tended to use explicit forecasts in formulating economic policies, but it argued that the policy stance should be more stable and hence less volatile. In addition, it tended to place much more emphasis on the importance of maintaining a stable and moderate growth rate in the money supply. Unfortunately, from its point of view, it was necessary to move policies toward a restrictive stance immediately after entering office because of the serious inflation under way. Hence, in the year 1969, monetary growth declined sharply and was not reversed until late February 1970, when sizable monetary growth was initiated. Thus, monetary policy has been anything but stable up to the present, so that investors utilizing the monetarist approach have had ample opportunity to make profitable investment decisions.

Even with a monetarist bent for placing much more importance on stabilizing monetary aggregates, there have been brief periods when it appeared that concern about interest rates and credit availability was foremost in the minds of recent policy makers. That was indeed the case, but for only brief periods of time. For example, on April 29, 1970 a large $16.6 billion government refunding was announced, with rates established which appeared at the time to be appropriate for the current state of the money market. But, alas, the Cambodian invasion broke two days later and the terms were no longer correct, suggesting that the $16.6 billion government issue would be a real turkey. The Federal Reserve promptly purchased large quantities of the issue; bank reserves surged, and so did the money supply. The alternative was not pleasant to contemplate. Hence, in that critical brief period the Federal Reserve promptly came to the aid of the Treasury and avoided a near financial crisis, even though it meant relaxing the objective of stabilizing monetary aggregates. But that is not the end of the story. After the near crisis had passed, the Federal Reserve promptly took money out of the economy until the growth rate dropped back to a more suitable range.

Again in June 1970, disclosure of bankruptcy proceedings by the Penn Central Railroad resulted in widespread fear of another type of liquidity crisis which could have had unfortunate implications for many corporations and the economy as a whole. The Federal Reserve moved promptly to allay those fears and to reduce the real threat to the economy. It had become increasingly evident before the Penn Central experience that the Federal Reserve was unhappy with the results of Regulation Q, which in fact prevented banks from buying domestic deposits in quantity. With relatively low interest rate ceilings imposed on commercial banks, astute corporate and individual investors were increasingly eschewing the banking system and investing in Treasury bills and commercial paper, where the returns were much higher. Disintermediation had become the byword of the day, and the banks were strapped for funds while the commercial paper market blossomed in size, if not quality. The Penn Central debacle immediately created quality fears in the minds of short-term investors, and there was a real threat that corporations would not be able to roll over their commercial paper when due. Since the total volume was then about $38 billion, the makings of a real financial crisis became evident. But again, alert action by the Federal Reserve averted disaster. They promptly suspended the ceiling on short-term bank CD's, making it possible for investors to place money in the banking system at the same time that they were scrambling out of the commercial paper market. In addition, the word was quietly passed to banks that the Federal Reserve discount window was readily available in the event banks needed reserves for extending loans to corporations which had been rudely closed out of the commercial paper market. Banks were able to provide the credit, and the adjustment was made without undue strain. Nonetheless, this experience once more confirmed the principle that interest rate controls seriously distort money flows and create the potential for serious credit difficulties. The Federal Reserve again demonstrated that its newly found interest in and dedication to stabilization of monetary aggregates did not prevent it from remaining mindful of its obligation to be concerned about credit markets and interest rates, even if the money supply ran out of control for a short period of time.

Some have concluded that recurring crises will make it impossible to achieve the major objective of stabilization of monetary growth at a moderate pace. This eventuality appears highly unlikely. Despite all the unusual disturbances in the first half of 1970, the annual rate of expansion of the money supply was 6 percent—just above the stated objective of Chairman Burns in his testimony before the Joint Economic Committee on February 18, 1970. Nonetheless, recent experience with monetary policy demonstrates that the art of central banking continues to develop, and alert analysts will recognize that monetary experience of the past may not be a perfect guide to the future.

In the prior postwar period, gold flows, balance of payments deficits, and fear of inflation or, alternatively, recession, have been powerful influences affecting the formulation of Federal Reserve policy. Guidelines, such as free reserves and short-term interest rates, sometimes provided clues as to what the Fed was attempting to do. But now the ball game appears to have changed significantly. The objective of stable growth in monetary aggregates has not yet been achieved because of the existence of first inflation and then recession in the early phase of the reorientation of policy. But what is likely to happen once inflation cools and stable economic growth resumes?

Based on present predilections rather than prior postwar experience, it appears very probable that much greater stability in monetary aggregates will be achieved. Monetarists argue that such a development would be desirable from the standpoint of encouraging stable economic growth in an environment of reasonably stable prices. But what will it do to investors who place reliance on monetary change as an important factor in formulating investment policies? We may be out of business and forced to search for new approaches. But let us not yet assume the millennium has arrived. Volatile monetary performance has been the hallmark of Federal Reserve action ever since its organization in 1914. It is difficult to believe that a complete break with the past will be achieved overnight, even though it might be desirable. In the meantime, recognition of monetarist principles should provide insurance against being trapped by volatile financial markets.

It should be pointed out that even with volatile monetary growth there are always arguments around the financial community as to why money does not matter "this time." Two recent examples should emphasize how insidious that can be, and how a careful monetary analyst must always keep his wits about him in order to avoid running with the crowd. The argument against selling stocks in 1969 ran something like this. The administration espoused only a "gradualist" policy in bringing the inflation under control. Some interpreted policy intent to mean that the correction could be achieved without significant economic pain. The "see through" theory argued that investors would look past the possible slight dip in profits to the glorious potentials of the 1970's. Therefore, there would be no correction in financial markets worth taking into account. Admittedly the argument was appealing, for it implied that inflation could be brought under control without the usual pains of a recession. But a careful continuing analysis of monetary policy in 1969 strongly suggested that policies would not work out that way. Beginning in the third quarter of 1968, monetary growth turned down again, and between the spring of 1969 and February 1970 little growth occurred. There was ample evidence that the economy was weakening. As early as the beginning of 1969 the leading indicators began to weaken, confirming the earlier monetary evidence. Yet businessmen insisted that profit expectations were firm and capital spending surveys suggested more spending ahead. What should a prudent investor have done? It all depended on how much he believed in money in contrast to the siren call of the expansionists. Certainly ample monetary evidence suggested a prudent paring in stock commitments no later than early 1969. By May 26, 1970, 36 percent from the high in the Dow Jones average, it was all too clear that monetary pressures had again called the tune.

In the spring of 1970 it was clear that a recession was under way, that capital spending was being reduced, and that optimism was conspicuous by its absence. Yet the money supply had begun to expand late in February. There was even talk of a cumulative decline in economic activity because of developing liquidity problems. Indeed the stock market continued to decline three months after the monetary expansion began. The lag was in the normal band of past history, but rather than investors promptly adjusting to easier money, as many had argued they would, their lag was a little on the long side of the average. By then, technical market factors had become very weak, and many observers were calling for 500 on the Dow—what was to be done? Again it depended considerably on how much confidence the investor had that an expanding money supply would restore liquidity and again induce typical market responses. Although monetarists had been considered overly bearish on the market and the economy in 1969 and early 1970, they were considered among the most optimistic by late spring and early summer, for they argued that a resumption in economic growth would occur in late 1970 and the market would start moving upward several months in advance of the recession bottom.

As indicated by the above discussion, reaching judgments on timing decisions in the marketplace is ever challenging and requires dedication to principles if decisions are to be reasonably good. Perfection is not sought, nor can it be obtained. In the final analysis, a decision to take a more aggressive stance concerning common stock purchases must be primarily a feeling for conditions backed up by knowledge concerning current policy intent and actions plus a great deal of faith that the basic experience of history will be repeated. In other words, both intuition and scientific analysis must enter into an investment judgment. An attempt must be made to think independently by trying to consider every relevant fact while avoiding being swept along by the crowd.

Even then, the decision can be only a tentative one, particularly in the early weeks of an aggressive investment policy. This may mean that the prudent solution would be to distribute new stock purchases over the two to four month period following what appears to be a new expansive trend in monetary growth. Such an action policy would not usually be a serious handicap, since stock prices frequently, but not always, form a fairly wide bottom before resuming a marked upward trend. Since investors always operate in a world of uncertainty, a hedge against the wrong decision is advisable. However, as the degree of uncertainty about an expansive monetary trend subsides, the investor should be more willing to make additional equity investments. On the other hand, if an apparent renewed monetary expansion becomes abortive, additional equity investments should cease. The same reasoning may be applied to reduction of equity holdings following a prolonged contraction in monetary growth. In other words, even if the investor is convinced that changing monetary trends exercise a pervasive influence on stock price trends, plenty of room remains for the exercise of judgment with respect to the speed of executing investment changes. The distribution of stock purchases or sales over time can be related to the investor's view as to the degree of uncertainty concerning continuation of the present monetary growth trend.

A careful and informed analysis of current economic and monetary policy trends is, nevertheless, likely to give an indication clear enough to enable an investor to profit from the changing monetary trend. It should be emphasized, if it is not already apparent, that the monetary growth, stock price, bond price relation under discussion is not a strict mechanistic approach, but calls for careful analysis of economic and monetary trends by an informed analyst. Suffice it to say that the necessary knowledge and judgment is not readily attained, but then most worthwhile accomplishments are difficult. If it were otherwise, we would all be happy, successful, and lazy!

Since the lead of a rising money supply over a reversal in a bear market and the beginning of a bull market is always fairly short, sometimes it is useful to be aware of other conditions that usually exist before a bull market begins. Remember, bear markets usually begin while the economy is in a boom prior to the beginning of either an economic pause or recession. Reduced liquidity brought on by monetary restraint causes investors to attempt to restore liquidity by selling assets, and both bond and stock prices decline, with the impact felt first in the bond market.

Although a bear stock market begins during the expansion phase of the business cycle, it inevitably ends in the contraction phase. In other words, stock prices not only lead at the upper turning point of a business cycle, but also they lead at the lower turning point. Therefore, not only must monetary growth become more expansionary before a bull market can get under way, but also the economy must be in a pause or recession before stocks are likely to reverse a bear market. Certainly stock prices usually continue downward for some time after the cycle weakens, profits sag, and unemployment starts to rise. It is at that time that many investors become concerned about their equity holdings and are tempted to sell at or near the lower turning point of a bear market. It is argued here that recognition of the fact that the economy has slowed is a good reason for becoming interested in acquiring equities, especially if monetary growth has begun to expand. In the post World War II period stock prices reached their trough five months, on the average, after the economy began the first four post World War II recessions (see Table 22). At the time of this writing, it appears that the economy peaked out in October or November 1969, and stocks reached their trough seven or eight months later in June 1970, on a monthly average basis.

In addition, it is worthwhile to note that bull markets in stocks do not occur before bull markets in bonds. There are good reasons why this should be true. During a recession the

TABLE 22
Business Peaks and Stock Market Troughs

Business Cycle Peak		Stock Market Trough		Time Lapse
November	1948	June	1949	7 months
July	1953	September	1953	2 months
July	1957	December	1957	5 months
May	1960	October	1960	5 months
October	1969*	June	1970	8 months
			Average:	5.4 months

* Estimate.
Source: Standard & Poor's, Department of Commerce.

first reaction by investors encouraged to make investments is to acquire the least risky type of asset. In the first instance this may be Treasury bills, but the impact is likely to spread through the entire bond spectrum. A declining business cycle usually entails some reduction in the demand for credit as consumers and businessmen cut their spending plans. Unless investors are quite convinced that serious inflation will continue to affect bond prices, these pressures bring somewhat lower interest rates and higher bond prices. If bond prices rise, the impact of lower rates either promptly or shortly is translated into a rising equity market. In other words, in attempting to detect whether a bear market is about to be reversed, it is useful to ask "Have bond prices begun to rise?" For the post World War II period, the average lead of a bull market trend in bonds over stocks has averaged about 4.7 months, or a range from zero months to nine months (see Table 23).

You will note that the average lead of an increase in money over a rising trend in stock prices is usually shorter than the lead of bond price increases over the trough in stock prices. This certainly need not be the case. Recognition of the development of a recession, easier money, and rising bond prices should help to strengthen the confidence and nerve of investors after participating in a bear market. In the judgment of the writer, an expanding money supply is by far most important. But

TABLE 23

Bull Market Relation—Bonds and Stocks

Bond Market Trough		Stock Market Trough		Time Lapse
October	1948	June	1949	8 months
June	1953	September	1953	3 months
September	1957	December	1957	3 months
January	1960	October	1960	9 months
September	1961	June	1962	9 months
September	1966	October	1966	1 month
June	1970	June	1970	0 months
			Average:	4.7 months

Source: Standard & Poor's.

if the economy is already in a pause or recession and interest rates are declining, the case for buying stocks is even stronger, based on both theoretical reasoning and the evidence of the past.

TAX FACTORS

Just as there are always good reasons, real or imagined, why an investor should not buy stocks at or near the low of a bear market, there are also many reasons why stocks are not sold when liquidity becomes unfavorable. For one thing, the economy is inevitably strong at bull market peaks and expectations by consumers, businessmen, and unfortunately many economists, are bullish. Economists or analysts who rely on the recent and prospective spending trend for capital spending are especially prone to maintain an optimistic view of the future for too long. As late as March 7, 1970, *Business Week* published the results of a survey of businessmen concerning their profit expectations. The results showed businessmen in manufacturing industries expected their profits to be up 6 percent in 1970, despite the fact that profits had been declining since the second quarter of 1969. Also, capital spending surveys in early 1970 showed an expected rise of about 11 percent. The new economists who rely on capital spending surveys as a major input in

their Keynesian framework were inclined to have a very bullish view of the economy, as were most businessmen. But
capital spending lags the economy, and plans for capital spending lag even more. Therefore, reliance on those tools will
always mislead the investor at the turning point and, of course,
peak stock prices will be long gone after the economy moves
into recession.

In addition to the generally bullish view of the economy
at upper turning points of bull markets, sloppy thinking about
taxes often contributes to lethargy and incorrect investment
decisions. How many times have you heard investors say "I
can't sell this stock because my capital gains tax would be too
large!" Apparently they would prefer to hold the stock during
a bear market so the tax liability would be less, but so would
the gain! For each $1 depreciation in a bear market, the in-
vestor suffers to a greater extent than the tax collector.

Although there can be no doubt that investors consider the
capital gains tax a major factor affecting investment decisions, there is legitimate doubt as to the correctness of this
widely held view.[3] In the minds of most investors, the existence
of a capital gains tax represents a major deterrent to taking
profits and either switching to another investment medium or
holding liquid funds until better investment buys are available.
Since the investment approach developed in this book involves
the taking of gains and reinvestment of funds in equities at a
later and, hopefully, more favorable market level, the effect of
the capital gains tax must be carefully considered. If the detri-
mental effects of the capital gains tax are as serious as generally
believed, much of the advantage of proper timing of stock
commitments would be dissipated. It should not be surprising
to find that this analysis concludes otherwise.

The capital gains tax has an effect on each of the two follow-

---

[3] For a detailed discussion of this matter see Beryl W. Sprinkel and B. Kenneth
West, "Effects of Capital Gains Taxes on Investment Decisions," *Journal of Business*
(Chicago, Ill.: University of Chicago Press, April, 1962).

ing investment choices: (1) the sale of currently held securities with the intention of repurchasing the same securities at a lower price, i.e., nonswitch decisions; (2) the sale of currently held securities with the intention of purchasing alternative investments which are expected to have a superior price and income performance over a given interval of time, i.e., switch decisions. Discussion will be limited to the nonswitch decision, but the principles are readily adaptable to the switch alternative.

Nonswitch decisions deal with the possibility of taking advantage of expected short-term fluctuations in the prices of securities presently held. Such situations arise during the course of a business cycle, but many investors pass up the opportunity to capitalize on an anticipated temporary market decline not only because of uncertainty that the price decline will actually materialize, but also because capital gains liabilities act as a deterrent to such action.

If a market decline is anticipated, there are two possibilities to be investigated. These depend on expectations as to the market action of the security subsequent to the decline.

1. If the security is expected to remain substantially depressed in price and exhibit poor investment performance relative to other investment alternatives after the decline, clearly sale of the issue at the current level would maximize profits.

2. The more interesting (and potentially more profitable) possibility to be examined is the situation in which a market decline is expected to be followed by a relatively attractive rise in the price of the security, either surpassing or falling short of the current level. In such circumstances, there seem to be misconceptions among investors as to how the sell or hold alternative should be measured in the face of an expected market decline.

It should be emphasized that for the investor to maximize his profits, judgments about the future price performance of his holdings must be made on a continuing basis. In the absence of these rather definite expectations, it is not possible to formalize what the impact of capital gains taxes on his decisions should be.

The typical case can best be demonstrated by an example. Suppose an investor held a security with a market value of $100. Suppose, also, that the original cost of this issue was $50, and that the investor's capital gains tax rate was 25 percent. Finally, assume that the holder expects the price of this security to fall temporarily to $95, to be followed by an eventual rise to $150, at which point he would sell. Should he hold, or should he sell and buy back at $95? Let us label these alternatives Case A and Case B, respectively.

Case A: Hold to $150 and sell.

Gross gain	$100	($150 — $50)
Capital gains tax	25	
Net gain	$ 75	

Case B: Sell at $100, pay taxes on gain, buy back at $95, and sell again at $150.

First transaction:

Sale proceeds	$100.00	
Less capital gains tax	12.50	($50 × 0.25)
Reinvestable funds	$ 87.50	
Net gain	37.50	($50 — $12.50)

Second transaction: Invest $87.50 at price of $95.

$$\text{Percentage gain} - \frac{150 - 95}{95} = 57.9\%$$

Gross gain — $87.50 × 57.9%	$50.66
Capital gains tax — $50.66 × 0.25	12.67
Net gain on second transaction	$37.99

Total profits = $37.99 + $37.50 = $75.49

In the example above, the investor would obtain slightly greater net benefits by following the procedure in Case B. It should be noted that a market decline of only 40 percent of the tax liability and 10 percent of the total gain yielded these results. This result will be surprising to those who believe the market value of a particular holding must decline by at least as much as the tax liability before sale and repurchase at the lower level becomes profitable.[4]

A thorough analysis of the impact of the capital gains tax involves consideration of several complicating factors: (1) In certain situations, the marginal capital gains tax rate can

---

[4] Although the algebra is a little tedious, it is possible to generalize this problem and find the break even point. That is, given the cost, the investor's tax rate, and his assumptions as to future market performance, it is possible to formalize the procedure for determining whether to sell and buy back at a lower level or to hold to the second sell point. This can be accomplished by equating the profits if held with the profits which would result if a sale were made and the security were repurchased at the lower level.

For the purposes of this analysis, let C = original cost; M = current market; M_2 = level to which market price is expected to fall in interim; M_3 = expected market at second sell point; R = reinvestable funds after payment of capital gains taxes.

It can be demonstrated that for a sale and repurchase to be profitable, the ratio of the current market value to reinvestable funds must be smaller than the ratio of the expected percentage rise from M_2 to M_3 divided by the percentage increase expected from M to M_3, i.e., $M/R\%$ rise from M_2 to $M_3/\%$ rise from M to M_3. The following table gives the proper decision under two assumptions as to the expected interim market decline in the example used previously.

TABLE 24

Decision Indicator

Expected Repurchase Point	Ratio, Current Market to Reinvestable Funds	Ratio, % Rise from M_2 to M_3/% Rise from M to M_3	Indicated Decision
$97.00	1.143	1.093	Hold
94.00	1.143	1.191	Sell & repurchase

The derivable break even point under the above assumptions is $95.48. From these relationships, several generalizations can be established: (1) The higher M_3, the lower must M_2 be for the investor to break even. (2) The higher the capital gains tax rate, the lower must M_2 be for the investor to break even. (3) The higher the current market, the higher M_2 may be for the investor to break even.

be as high as 35 percent by 1972 under the 1969 Tax Reform Act, but in most cases is less than 25 percent. (2) If stocks are sold before being held six months, the gain must be reported as income subject to full income tax rates. (3) If an investor chooses to sell and later repurchase a stock, his income stream will differ from that which would have been experienced if the security were to be held straight through the price dip. (4) Because of the altered timing of the flows introduced by the income stream consideration, precise measurement of the alternatives necessitates a discounting of the income streams (including capital gains) to arrive at an accurate present value of the anticipated income flow alternatives. (5) Brokerage costs also must be taken into account if a sale and repurchase is contemplated. These complications modify but do not negate the basic conclusions.

SUMMARY REMARKS ON TAXES

Capital gains taxes clearly reduce the investor's flexibility in taking advantage of security price fluctuations and in switching to alternative investments. However, investors frequently overestimate the extent of the "lock in" effect. A stock need not decline by a percentage equal to the capital gains tax rate after sale before the investor is even, as is often naively stated. More important, a stock need not decline by the full amount of the existing capital gains tax liability for a sale and repurchase to be profitable. As demonstrated in the example, a sale and repurchase in anticipation of a decline in price of less than one-half of the tax liability may be profitable. It was argued that a sale and repurchase would prove profitable if the ratio of the current market value to reinvestable funds is smaller than the ratio of the percentage rise from the repurchase point (to the ultimate sale point) divided by the percentage increase from the current price (to the ultimate sale point).

The investor frequently forgets that a contingent tax liability exists whether or not a capital gain is actually realized. The tax must eventually be paid unless the security is held until death and the estate benefits from a lower tax rate, or unless the security is given away and the estate benefits from gift taxes.[5] By not realizing a gain, an investor in effect enjoys any income or further capital gain which may accrue to that portion of his assets which represent a contingent capital gains tax. However, a sale and repurchase is profitable so long as the percentage rise from the buy-back price to the final sale price is sufficiently large to offset the reduced capital available for investment after payment of taxes. Although the payment of capital gains taxes will significantly reduce investment results, the existence of the tax will not seriously affect the correctness of a particular investment decision.

All these alternatives can be affected by various complicating factors, including income differentials, brokerage charges, and shifting marginal tax rates. However, these factors can be taken into account. Notwithstanding the existence of these considerations, the basic premise still stands. The impact of capital gains taxes on investment decisions has been over-emphasized by many investors. It is also clear that the existence of capital gains taxes will not seriously dissipate the advantage of basing investment decisions upon changes in liquidity as measured by changes in the rate of monetary growth.

---

[5] Since profit sharing and pension trusts need not pay capital gain taxes, tax factors do not interfere with investment decisions. This fact means, in effect, that the manager of one of these accounts should ask himself each morning if the portfolio he holds promises the optimum return within the risk constraints imposed by the account. If not, the portfolio should be changed until it does represent the optimum allocation of investment funds.

11

Monetary Policy
and the 1970's

Short-range forecasting is hazardous and frustrating and is seldom achieved with a high degree of precision. The forward projection of past trends is relatively easy, and in fact may give satisfactory results most of the time. However, for most private and governmental decisions, we are interested in the turning points of the business cycle, and extrapolation of the past inevitably leads to serious misses at the very points in time where being correct is of maximum importance. It has been argued that utilization of the monetarist theory espoused in this book, accompanied by careful integration of the leading, co-incident, and lagging indicators of economic activity, will significantly reduce the error at turning points.

But if business cycle forecasting is difficult, longer-range prediction is even more complicated. It is relatively easy to estimate *potential* for real economic growth in the years ahead, since most of the ingredients are subject to only very slow change. Various economists have tried their hands at this game and the results are, not too surprisingly, rather similar. In

January 1970, the Council of Economic Advisers, under Chairman Paul W. McCracken, published its views as to the prospects for potential real growth in the years ahead, and few analysts would quarrel with its results.[1] It estimated that potential growth will rise by about 4.3 percent per year in real terms. In other words, potential real production and, hence, incomes should continue to increase at the pace of recent years, well above the approximate 3 percent for the past half century. This result is derived from a projected growth in the labor force of 1¾ percent per year, a decline in annual average hours of work per person of 1 percent per year, and an increase of output per man hour in the total economy of 2.8 percent per year. In 1969 dollars, potential real output under these conditions should increase to $1.2 trillion by 1975, 29 percent above 1969. Since no real growth occurred in 1970, utilization of potential resources declined, thereby creating the possibility of even greater real growth in the years immediately ahead.

But will this potential be realized? And what about inflation, interest rates, equity prices, and the frequency of business recessions when actual output will be well below potential? Estimating these variables in which most investors, concerned individuals, and government officials are most interested is difficult indeed. As argued previously, the outcome for these factors depends on total demand for goods and services that is evident in the marketplace which, in turn, is determined, according to monetarist views, by the trend in monetary growth. If we are to have highly volatile growth in the money supply similar to recent years, volatile economic performance will certainly follow, just as it has since 1965. Economic pauses and recessions will be interspersed with growing inflationary pressures, high and rising interest rates most of the time, and

---

[1] *Economic Report of the President, February 1970* (Washington, D.C.: U.S. Government Printing Office), pp. 78–84.

poor stock market performance. Is there any reason for believing that our economic future may be more fulfilling than we have been able to realize of late? Or must our performance remain well below our aspirations as well as our potential?

One can be quite confident in asserting that regardless of which political party rules in Washington, a protracted economic collapse with attendant economic and human costs will not be permitted. We now know enough to avoid another economic holocaust like the decade of the 1930's and, more importantly, political pressures will make sure that this knowledge is utilized in the formulation of policies pursued. This does not mean that occasional recessions are a thing of the past. From time to time, like the recent past, policy mistakes will result in a serious recession when actual production and employment will run well below capacity and financial markets will be characterized by great turbulence.

But what if the monetarists are right? What implications flow from the arguments that monetary growth is the critical policy variable for influencing total demands for goods and services? What if, for the first time in the history of this republic, monetary policy makers choose as their main objective stabilization of the growth rate of monetary aggregates like the money supply at a moderate pace? Will this make any significant difference? Obviously, if you believe the preceding arguments, you must conclude that it will indeed!

What difference? Monetarists contend that the growing inflation of recent years was due largely to an excessive growth in the money supply. Without rapid growth in money, serious inflation would not have occurred. They also attribute the trend toward high and rising interest rates to the growing inflation brought about by excessive monetary growth. Furthermore they claim that volatility in monetary growth similar to the period since mid 1965 was a major contributor to economic instability characterized by recurring stop-go economic performance with adverse implications for corporate earnings growth. But what if monetary growth in coming years is relatively stable and continues to increase at a moderate pace of 3–5 percent?

Is there any reason to believe that this is a realistic possibility? The answer is clearly yes. As previously noted, there has been a profound swing in professional and governmental thinking toward monetarist thinking and away from Keynesian prescriptions. There is nothing more important than an idea whose time has arrived. It would appear that monetarist theories and prescriptions are topical, relevant, valuable, and increasingly popular. These views are achieving dominance, not because of the overwhelming persuasiveness of the research results, and not even because of the articulate presentation of the monetarists, but rather because of the poor performance of the economy when it was managed according to new economics doctrine. The failure of the 1968 tax increase to slow the economy was an especially influential event which led many observers to change their minds about the relative impact of monetary and fiscal policies on demands for goods and services.

Policy makers have also joined the march toward monetarism. The Joint Economic Committee has for several years asked that monetary growth remain in the 2 percent to 6 percent range of rise.[2] At the insistence of the Joint Economic Committee, the Federal Reserve must report each quarter for the purposes of explaining its policies and objectives, and the Committee has been particularly insistent on explanations when the growth pattern fluctuated outside the 2 percent to 6 percent range.

The Council of Economic Advisers is also leaning toward the monetarist camp. Before appointment as chairman, Pro-

---

[2] *Report of the Joint Economic Committee on the January 1967 Economic Report of the President* (Washington, D.C.: U.S. Government Printing Office), p. 14.

fessor Paul W. McCracken indicated that although he was not a Friedmanite, he was much more Friedmanesque than previously.[3] Analysis of the economy by the Council has leaned consistently toward the monetarist view, and prescriptions for cushioning the 1970 recession called for greater monetary growth while cautioning that excessive monetary expansion similar to late 1966 and 1967 would renew inflation.

Nor is the Federal Reserve System impervious to monetarist views, even though it was one of the last remaining holdouts. Throughout the history of the Federal Reserve System, officials displayed great interest in credit conditions and interest rates, and only lately have become interested in monetary aggregates like the money supply. For many years the St. Louis Federal Reserve Bank has guided its research and policy prescriptions by the theoretical framework of the quantity theory of money. But until recently it was known as the renegade of the System. At present the Federal Reserve Board appears to have moved considerably toward the monetarist view of the economy, and more importantly, policy objectives are now formulated to a considerable extent in terms of monetary aggregates instead of interest rates and credit conditions. As indicated previously, this move toward the aggregates has not eliminated devotion and attention to the obligation of the Federal Reserve System to perform its critical role of lender of last resort, but it has shifted its emphasis toward the aggregates. Now that the inflation is being brought under control and a deep recession has been avoided, the Federal Reserve Board appears to be attempting to achieve a moderate and stable expansion in the money supply. Surely it is receiving encouragement in attempting to achieve this objective from the President, who leans toward the monetarist view, by the Council of Economic Advisers, by the influential Joint Economic Committee of

---

[3] "A Centrist for CEA," *Business Week,* December 7, 1968, p. 35.

Congress, and by a growing number of private economists who subscribe to monetarist doctrine.

Let us suppose that the Board sticks to its guns and indeed does achieve stable and moderate monetary growth. This assumption of course implies that outside forces such as renewed wars and/or federal deficits do not seriously interfere with the achievement of that objective. Monetarists do not contend that money is the only factor that matters, but that it has very significant implications for economic stability, inflation, interest rates, and financial markets.

First, stable monetary growth would imply reasonably stable growth in final demands as well as stable growth in corporate profits. Stop-go patterns of economic performance would be much less likely to occur. There has been no pause, recession, or depression that was not preceded by monetary restraint. Monetarists contend that this observed relation is causal, with money being the motivating force. If we could be certain that moderate monetary growth would continue indefinitely, it would be tempting to argue that recessions would be an experience only of the past, not the future. But it is certainly possible that nonmonetary factors could bring on a moderate decline in economic activity, even though no such development has been observed in modern times. Nonetheless, economic growth and performance would be much more stable than the average in the postwar years, even though some variability would undoubtedly remain. Expectations of consumers and businessmen would become more stable once they built confidence in the persistence of a predictable and stable monetary policy.

If the potential for real economic growth of about $4\frac{1}{3}$ percent per year continues, along with moderate and stable expansion in the money supply, there will be little room for inflation. As reflected in the long-term data for the United States and also for many foreign countries, serious inflation develops only when the money supply per unit of output rises significantly, not when it is stable. Much of the nonwar history of the United States has been characterized by relatively stable money per unit of output, and we have thus enjoyed reasonably stable prices. Only in recent years when monetary policy became highly expansive under the influence of the new economics doctrine did inflation become a serious problem. Therefore we can conclude that less inflation appears probable if moderate monetary growth is sought and achieved.

However, if the rate of inflation recedes and expectations adjust accordingly, market interest rates should drop back toward the real rate of interest. The inflation premium in interest rates would be much less than in recent years, and one of the goals of modern liberals and populists would be achieved. Lenders would no longer insist on a sizable hedge against inflation, and borrowers would not be willing to pay premium rates in the expectation that the value of money would recede significantly in future years.

What can we say about the equity market in such an environment of relatively stable economic growth, more stable growth in corporate profits, reduced inflation, and lower interest rates? First, let us recognize that there has been no major stock market break in modern times that was not preceded or accompanied by a sharp reduction in monetary growth. Stable growth in the money supply would indeed eliminate one of the major market hazards. Investors could then concentrate their attention on choosing the stocks that promise to provide the most satisfactory return within the constraints provided by investment objectives.

But if inflation recedes, what will this do for equity prices? Isn't it well known that equities provide a good hedge against inflation and hence do well in that sort of environment? The inflation hedge theory is well known, but largely fallacious. Certain types of stocks indeed do well during inflation, especially those of companies that finance heavily by debt and hold real assets on the left hand side of the balance sheet. In other words, this is a special case of debtors gaining from inflation if they have their assets invested in real rather than financial assets. But, in general, stocks do not thrive in an inflationary environment. Note the past 25-year period. Serious inflation characterized the 1945–48 period, and stocks declined. They showed modest gain during the brief inflationary spurt accompanying the Korean War, but the sizable postwar bull market made little progress until price stability was restored in the 1950's. From 1951 to mid 1965 consumer prices rose only 1.4 percent per year and wholesale prices increased only 0.6 percent annually. Despite three cyclical interruptions from 1951 to 1960, stock prices more than doubled. Prices remained steady in the first half of the 1960's, and stock prices nearly doubled again. Inflation became a serious matter in the last half of the decade, and stock prices encountered increasing difficulties with the low in the market on May 26, 1970 falling to a level first achieved in March 1961. One of the reasons that stock prices encounter difficulties during inflation is that policy makers in the United States inevitably react either promptly or eventually, and a tighter monetary policy extracts its toll from the equity market.

The story doesn't end nor start there. Anticipated inflation, which becomes inevitable as actual inflation develops, results in higher interest rates. As interest rates rise, the discount rate applied to expected earnings flows also increases. This fact tends to depress equity prices unless earnings are inflated proportionately, which is often not the case, as previously argued. Furthermore, a tighter monetary policy in response to a rising inflation further increases interest rates in the shorter run. In addition, the inevitable liquidity squeeze accompanying a tighter monetary policy, i.e., reduced monetary growth, increases selling pressure on stock prices. Finally, reduced monetary growth followed by slower growth in total spending extracts a toll from

corporate profits. Hence, stock prices weaken further. Therefore, we can see that inflation is bad news for the stock market
for several reasons. First, interest rates rise as inflation develops
but earnings may also rise for a period. A tighter money policy
to combat inflation raises rates further in the short run and
price increases become more difficult while costs continue the
upward march. Increased liquidity pressures depress stock
prices, and the decline in corporate earnings further depresses
the stock market. To put it differently, changing monetary
growth exerts a *direct* effect on stock prices via the liquidity
effect and also *indirect* effects through the impact on inflation,
interest rates, and finally corporate profits.

This brief analysis suggests that a decade of reduced inflation should be favorable for the equity market. Since less
inflation will undoubtedly bring lower interest rates, this pros-
pect bodes well for the stock market since the earnings discount factor will decline. Price earnings ratios in recent years
have undoubtedly been restrained by high and rising interest
rates. A reversal of the recent interest rate pattern should serve
to bolster PE ratios.

But what about earnings? Doesn't restrained and moderate
monetary growth mean sluggish economic growth and hence
poor earnings performance? In the view of the monetarists, the
answer is clearly no. At the trough of the recent recession, unemployment of labor was about 6 percent, and utilization of
manufacturing capacity had declined to near the 73 percent
rate. These facts mean that the capacity of the economy for real
growth in the next few years will be well above the normal $4\frac{1}{3}$
percent. Cost control combined with increased productivity and
increased volume of sales resulting from stable but moderate
monetary growth will exert tremendous stimulus to corporate
profits in the early stages of the expansion. Eventually, capacity
utilization of resources will approach practical full employment
of resources and further growth will be contingent on realiza-

tion of increased potential. But if inflation and costs are held under control as posited, profits can continue to make satisfactory progress. Stable economic growth promotes stable corporate profits growth. In other words, maintenance of a stable and largely predictable monetary environment will permit realization of the vast economic potential of the United States economy.

In summary, a decade of stable and moderate monetary growth would favorably affect the fundamental factors influencing stock prices. The *direct* effect of liquidity upon stock prices would be favorable since volatility in monetary growth would be conspicuous by its absence. Stable growth in the economy in response to stable monetary growth would *indirectly* enhance growth in corporate profits. Finally, the *indirect* effect of only moderate growth in the money supply would gradually reduce inflation and interest rates, i.e., the discount rate applied to corporate earnings would decline. Absence of adverse liquidity pressures, rising corporate profits, and reduced interest rates all point to higher prices for equity investments.

In conclusion, it should be recognized that elimination of monetary instability will contribute to improved economic performance, but it will not usher in Utopia. Economic growth will still depend on population growth, savings and capital formation, technological improvements, and a constant striving to improve the quality of the labor force. Many of our pressing national problems in turn bear only a modest relation to economic growth. Solving and preventing wars, reducing racial strife and discrimination, upgrading the quality of marginal workers, creating the proper incentives in our welfare programs, reducing air and water pollution, achieving better control over crime, and arresting the disaffection of our youths are all serious national problems. Unfortunately, their solution is far from obvious, but clearly we need to have not only a better understanding of the sources of the difficulties but also the resources to energetically attack them. Maintenance of stable monetary growth will help assure that our economic performance will better match our potential so that resources for improving the quality of our lives will be available.

CHAPTER 12

Summing It All Up

If you aren't convinced by now, you need not prevail further. But a brief recapitulation of the monetarist theory and arguments, which consumed the foregoing pages, may be useful.

It was argued that causation runs from changes in money to changes in spending on assets, consumer and producers' goods, to inflation, and to interest rates. In contrast, fiscalists or new economists argue causation runs from fiscal and investment change to spending to inflation. Interest rates in their approach are determined by the money supply and the demand for money, and the Keynesian theory predicts that more money yields lower interest rates. The monetarist and fiscalist theories are equally logical and internally consistent and espoused by able and articulate spokesmen. But it was argued that the monetarist approach is more consistent with the facts of the past, and that this approach to economic forecasting has scored notable victories over the Keynesian approach in recent years.

Since change in the money supply is the critical variable in the monetarist theory, it is comforting to conclude, after a tedious chapter analyzing factors affecting the quantity of money, that the Federal Reserve in effect determines money creation and destruction. This fact makes possible a purposeful monetary policy aimed at achieving economic growth within the framework of high employment and stable prices. Since the money supply is easier to manipulate than federal spending and revenue, it is fortunate that changes in money are usually the dominant influence determining income change.

Monitoring and measuring monetary change is not easy. To make this exercise meaningful, data must be adjusted so that trends become evident. The analysis must be carried on amid a continuing understanding of government policy objectives as well as knowledge concerning the state of the economy.

Various studies have demonstrated that changes in money are associated with changes in the economy in a causal and predictable manner. Integration of monetary analysis with the NBER indicator approach insures that a careful analyst will not be seriously misled concerning the current state of the economy nor the near term outlook. Concentration on the causal money variable and the leading indicators has enabled careful analysts to call every cyclical turn since the early 1950's.

Excessive monetary growth, in the view of the monetarist, has accounted for all known sizable inflations, domestic and foreign, modern and ancient. A rising trend in money per unit of real output has inevitably brought inflation, whereas stabilization of money growth in line with output growth has brought price stability. Price series vary in their sensitivity to changing demand pressures, with sensitive commodity and wholesale prices reacting first while wage rate change lags the parade.

Monetarists argue that interest rates should be viewed in two parts, the real rate of interest plus the price expectation component. Most fluctuations in interest rates can be explained by changing inflationary expectations rather than changes in the real rate. Easy money brings higher, not lower, interest rates since more money means more spending, more income, and ultimately more inflation. Knowledge of changing inflationary pressures enables the careful analyst to predict interest rate trends with reasonable accuracy.

Since changing monetary growth establishes incentives to either acquire or expend liquidity, it is not surprising that changes in money exert a *direct* influence on stock market fluctuations. Furthermore, the *indirect* effects of monetary change are even more dramatic and influential. Monetarists argue that monetary growth is the major variable influencing trends in corporate profits and interest rates. Expectations concerning inflation, hence interest rates, and corporate earnings exert a major influence on equity prices since these prices are determined by the discounted value of expected earnings. Rising corporate earnings enhance equity prices whereas lower corporate earnings depress equities. Rising inflationary expectations cause higher interest rates as does the short-run impact of a tighter monetary policy, and these influences depress equity prices unless inflationary expectations also enhance earning growth. Lower interest rates exert a bullish influence on common stock prices.

Using monetary growth as a basic factor influencing the timing of investment decisions is not without complications. Hindsight demonstration of the relation between money and financial markets is considerably easier than foresight prediction. At or near turning points in markets, the psychology of the marketplace inevitably reduces nerve and confidence. It is at such turning points that full knowledge of the strengths and weaknesses of the monetary approach is critically important. Although there are always numerous available arguments why money won't work "this time," it usually does!

The current trend in economic thinking and policy making toward the monetarist approach establishes the potential for much better economic performance in the future than in the recent past. Stable monetary growth in line with output potential raises the welcome possibility of less inflation and lower interest rates along with stable economic growth and better corporate profit performance. In that kind of environment, financial markets (both stocks and bonds) should thrive.

The adoption and successful execution of the foregoing principles does not assure an easy road to wealth or plenty, either personally or on a national scale. But by now you must believe, or at least suspect, that monetarism is not akin to imaginative star gazing. Rather, the monetarist view is based on a well-tested body of economic thought. It is hoped that this approach represents a significant step toward better analysis, better public policies, and more successful investing. If the foregoing economic relations survive the onslaught of the future, as I expect, the Age of Aquarius may become more aptly known as the Age of Monetarism!

Appendix

In order to derive a monetary series unaffected by seasonal movements, seasonally adjusted data for demand deposits + currency were used. In order to remove the secular trend from the data, rates of change were computed; that is, the percentage change this month from last month. For example, if the money stock rose from $100 billion last month to $101 billion this month, the rate of change was + 1 percent. If, on the other hand, it fell from $100 billion to $99 billion, the rate of change was − 1 percent.

Unfortunately, month-to-month changes in the stock of money are erratic, and observation of only the monthly rate of change sometimes makes it difficult to detect the prevailing trend. Consequently, a six month moving average of the monthly rate of change was computed. This six month moving average reduces the sensitivity of the monetary growth rate series but removes much of the erratic movement. The six month moving average was computed by averaging the monthly rate of growth for the past six months. The following month, the data for the latest month was added, the seven-month-old data was removed, and a new average six-month rate of growth was computed. This procedure was followed for each month. Since, for some purposes, an annual rate of change was desired, each of the six month average rates of change was converted to average annual rates of change by multiplying by 12. The annualized six-month moving average rates of change in the stock of money were plotted on charts reflecting the monetary growth rate. The resulting series is seasonally adjusted, reasonably free of erratic movements, yet sensitive to broad cyclical movements. The above procedure was followed in deriving the data for all charts containing the rate of growth in the money stock.

Monetary stock data for the period prior to 1946 were taken from *Monetary Statistics of the United States* by Milton Friedman and Anna Schwartz.[1] A monthly, seasonally adjusted official series does not exist for the earlier period. The data used for the period 1946 to the present are the latest official series available from the Board of Governors of the Federal Reserve System.

The following table presents the stock of money data from 1920 to 1970. Also, the monthly rate of change and the annualized six-month moving average rate of change are presented.

---

[1] Milton Friedman and Anna Schwartz, *Monetary Statistics of the United States*. (New York: National Bureau of Economic Research, Columbia University Press, 1970.)

Period Ending		Money Supply in Millions of $	Month-to-Month Percentage Change	Annual Rate of Change*
Year	Month			
1920	1	23.5	—0.89	13.25
	2	23.9	1.49	13.62
	3	24.1	1.26	13.21
	4	24.0	—0.50	8.57
	5	24.0	—0.17	5.90
	6	23.8	—0.63	1.09
	7	23.8	—0.04	2.76
	8	23.8	—0.21	— 0.59
	9	23.7	—0.17	— 3.43
	10	23.6	—0.72	— 3.86
	11	23.1	—1.78	— 7.07
	12	23.4	0.99	— 3.89
1921	1	22.7	—2.87	— 9.51
	2	22.5	—0.93	—10.95
	3	22.0	—2.31	—15.20
	4	21.6	—1.50	—16.80
	5	21.6	—0.23	—13.75
	6	21.2	—1.95	—19.75
	7	20.9	—1.09	—16.06
	8	21.0	0.29	—13.78
	9	20.8	—1.14	—11.32
	10	20.9	0.58	— 7.18
	11	20.9	0.24	— 6.27
	12	20.9	—0.29	— 2.87
1922	1	20.7	—0.91	— 2.49
	2	20.9	0.92	— 1.25
	3	20.9	0.19	1.44
	4	21.4	2.58	5.47
	5	21.6	0.84	6.69
	6	21.8	1.02	9.31
	7	21.0	0.50	12.06
	8	21.0	—0.00	10.17
	9	22.3	1.41	12.58
	10	22.3	0.36	8.24
	11	22.3	—0.18	6.18
	12	23.1	3.41	11.04
1923	1	22.9	—0.61	8.70
	2	23.0	0.39	9.43
	3	22.6	—1.74	3.09
	4	22.9	1.28	4.93
	5	23.0	0.57	6.40
	6	22.9	—0.69	— 1.66
	7	22.8	—0.09	— 0.61
	8	22.8	—0.18	— 1.75
	9	23.0	0.61	2.98
	10	23.0	0.39	1.22
	11	23.1	0.17	0.44
	12	23.2	0.39	2.62

* Six-month moving average.

Period Ending		Money Supply in Millions of $	Month-to-Month Percentage Change	Annual Rate of Change*
Year	Month			
1924	1	23.0	—0.82	1.13
	2	22.9	—0.36	0.96
	3	23.0	0.36	0.26
	4	23.1	0.49	0.26
	5	23.2	0.74	1.39
	6	23.5	1.09	2.60
	7	23.8	1.36	6.84
	8	24.1	1.30	9.98
	9	24.4	1.12	11.69
	10	24.5	0.41	11.66
	11	24.8	1.60	13.39
	12	24.6	—0.81	9.69
1925	1	25.0	1.30	9.77
	2	25.2	0.86	8.72
	3	25.0	—0.44	5.58
	4	25.2	0.52	5.80
	5	25.4	0.85	4.17
	6	25.6	1.05	7.66
	7	25.7	0.49	5.87
	8	26.2	1.83	8.05
	9	26.5	1.25	11.21
	10	26.5	—0.04	10.02
	11	26.4	—0.30	7.86
	12	26.3	—0.23	5.51
1926	1	26.3	0.18	4.88
	2	26.4	0.48	2.05
	3	26.3	—0.48	— 0.98
	4	26.1	—0.97	— 2.65
	5	26.4	1.00	— 0.08
	6	26.3	—0.23	— 0.08
	7	26.1	—0.84	— 1.90
	8	26.2	0.42	— 1.83
	9	26.1	—0.37	— 1.60
	10	25.9	—0.80	— 1.45
	11	26.0	0.25	— 3.13
	12	25.7	—1.04	— 4.75
1927	1	25.8	0.45	— 2.38
	2	25.9	0.50	— 2.24
	3	26.1	0.76	— 0.39
	4	26.0	—0.42	0.39
	5	26.4	1.79	3.48
	6	26.0	—1.40	2.70
	7	26.1	0.25	2.30
	8	26.2	0.54	2.38
	9	26.1	—0.67	— 0.08
	10	26.2	0.48	1.53
	11	26.6	1.80	1.76
	12	26.0	—2.58	— 0.46

* Six-month moving average.

Period Ending		Money Supply in Millions of $	Month-to-Month Percentage Change	Annual Rate of Change*
Year	Month			
1928	1	26.4	1.50	2.21
	2	26.4	0.30	1.75
	3	26.5	0.04	2.97
	4	26.8	1.36	4.93
	5	26.6	—0.75	— 0.15
	6	26.0	—2.33	0.15
	7	26.2	0.77	— 1.29
	8	26.0	—0.61	— 3.10
	9	26.3	0.88	— 1.44
	10	26.4	0.65	— 2.89
	11	26.6	0.72	0.08
	12	26.7	0.11	5.03
1929	1	26.3	—1.24	0.99
	2	26.5	0.57	3.33
	3	26.5	0.08	1.74
	4	26.6	0.26	0.98
	5	26.3	—1.09	— 2.64
	6	26.4	0.49	— 1.89
	7	26.9	1.89	4.39
	8	26.7	—0.78	1.66
	9	26.6	—0.22	1.05
	10	28.5	6.98	14.52
	11	25.7	—9.68	— 4.01
	12	26.7	3.65	2.01
1930	1	25.9	—2.81	— 7.30
	2	26.2	1.04	— 3.75
	3	26.6	1.56	— 0.23
	4	26.2	—1.54	—17.29
	5	25.6	—2.25	— 0.99
	6	25.6	—0.12	— 8.40
	7	25.7	0.43	— 1.84
	8	25.4	—1.25	— 6.39
	9	25.4	—0.04	— 9.67
	10	25.3	—0.20	— 6.94
	11	25.4	0.16	— 2.04
	12	25.2	—0.39	— 2.59
1931	1	24.9	—1.39	— 6.22
	2	25.1	0.68	— 2.38
	3	25.1	0.20	— 1.90
	4	24.6	—2.03	— 5.56
	5	24.3	—1.42	— 8.70
	6	24.3	0.04	— 7.88
	7	24.2	—0.33	— 5.75
	8	23.8	—1.53	—10.17
	9	23.8	—0.21	—11.08
	10	23.1	—2.78	—12.42
	11	22.8	—1.51	—12.55
	12	22.3	—2.02	—16.66

* Six-month moving average.

Period Ending		Money Supply in Millions of $	Month-to-Month Percentage Change	Annual Rate of Change*
Year	Month			
1932	1	21.9	—1.70	—19.46
	2	21.7	—0.87	—18.22
	3	21.5	—0.92	—19.82
	4	21.3	—1.02	—16.20
	5	21.0	—1.64	—16.42
	6	20.9	—0.38	—13.13
	7	20.6	—1.44	—12.53
	8	20.6	0.19	—10.49
	9	20.6	0.15	— 8.39
	10	20.7	0.15	— 6.05
	11	21.0	1.45	0.19
	12	20.8	—1.00	— 1.06
1933	1	21.1	1.40	4.63
	2	20.4	—3.09	— 2.02
	3	19.5	—4.56	—11.27
	4	19.5	—0.10	—11.87
	5	19.9	2.11	—10.90
	6	19.6	—1.11	—11.10
	7	19.5	—0.66	—15.41
	8	19.6	0.15	— 8.72
	9	19.6	0.31	1.33
	10	19.8	0.76	3.06
	11	20.0	1.27	1.42
	12	20.2	1.10	5.89
1934	1	20.2	—0.15	6.88
	2	20.8	2.87	12.37
	3	21.2	2.21	16.22
	4	21.4	0.61	15.81
	5	21.5	0.61	14.44
	6	21.6	0.37	12.93
	7	22.0	2.18	17.53
	8	22.6	2.68	17.37
	9	22.5	—0.44	11.97
	10	23.1	2.35	15.49
	11	23.6	2.12	18.53
	12	23.3	—1.19	15.06
1935	1	24.2	3.82	18.55
	2	24.9	2.90	19.22
	3	24.8	—0.40	18.91
	4	25.1	1.37	17.03
	5	25.3	0.72	14.24
	6	25.7	1.70	19.85
	7	26.0	0.93	14.33
	8	27.3	5.28	19.46
	9	26.9	—1.54	16.66
	10	27.2	1.26	16.43
	11	27.8	2.02	19.01
	12	27.6	—0.86	13.72

* Six-month moving average.

Period Ending		Money Supply in Millions of $	Month-to-Month Percentage Change	Annual Rate of Change*
Year	Month			
1936	1	27.6	0.11	12.01
	2	28.1	1.78	5.47
	3	28.1	0.11	8.72
	4	28.7	2.03	10.31
	5	29.5	2.86	12.16
	6	30.2	2.31	18.55
	7	30.3	0.53	19.17
	8	30.2	—0.33	14.82
	9	30.7	1.62	17.76
	10	30.7	—0.13	13.42
	11	31.0	0.85	9.58
	12	31.4	1.39	7.86
1937	1	31.1	—0.80	5.14
	2	31.4	0.90	7.58
	3	31.6	0.60	5.60
	4	31.5	—0.28	5.26
	5	31.1	—1.24	1.09
	6	31.1	—0.03	— 1.72
	7	31.0	—0.19	— 0.51
	8	30.8	—0.64	— 3.58
	9	30.7	—0.55	— 5.90
	10	30.1	—1.89	— 9.08
	11	29.9	—0.70	— 7.98
	12	29.6	—0.87	— 9.67
1938	1	29.9	0.78	— 7.84
	2	30.1	0.70	— 5.17
	3	30.2	0.30	— 3.46
	4	30.0	—0.56	— 0.73
	5	29.6	—1.20	— 1.74
	6	29.7	0.34	0.67
	7	30.1	1.11	1.34
	8	30.8	2.50	4.94
	9	31.2	1.17	6.72
	10	31.6	1.22	10.32
	11	32.2	1.93	16.59
	12	32.4	0.62	17.02
1939	1	32.3	—0.15	14.35
	2	32.2	—0.34	8.76
	3	32.7	1.49	9.45
	4	33.0	0.89	8.82
	5	33.2	0.61	6.23
	6	33.3	0.33	5.64
	7	34.2	2.70	11.41
	8	35.1	2.63	17.41
	9	35.8	2.17	18.83
	10	36.3	1.17	19.30
	11	37.2	2.59	23.27
	12	36.8	—0.97	20.17

* Six-month moving average.

Period Ending		Money Supply in Millions of $	Month-to-Month Percentage Change	Annual Rate of Change*
Year	Month			
1940	1	37.4	1.49	17.88
	2	37.9	1.42	15.59
	3	38.5	1.45	14.25
	4	38.3	—0.39	11.03
	5	39.1	2.06	10.14
	6	39.7	1.56	15.15
	7	40.2	1.18	14.55
	8	40.3	0.37	12.42
	9	40.8	1.26	12.09
	10	41.5	1.66	16.15
	11	42.1	1.40	14.99
	12	42.9	1.76	15.44
1941	1	43.6	1.66	16.41
	2	44.8	2.71	21.11
	3	45.4	1.47	21.45
	4	45.6	0.46	18.90
	5	46.5	1.97	19.97
	6	46.3	—0.47	15.36
	7	47.5	2.66	17.46
	8	47.6	0.19	12.47
	9	48.2	1.11	11.78
	10	48.0	—0.31	10.13
	11	48.8	1.54	9.37
	12	49.0	0.51	11.27
1942	1	50.2	2.53	11.21
	2	51.0	1.45	13.74
	3	51.6	1.16	13.82
	4	52.7	2.27	18.97
	5	53.8	1.95	19.83
	6	54.1	0.69	19.97
	7	56.1	3.57	22.29
	8	57.4	2.34	24.06
	9	58.7	2.37	26.42
	10	60.8	3.46	28.96
	11	61.9	1.88	28.66
	12	63.3	2.33	31.67
1943	1	65.1	2.79	30.42
	2	67.9	4.22	34.28
	3	69.9	2.95	35.36
	4	69.0	—1.25	25.40
	5	69.8	1.16	23.85
	6	73.5	5.37	30.23
	7	76.3	3.78	32.40
	8	80.0	4.77	34.06
	9	72.6	—9.19	7.53
	10	73.8	1.57	12.95
	11	77.2	4.61	19.80
	12	80.5	4.30	18.34

* Six-month moving average.

Period Ending		Money Supply in Millions of $	Month-to-Month Percentage Change	Annual Rate of Change*
Year	Month			
1944	1	79.0	—1.88	6.88
	2	80.0	1.25	— 0.03
	3	81.3	1.68	22.50
	4	83.0	2.08	23.49
	5	85.0	2.48	19.69
	6	83.9	—1.39	8.32
	7	84.6	0.91	13.80
	8	87.2	3.03	17.43
	9	89.0	2.03	18.20
	10	91.5	2.88	19.97
	11	93.8	2.54	20.24
	12	91.3	—2.72	16.80
1945	1	94.3	3.34	21.68
	2	95.9	1.64	19.08
	3	97.8	1.97	19.04
	4	98.6	0.83	15.03
	5	99.2	0.64	11.29
	6	98.1	—1.16	14.10
	7	99.7	1.64	10.98
	8	100.9	1.24	10.24
	9	102.4	1.45	9.29
	10	103.1	0.75	9.14
	11	103.7	0.57	8.99
	12	103.0	—0.67	9.83
1946	1	102.6	—0.47	5.66
	2	103.8	1.20	5.61
	3	103.5	—0.28	2.19
	4	105.7	2.14	4.98
	5	106.8	1.05	5.96
	6	107.5	0.67	8.63
	7	108.0	0.46	10.44
	8	108.0	0.01	8.05
	9	108.5	0.38	9.30
	10	108.7	0.19	5.51
	11	108.7	—0.00	3.43
	12	108.4	—0.27	1.55
1947	1	109.5	1.03	2.69
	2	109.7	0.18	3.04
	3	110.3	0.55	3.38
	4	111.1	0.73	4.45
	5	111.7	0.54	5.53
	6	112.1	0.36	6.76
	7	112.2	0.09	4.88
	8	112.6	0.36	5.22
	9	113.0	0.36	4.84
	10	112.9	—0.09	3.21
	11	113.3	0.35	2.85
	12	113.1	—0.18	1.77

* Six-month moving average.

Period Ending		Money Supply in Millions of $	Month-to-Month Percentage Change	Annual Rate of Change*
Year	Month			
1948	1	113.4	0.27	2.13
	2	113.2	—0.18	1.06
	3	112.6	—0.53	— 0.71
	4	112.3	—0.27	— 1.06
	5	112.1	—0.18	— 2.12
	6	112.0	—0.09	— 1.95
	7	112.2	0.18	— 2.13
	8	112.3	0.09	— 1.60
	9	112.2	—0.09	— 0.71
	10	112.1	—0.09	— 0.36
	11	111.8	—0.27	— 0.53
	12	111.5	—0.27	— 0.89
1949	1	111.2	—0.27	— 1.79
	2	111.2	—0.00	— 1.97
	3	111.2	—0.00	— 1.79
	4	111.3	0.09	— 1.43
	5	111.5	0.18	— 0.54
	6	111.3	—0.18	— 0.36
	7	111.2	—0.09	— 0.00
	8	111.0	—0.18	— 0.36
	9	110.9	—0.09	— 0.54
	10	110.9	—0.00	— 0.72
	11	111.0	0.09	— 0.90
	12	111.2	0.18	— 0.18
1950	1	111.5	0.27	0.54
	2	112.1	0.54	1.98
	3	112.5	0.36	2.88
	4	113.2	0.62	4.12
	5	113.7	0.44	4.83
	6	114.1	0.35	5.16
	7	114.6	0.44	5.49
	8	115.0	0.35	5.12
	9	115.2	0.17	4.74
	10	115.7	0.43	4.37
	11	115.9	0.17	3.84
	12	116.2	0.26	3.65
1951	1	116.7	0.43	3.64
	2	117.1	0.34	3.63
	3	117.6	0.43	4.13
	4	117.8	0.17	3.60
	5	118.2	0.34	3.94
	6	118.6	0.34	4.09
	7	119.1	0.42	4.08
	8	119.6	0.42	4.23
	9	120.4	0.67	4.73
	10	121.0	0.50	5.38
	11	122.0	0.83	6.36
	12	122.7	0.57	6.83

* Six-month moving average.

Period Ending		Money Supply in Millions of $	Month-to-Month Percentage Change	Annual Rate of Change*
Year	Month			
1952	1	123.1	0.33	6.62
	2	123.6	0.41	6.59
	3	123.8	0.16	5.57
	4	124.1	0.24	5.05
	5	124.5	0.32	4.06
	6	125.0	0.40	3.72
	7	125.3	0.24	3.55
	8	125.7	0.32	3.38
	9	126.4	0.56	4.17
	10	126.7	0.24	4.15
	11	127.1	0.32	4.14
	12	127.4	0.24	3.81
1953	1	127.3	—0.08	3.16
	2	127.4	0.08	2.68
	3	128.0	0.47	2.52
	4	128.3	0.23	2.51
	5	128.5	0.16	2.19
	6	128.5	0.00	1.72
	7	128.6	0.08	2.03
	8	128.7	0.08	2.03
	9	128.6	—0.08	0.93
	10	128.7	0.08	0.62
	11	128.7	—0.00	0.31
	12	128.8	0.08	0.47
1954	1	129.0	0.16	0.62
	2	129.1	0.08	0.62
	3	129.2	0.08	0.93
	4	128.6	—0.46	— 0.16
	5	129.7	0.86	1.55
	6	129.9	0.15	1.70
	7	130.3	0.31	2.01
	8	130.7	0.31	2.47
	9	130.9	0.15	2.62
	10	131.5	0.46	4.46
	11	132.1	0.46	3.68
	12	132.3	0.15	3.67
1955	1	133.0	0.53	4.11
	2	133.9	0.68	4.86
	3	133.6	—0.22	4.08
	4	133.9	0.22	3.62
	5	134.6	0.52	3.76
	6	134.4	—0.15	3.14
	7	134.8	0.30	2.69
	8	134.8	—0.00	1.34
	9	135.0	0.15	2.08
	10	135.2	0.15	1.93
	11	134.9	—0.22	0.45
	12	135.2	0.22	1.19

* Six-month moving average.

Period Ending		Money Supply in Millions of $	Month-to-Month Percentage Change	Annual Rate of Change*
Year	Month			
1956	1	135.5	0.22	1.04
	2	135.5	0.00	1.04
	3	135.7	0.15	1.04
	4	136.0	0.22	1.18
	5	135.8	—0.15	1.33
	6	136.0	0.15	1.18
	7	136.0	0.00	0.74
	8	135.7	—0.22	0.29
	9	136.2	0.37	0.74
	10	136.3	0.07	0.44
	11	136.6	0.22	1.18
	12	136.9	0.22	1.32
1957	1	136.9	—0.00	1.32
	2	136.8	—0.07	1.61
	3	136.9	0.07	1.02
	4	136.9	—0.00	0.88
	5	137.0	0.07	0.58
	6	136.9	—0.07	— 0.00
	7	137.0	0.07	0.15
	8	137.1	0.07	0.44
	9	136.8	—0.22	— 0.15
	10	136.5	—0.22	— 0.58
	11	136.3	—0.15	— 1.02
	12	135.9	—0.29	— 1.46
1958	1	135.5	—0.29	— 2.20
	2	136.2	0.52	— 1.32
	3	136.5	0.22	— 0.44
	4	137.0	0.37	0.73
	5	137.5	0.36	1.76
	6	138.4	0.65	3.66
	7	138.4	—0.00	4.24
	8	139.1	0.51	4.22
	9	139.5	0.29	4.35
	10	140.1	0.43	4.48
	11	140.9	0.57	4.90
	12	141.1	0.14	3.87
1959	1	141.8	0.50	4.84
	2	142.2	0.28	4.40
	3	142.8	0.42	4.68
	4	143.1	0.21	4.24
	5	143.6	0.35	3.80
	6	143.8	0.14	3.80
	7	144.6	0.56	3.92
	8	144.1	—0.35	2.66
	9	143.8	—0.21	1.40
	10	143.5	—0.21	0.56
	11	143.3	—0.14	— 0.41
	12	142.6	—0.49	— 1.67

* Six-month moving average.

Period Ending		Money Supply in Millions of $	Month-to-Month Percentage Change	Annual Rate of Change*
Year	Month			
1960	1	142.4	—0.14	— 3.06
	2	141.9	—0.35	— 3.07
	3	141.6	—0.21	— 3.08
	4	141.5	—0.07	— 2.80
	5	141.0	—0.35	— 3.23
	6	140.9	—0.07	— 2.40
	7	141.2	0.21	— 1.69
	8	141.7	0.35	— 0.28
	9	141.8	0.07	0.29
	10	141.8	0.00	0.43
	11	141.6	—0.14	0.85
	12	141.7	0.07	1.13
1961	1	141.9	0.14	0.99
	2	142.4	0.35	0.99
	3	142.8	0.28	1.41
	4	143.2	0.28	1.97
	5	143.5	0.21	2.67
	6	143.8	0.21	2.95
	7	143.9	0.07	2.80
	8	144.3	0.28	2.65
	9	144.6	0.21	2.51
	10	145.1	0.35	2.64
	11	145.7	0.41	3.05
	12	146.0	0.21	3.04
1962	1	146.2	0.14	3.18
	2	146.4	0.14	2.89
	3	146.8	0.27	3.02
	4	147.1	0.20	2.74
	5	147.1	0.00	1.91
	6	147.1	0.00	1.50
	7	146.9	—0.14	0.96
	8	146.8	—0.07	0.55
	9	146.7	—0.07	— 0.14
	10	147.2	0.34	0.14
	11	147.6	0.27	0.68
	12	148.1	0.34	1.36
1963	1	148.8	0.47	2.58
	2	149.2	0.27	3.25
	3	149.6	0.27	3.92
	4	150.0	0.27	3.77
	5	150.6	0.40	4.03
	6	151.1	0.33	4.02
	7	151.7	0.40	3.87
	8	151.9	0.13	3.59
	9	152.1	0.13	3.32
	10	152.9	0.53	3.84
	11	153.9	0.65	4.35
	12	153.6	—0.19	3.29

* Six-month moving average.

Period Ending		Money Supply in Millions of $	Month-to-Month Percentage Change	Annual Rate of Change*
Year	Month			
1964	1	154.1	0.33	3.15
	2	154.5	0.26	3.40
	3	155.0	0.32	3.79
	4	155.2	0.13	2.99
	5	155.9	0.45	2.59
	6	156.4	0.32	3.62
	7	157.5	0.70	4.37
	8	158.4	0.57	5.00
	9	159.1	0.44	5.23
	10	159.7	0.38	5.73
	11	160.3	0.38	5.58
	12	160.5	0.12	5.19
1965	1	160.9	0.25	4.28
	2	161.3	0.25	3.63
	3	161.7	0.25	3.25
	4	162.0	0.19	2.86
	5	162.3	0.19	2.48
	6	163.1	0.49	3.22
	7	163.7	0.37	3.46
	8	164.3	0.37	3.69
	9	165.2	0.55	4.29
	10	166.4	0.73	5.37
	11	166.9	0.30	5.60
	12	168.0	0.66	5.94
1966	1	168.9	0.54	6.27
	2	169.7	0.47	6.49
	3	170.5	0.47	6.33
	4	171.7	0.70	6.29
	5	171.6	−0.06	5.57
	6	171.7	0.06	4.37
	7	171.0	−0.41	2.48
	8	171.2	0.12	1.77
	9	171.9	0.41	1.64
	10	171.4	−0.29	− 0.35
	11	171.2	−0.12	− 0.46
	12	171.7	0.29	0.01
1967	1	171.1	−0.35	0.12
	2	173.1	1.17	2.23
	3	174.6	0.87	3.14
	4	174.1	−0.29	3.15
	5	175.9	1.03	5.45
	6	177.5	0.91	6.69
	7	178.9	0.79	8.96
	8	180.0	0.61	7.85
	9	180.9	0.50	7.12
	10	181.7	0.44	8.58
	11	182.4	0.39	7.28
	12	183.1	0.38	6.23

* Six-month moving average.

Period Ending		Money Supply in Millions of $	Month-to-Month Percentage Change	Annual Rate of Change*
Year	Month			
1968	1	183.6	0.27	5.20
	2	184.7	0.60	5.17
	3	185.8	0.60	5.36
	4	186.6	0.43	5.33
	5	188.7	1.13	6.82
	6	190.2	0.79	7.64
	7	191.6	0.74	8.56
	8	192.7	0.57	8.51
	9	193.6	0.47	8.26
	10	194.3	0.36	8.12
	11	196.0	0.87	7.62
	12	197.4	0.71	7.46
1969	1	198.1	0.35	6.69
	2	199.3	0.61	6.76
	3	200.1	0.40	6.63
	4	201.0	0.45	6.80
	5	201.6	0.30	5.65
	6	202.4	0.40	5.01
	7	203.1	0.35	5.00
	8	202.6	—0.25	3.29 _Aug._
	9	202.8	0.10	2.69 _Sept._
	10	203.2	0.20	2.18 _Oct_
	11	203.5	0.15	1.88 _Nov_
	12	203.6	0.05	1.18 _Dec_
1970	1	205.2	0.79	2.06
	2	204.5	—0.34	1.87
Period	3	206.6	1.03	3.73
	4	208.3	0.82	4.98
	5	209.2	0.43	5.55
	6	209.6	0.19	5.84
	7	210.6	0.48	5.22
	8	211.8	0.57	7.04
	9	212.8	0.47	5.93
	10	213.0	0.09	4.47
	11	213.7	0.33	4.26
	12	214.6	0.42	4.72

* Six-month moving average.

Index

This book has been set in 12 and 11 point Granjon, leaded 2 points. Chapter numbers and titles are in Lydian. The size of the type page is 24 by 42 picas.